FINLAND

St. Petersburg

Moscow

R U S S I A

Warsaw
LAND

NGARY
Belgrade
ROUMANIA
SERVIA
Bucharest
Black Sea
Caspian Sea

BULGARIA
Sofia
TURKEY
Constantinople

GREECE
Athens

TURKEY IN ASIA

Cyprus
(Br.)

an Sea

LI
EGYPT

EUROPE
IN 1914

0   100   200   300   400
Miles

BRITAIN —
TWENTIETH CENTURY

BRITAIN — TWENTIETH CENTURY

The Story of Social Conditions

MARY CATHCART BORER

*With line illustrations in the text
by Norman and Lilian Buchanan,
9 drawings from 'Punch'
and 24 pages of photographs*

FREDERICK WARNE & CO. LTD. LONDON
FREDERICK WARNE & CO. INC. NEW YORK

© Frederick Warne & Co. Ltd.

London, England

1966

The publishers wish to thank the following for their kind permission to reproduce photographs used in this book: Fox Photos Ltd. for photographs on Plates 1, 4 (above), 8, 9 (left), 10, 12, 13 (left), 14, 15, 16, 17, 18, 19 (below, right), 20 (right), 21 (above), 22 (left), 23 and 24 (above); the G.L.C. for photographs on Plates 2, 3, 5 (below) and 11; 'Topix' for photographs on Plates 4 (below), 5 (above), 6, 7, 9 (above and below), 13 (below), 19 (above and below, left), 20 (above), 21 (below), 22 (below) and 24 (right). Grateful thanks are given to the authors and publishers mentioned in the text for extracts quoted in this book. The publishers also wish to acknowledge the following: the Executors of H. G. Wells for an extract from 'Kipps'; the Society of Authors as the literary representative of the Estate of the late Laurence Binyon for an extract from 'For the Fallen'; Messrs. John Murray Ltd. for an extract from W. N. Hodgson's 'Verse and Prose in Peace and War'; Robert Nichols for an extract from 'Such was My Singing'; Messrs. Faber and Faber and Messrs. Harcourt Brace & World Inc. (U.S.A.) for extracts from T. S. Elliot's 'Collected Poems 1909–1962'; Messrs. Victor Gollancz Ltd. for an extract from Ellen Wilkinson's 'The Town That Was Murdered'; Messrs. George Allen & Unwin Ltd. for an extract from C. A. Oakley's 'Where We Came In'; Messrs. Harper & Row, American publishers of 'England' by Wilhelm Dibelius; and Messrs. Houghton Mifflin Co., American publishers of 'The Gathering Storm' by Winston Churchill.

LIBRARY OF CONGRESS CATALOG
CARD NO 67–10966

Printed in Great Britain by
William Clowes and Sons, Limited
London and Beccles
119/666

Contents

CHAPTER ONE

The End of the Nineteenth Century

In a great, high-canopied bed, richly curtained, a little old lady, tired and very frail, lay sleeping. She sighed and then a smile lit her sad, exhausted face. The doctors, her children and grandchildren, sitting motionless in the dark, silent room on that bleak January morning of 1901, leant forward to await the moment of her awakening, but it never came. She was far away, dreaming not of the new century into which she had just survived but of the long span of years stretching back to the days of her childhood, days when Napoleon had been alive, living out his last, frustrated years on St. Helena, when George IV and William IV had been kings of England and the Duke of Wellington the Prime Minister. Her thoughts drifted on to that midsummer dawn of 1837 when, as a girl of eighteen, she had been roused from sleep, in her bedroom at Kensington Palace, to be told that her Uncle William was dead and that she was now Queen of England.

She lived again that morning, less than three years later, when she had become the bride of her German cousin, Prince Albert. That had been the happiest of all her days, for she had loved him tenderly and passionately. They had had twenty years together and she had borne him nine children. His untimely death brought her no sorrow now but peace, for the forty unforgetting years of loneliness, the solitariness of widowhood added to the isolation of her throne, were nearly over and in these last moments she felt very close to him.

Three of her children had died before her and her eldest daughter, her dearest Vicky, had been widowed, like herself; but Vicky's son, her favourite grandchild, Kaiser Wilhelm II, the Emperor of Germany, was, she knew, close by her bedside at this moment, watching and waiting, and so was Bertie, her eldest son, the Prince of Wales, the one who had given her so much anxiety and heartache. Bertie would be King of England now. He had waited a long time. "I feel so sad and anxious about him. He is so idle and weak," she had once written to Vicky, but that was a long time ago. During the last few years she had come to understand him a little better, and his marriage to dear Alexandra, his beautiful Danish princess, had given her great happiness.

Her thoughts drifted on to the friends and counsellors of her long reign: Lord Melbourne, who had been so kind during the early years, Sir Robert Peel, the Duke of Wellington, Lord John Russell, Lord Derby, Lord Beaconsfield and Mr. Gladstone. She had outlived them all, but now her own time had come and soon, like them, she would be only a name in the history books.

Later that day Queen Victoria died, peacefully and painlessly, in the arms of Kaiser Wilhelm. Not only the people of England but the whole world had been awaiting the news, and when it came the great bell of St. Paul's Cathedral tolled solemnly for two long hours across the spires and wharves, the offices and marts of the City of London, and from every parish church throughout the country the passing bell pealed, echoing through every hamlet and village, town and city in the kingdom, so that none could fail to hear it. It was the death knell not only of a well-loved queen but of an epoch.

"Things will never be the same, now that the old queen's gone," they said in the clubs of St. James's, in the drawing rooms of country vicarages, in shops and factories, cottages and tenements, and her passing did indeed mark the end of a period of peaceful and leisured prosperity for many, who in the troubled years ahead were to look back on the close of the nineteenth century with a hopeless, desperate nostalgia; and the fact that much of the abundant affluence had been built on the ill-paid toil and privations of the millions of Britain's labouring population, who each year were growing more actively resentful of their unenviable lot, was temporarily lost in the mists of sentiment and time.

It was at her favourite home, Osborne House in the Isle of Wight, that the old queen had died, and her coffin was carried across the Solent to Portsmouth and brought up by train to Victoria Station. Then began the long, sad procession across London to Paddington and the train journey to Windsor for the funeral service and the final burial in the mausoleum at Frogmore, by the side of her husband. The bier was covered with crimson velvet and the pathetically small coffin was draped in a gold-embroidered white satin pall on which all the glittering panoply of state was laid—the crown, the orb and the insignia of the Garter. A million Londoners lined the hushed streets to watch her passing and behind her rode Edward VII, the Emperor of Germany and a score of European rulers and princes who were her close relatives.

Only the hollow clatter of the horses' hoofs, the chilling rumble of the wheels of the gun-carriages and the heartbreakingly melancholy music of Chopin's funeral march broke the silence of that last journey through London. The heart of the British Empire had stopped beating for a moment. Rich men on the crest of the wave of their prosperity, men of middling fortune who were yet well content, men who had grown weary of the struggle to maintain the Victorian façade of affluence with inadequate means, and men so poor that they had lost all hope, stood side by side on the London pavements, their differences momentarily forgotten as they briefly shared the sharp sting of emotion which the solemn, warning pomp of death must always bring.

Thousands of words were to be said and written about Victoria, many in affection and gratitude, for she had served England well, but some, by a later generation, in scorn and ridicule of that "plump little hausfrau, the widow of Windsor", to whom they attributed all that was false and bad in Victorian culture and few of its solid achievements. But no one forgot her, for Queen Victoria had become an institution and most of her subjects had known no other monarch.

Her reign had begun inauspiciously. Her Hanoverian uncles, George IV and William IV, had died unlamented, though some had had a mild affection for the kindly, ineffectual old William. Few had had any love for her handsome young German husband when he first arrived in England, most people regarding him as too austere, aloof and formal. At the time of Victoria's accession there was a strong body of opinion in England which resented the expense of the upkeep of the monarchy and openly advocated a republic. With the passing years of the nineteenth century, however, throughout the rapid growth of material prosperity and imperial power, the queen undertook her duties as head of state with such intelligent and meticulous devotion that not only did the antagonism fade away but the institution was recognized as a new and important force in maintaining the unity of the country and the Empire. Victoria became a symbol of British solidarity and allegiance to the "Great White Queen across the waters" an emotional force helping to link the widely differing races who were to become members of the Empire.

3

During the early years of her reign the court had been gay, for she was very young and was enjoying the freedom from her mother's over-careful vigilance; but on her marriage she took less part in the social round, and after her widowhood none at all. Although she had little contact with fashionable English society, of which some members had begun to resent the sober ways of her court, she never lost touch with the people, and in her dealings with simple folk she showed humanity and understanding. Her people truly mourned her on that cold, sad January day and many wept for a friend who had never spared herself on their behalf. They had loved her and would miss her sorely.

Now the Edwardian era had begun, the true beginning of the twentieth century. Victoria's long reign had seen bewildering changes in England. At its opening, though the inventions of the Industrial Revolution had already wrought their changes in the North and the Midlands, most of her people had lived in a peaceful, rural tranquillity. In 1800 the population had been less than nine million. With new discoveries in medicine, the development of new techniques in surgery, including the use of anaesthetics, and improved social hygiene, which reduced the danger of infectious diseases, the death rate declined and the population began to rise with startling rapidity. By the year of the queen's accession, in 1837, it was nearly fourteen million, and at her death, by which time Britain had become the greatest industrial and manufacturing country in the world, it was more than thirty-two million. Now the changes were to come ever faster, with a speed which is still accelerating, and producing results which a few far-sighted Victorians had rightly predicted would bring disaster in their train as well as material progress.

In 1901 Great Britain ruled a vast empire and her power seemed invincible. At the beginning of Victoria's reign that empire had been in its infancy. Britain had turned her trade rivals, the French, out of both India and Canada after the Seven Years War in the mid-eighteenth century, and a few years later Captain Cook had claimed for Britain all the lands he touched in the course of his South Sea voyages, including Australia and New Zealand. Britain had lost her American colonies but less than forty years later had taken over Cape Colony from the Dutch, at the end of the Napoleonic wars.

At this time, however, Britain had no imperial policy. The American colonists, the government argued, had shown base ingratitude and

4

colonies appeared to be costly and unrewarding enterprises for which Britain had little use and which she could well do without. Australia was an unexplored continent with a fringe of coastal settlements, used mainly as a convenient dumping ground for convicts. As for Canada, Manitoba, British Columbia and the north-west were an unknown wilderness. The British government would not have minded if the immigrants to these far-distant continents had followed the way of the Americans. Cape Colony was very small but served as a useful trading station and port of call for British ships on their way to India and the Far East. West Africa meant nothing to most people but a chain of widely separated coastal trading stations, with an appalling climate which few Englishmen were able to survive for more than a year or two. In India, territories which Clive had won had been brought under some measure of order by Warren Hastings of the East India Company, but there were constant costly disturbances amongst the Gurkhas and Mahrattas, who bitterly resented the intrusion of foreigners.

Colonies, far from being an asset, were a liability, said the politicians, and trading stations at strategical points throughout the world were all that was needed for the maintenance of Britain's rapidly developing commerce. This opinion became so strong that by 1860 there was a movement from both Conservatives and Liberals for the actual dismemberment of the Empire. However, the politicians had reckoned without the colonists themselves, Englishmen and Scots, Irish and Welsh who for the most part felt strong bonds of loyalty both to Great Britain and the queen. It was Sir John Macdonald who spoke for the conception of the Empire and Disraeli who, to the discomfiture of the Little Englanders, inspired not only his own party but ultimately the whole country with the principle of imperialism.

Britain had lost the American colonies through trying to govern them from London, an ocean's width away from contact and understanding of people, most of whom by this time had been born in America and knew little of the country of their parents and grandparents. As the nineteenth century progressed and the new colonies developed in Australia, New Zealand and Canada, with an ever-increasing flow of immigrants, the British government steered its way through such difficulties as arose with far greater tolerance and success.

In Australia the pioneers on the south-east coast, around Sydney, at last managed to cross the Blue Mountains and make a first settlement in the interior, at Bathurst. By 1839 the transportation of convicts to New South Wales had ceased and the industry of sheep-rearing grew steadily, as more free colonists arrived each year. By 1851, the year of Prince Albert's great exhibition at the Crystal Palace in Hyde Park, New South Wales had a population of 190,000 and Victoria and South Australia each had 77,000. This was the year that gold was discovered in New South Wales and Victoria, giving a sudden impetus to immigration, so that at the peak of the gold rush people were arriving at the rate of two thousand a week. Fifty years later, in 1901, the various colonies of Australia had joined in an independent federation of states, with a governor-general who represented the British Government.

Missionaries and traders had arrived in New Zealand early in the century. By 1840 the first two thousand colonists had arrived and twenty years later, by which time their numbers had risen to 100,000 —most of them engaged, as in Australia, in sheep-rearing and the woollen industry—they received their right of self-government within the Empire.

Canada's history had been turbulent. During the American War of Independence some 35,000 people who remained loyal to Britain had fled there, and the British government had allotted them land, tools and a guarantee of two years' supply of food. The Loyalists settled in Nova Scotia and New Brunswick, south of the French province of Quebec, which had also remained loyal to Britain, and in Ontario to the west. During the Napoleonic wars America invaded Canada, but French and British Canadians united to repulse them. After the war there was serious unemployment in Britain and thousands of Scottish and English emigrants set sail for Canada, in particular for Ontario, but they were soon at loggerheads with the old-established Empire Loyalists. In 1839 William Mackenzie organized a rebellion against the government and a group of French Canadians attempted to establish a French republic on the St. Lawrence. Lord Durham was sent out to report on the situation and advised a union of British and French Canada, with ultimate self-government. The Act of Union was passed in 1840 and Lord Sydenham became the first governor of a united Canada. By 1867 the four provinces of Ontario, Quebec, New Brunswick and Nova Scotia were united in the Dominion of Canada. Manitoba, British Columbia and Prince Edward Island were soon included and in 1878 it was declared that all British possessions in North America, whether inhabited or not, were part of the Dominion.

In India, after the subjugation of the Mahrattas, Britain assumed direct rule in a number of inland states, moved towards a defensible frontier in the north-west and, in the east, conquered Burma. After the Indian Mutiny of 1857 the East India Company was formally disbanded and Queen Victoria declared sovereign of India, twenty years later being proclaimed empress.

It was mainly to protect her interests in India that Britain allowed herself to become involved in the disastrous and tragically futile Crimean War. Imperial Russia was becoming increasingly aggressive and Czar Nicholas I was casting covetous eyes on the crumbling Turkish Empire and Constantinople. In France, after the revolutions, Napoleon III, a nephew of Napoleon Buonaparte, was elected president, and in 1852 became emperor. He set about rebuilding the old, seventeenth-century Paris and then dreamed of a new imperial France. As Russia's designs on Turkey and the Near East became apparent, France viewed them with alarm and Great Britain saw an ultimate threat to India.

Russia reasserted her right to send representatives of the Greek Orthodox Church to Jerusalem, to help protect the Holy Sepulchre and the Chapel of the Nativity. Palestine, however, was part of the Turkish Empire and Turkey had assigned this privilege to the French. The Russian insult to France lit the spark which ignited the Crimean War. France joined with Turkey against Russia. Britain, though having no direct concern with the quarrel between Russia and France, was uncertain of Russia's ultimate motives, and was drawn in on the side of France in order to protect India, while Germany supported Russia. The Crimean War achieved nothing for either side but indicated the direction in which the alignment of the great powers might fall in future struggles to maintain the balance of power in Europe, though in the event it proved to be very different.

In South Africa the story had been troubled since the Napoleonic wars, when the Boers of South Africa, who had been established there since the Dutch East India Company had founded a trading station at the Cape in the seventeenth century, had allied themselves with France. The British had landed and at the Congress of Vienna in 1815, when the war with France was at last over, Cape Colony had been ceded

7

to Great Britain on payment of an indemnity of £6 million to Holland. With the arrival of the first British settlers a few years later, the Boers had trekked northwards into the interior of the continent, resenting both the British themselves and their championship of the rights of the Bantu, to all of whom living in the Cape had been granted, in 1828, every right to which the Europeans were entitled.

The Boers founded the Transvaal and the Orange River Colony, where they declared their intention to live in complete independence, despite insistent reminders from the British government at Cape Town that they were still British subjects. Throughout the nineteenth century there had been incessant quarrels with the Boers over frontier problems and the rights of the Bantu, which were stoutly defended by the Victorian British, particularly the missionaries. At length, after the British defeat at the battle of Majuba Hill in 1880, the Transvaal won its independence and Kruger was proclaimed president of the independent South African Republic.

With the discovery of gold in the eastern Transvaal a few years later, however, and the establishment of the mining town of Johannesburg on the main reef, more trouble had arisen. There was a rush of prospectors and mining engineers from Europe, who brought the Boers undreamed-of prosperity. They sold large tracts of the Transvaal to the immigrants, the Uitlanders, and by 1892 it was estimated that between half and three-quarters of the inhabitants of the country were Uitlanders, paying between them nearly 90 per cent of the taxes, but receiving no civic rights in return. They were given no say in the spending of the money, nor were they allowed to publish their grievances or hold public meetings without permission from the Transvaal government. There was a ten-year residence qualification for naturalization and no Roman Catholic or Jew could ever hope to hold government office. The speaking of English was forbidden at public meetings and amongst older children in the schools. Offenders were not allowed trial by jury.

The Uitlanders appealed in vain to Kruger and then turned to Cecil Rhodes for help. The immediate result was the fiasco of the Jameson raid of 1896, which served only to worsen the lot of the Uitlanders and harden the hearts of the Boers, whose government was controlled increasingly from Holland and each year allied itself more closely with the interests of Germany, which had recently annexed territories in

8

South-west Africa, Cameroon and Togoland. Kruger's government was bigoted and unprogressive and all the appeals of the Uitlanders were rejected. Throughout the summer of 1899 tension mounted. British troops were sent from India to Natal and two battalions were ordered to South Africa from the Mediterranean. On 9th October the Boers sent a note demanding their immediate withdrawal, which was rejected, and two days later war broke out.

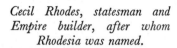

Cecil Rhodes, statesman and Empire builder, after whom Rhodesia was named.

Well equipped and with tenacious courage, the Boer farmers and their sons left their farms and went into battle, planning to attack all the important British towns near their frontiers. They sent a large force against the British garrison in Natal, another to surround Mafeking, where Cecil Rhodes was living, and a third, from the Orange Free State, to the siege of Kimberley. By the end of the month the British had been forced back to Ladysmith, with the enemy pressing from the north, west and east. It was a bitter blow to Britain's imperial pride. General Buller was placed in supreme command of the British forces in South Africa and arrived to find Mafeking and Kimberley besieged and the Ladysmith garrison almost surrounded. The Boers in the Cape were on the point of rebellion and there was news of an impending Dutch invasion to support them.

General Buller at once sent troops to relieve Kimberley and Ladysmith but was obliged to keep back a brigade to protect the Cape. The next month the Dutch invasion took place and in London the full seriousness of the situation was realized at last. To the younger generations of British people this was their first experience of war, the first threat to a lifetime of peaceful security. All reserves were called up. The soldiers of the Queen, in their new khaki uniforms, so much less conspicuous on the parched, dusty South African veld, under its hot blue skies and burning sun, than the scarlet uniforms which had been worn in the Crimea some forty years earlier, were dispatched to South Africa as quickly as possible, and volunteers arrived from Canada, Australia and New Zealand to help the Empire in its trouble.

General Buller collected forces for an attack on the Boers surrounding Ladysmith. He failed to relieve the town but the garrison refused to surrender and hung on. Lord Roberts was now appointed to the supreme command with Lord Kitchener as Chief of Staff. Mafeking, Kimberley and Ladysmith were still in a state of siege, food was running short and the inhabitants becoming weak and ill. In the Cape, General French was holding the Boer invaders at bay and Ladysmith beat off another attack. Buller made a second attempt to relieve Ladysmith but at the battle of Spion Kop he suffered another defeat. He tried a third time and failed, but a few weeks later Lord Roberts managed to fight his way through to the relief of Kimberley. Encouraged by the news, Buller made a fourth attempt on Ladysmith and again failed, but the fifth time he succeeded and the 22,000 people imprisoned there, almost at the end of their endurance, were at last freed. With Kimberley and Ladysmith relieved, the Boers retired from Natal to the mountains and at the same time began a retreat from Cape Colony. In March 1900, Lord Roberts marched into the Orange Free State capital, Bloemfontein, and the country was officially proclaimed to be under British protection. On 1st May he moved into the Transvaal and in less than three weeks Mafeking was relieved.

At the long-awaited news Britain rejoiced, and in the sober lanes and courts of the City of London bankers and merchants, brokers, jobbers and humble clerks linked arms and danced in the streets, flinging their Victorian top hats in the air with joyful abandon. By the beginning of June 1900, Lord Roberts had reached Johannesburg and Kruger had fled with the state documents to Europe. The Transvaal, like the Orange Free State, was made a British possession and the fiercest fighting of the war was over. It dragged on, however, for another two years, in spasmodic guerrilla fighting which was to cost many more lives on both sides.

Lord Kitchener was now left in charge of operations and at the beginning of 1901, as the old queen lay dying, he began a new system of attack. The British gradually gained the upper hand. The gold mines began to work again and a government was established at Johannes-

Lord Roberts, who took command in the war against the Boers.

Paul Kruger, President of the South African Republic at the time of the Boer War.

burg. Kitchener's concentration camps became full of Boers, either captured or surrendered, but all sullen and resentful. By 1902 there were still 25,000 of them in the field against the British army, but another drive by Kitchener at last convinced them that it was useless to hold out any longer. On 23rd March 1902, representatives, still in truculent mood, came to Pretoria to make overtures of peace. Negotiations were difficult and protracted and both sides wearied of the arguing. The Boers insisted that the peace treaty should include the promise of ultimate self-government for the Orange Free State and the Transvaal, and this provision was included and honoured, but they resolutely refused to consider the rights of the Africans in their territories, as the British had done in the Cape. Unfortunately, in the interests of expediency and a desire for a speedy settlement of the quarrels which had brought about the war, Britain did not press the matter. It was dropped and thereby were sown the seeds of the current problems and sufferings in South Africa.

This, then, was the British Empire in 1901. Australia, New Zealand and Canada were loyal and prosperous. India was over-populated and desperately poor, her princes loyal but her people already beginning to dream of ultimate independence. South Africa was still at war but the end was in sight.

Half the world was in British hands, countries which were already yielding bountifully in food and raw materials, but whose vast potential wealth had hardly yet been tapped. Great Britain had become a great commercial and industrial power with ever-increasing millions of industrial and factory workers. She had turned her back on the land and adopted a deliberate policy of importing food from the Empire and America, which with the introduction of refrigeration had become practical and cheap. Half a million labourers were turned off their farms to swell the ranks of industry, but it mattered little to the commercial world and the overall economy of the country, for British manufactured goods were in universal demand and overseas markets assured, not only in the rapidly developing countries of the Empire but in every corner of the world.

The London docks, already the largest in the world, had to be rebuilt, for they had become too small to accommodate the vast flow of traffic which now passed through them: wool, mutton, lamb, cheese and butter from New Zealand and Australia; beef from the Argentine; coffee from Brazil; wheat and timber from Canada; wheat and tobacco from America; sugar, bananas and rum from the West Indies; tea from India and Ceylon; wines and fruits from the countries of southern Europe; the mahogany so well loved by Victorian furniture makers from West Africa; the ostrich feathers, ivory and tortoiseshell which were so popular from South Africa; and carpets from India, Persia, Turkey and China. From London and other ports of Great Britain went manufactured goods of all kinds, cotton and woollen cloth, machinery, hardware,

> Road-rail, pig-lead,
> Firewood, iron-ware, and cheap tin trays.

The City of London was the financial centre of this enormous trade, providing sterling capital and doing business throughout the world. Lloyd's provided the insurance cover, the Baltic Exchange arranged the shipping. The London bullion market fixed the price of gold and all the nations of the earth found that British sterling was the most convenient currency in which to do their business and their shopping. The merchant bankers of London, Baring, Schroeder, Lazard and Rothschild, skilfully playing the markets on the London Stock Exchange, grew enormously rich and provided money for the floating of new companies and commercial enterprises in whatever part of the globe they might be needed. It was London money which financed the building of the Trans-Caucasian railway for Russia and supplied the capital for industrial development in South America, China and many of the countries of Europe. The whole world was quickly awakening to the demands of the new century and at this moment of time it was to the City of London it turned for financial help.

This was Britain at the turn of the century—wealthy, busy, powerful, the workshop of the world and the hub of a great empire. In international politics, apart from a few foreign trade agreements, her Unionist government under Lord Salisbury, of Conservatives supported by Liberal Unionists, was following a policy of isolationism. Britain had no need of foreign alliances for she was supreme and impregnable. The only forms of enemy attack she then knew were by land or sea. With a mighty navy to safeguard her island shores, she was far safer than any country in Europe which was compelled to maintain a large army to defend its frontiers.

CHAPTER TWO

The People

Social history, which is an account of changing manners, customs and material culture, is also a record of people's intellectual and spiritual development, and their changing attitudes to their families, their work, their country, their Church and their fellow men. The infinite ramifications of the mechanical inventions of the Industrial Revolution and the subsequent sudden increase in the speed of communication came too quickly for many English people to assimilate, except after many years, the full significance of the social revolution which must inevitably follow it. Come it did, however, at first with painful slowness, but with steadily growing momentum.

By the end of the nineteenth century, though the material foundations of the twentieth-century way of life had been firmly laid, the spiritual and mental progress of the British people into the new age was extremely uneven, as indeed it still is. To understand the tensions and problems of the present time, we must know something of the origins of the revolution through which Britain has been passing.

At the end of Victorian times and throughout the Edwardian era Britain was still a class-conscious country, the various sections of the community being sharply divided by birth, wealth and education. Social classes have never been inflexible. They were brought about in the first place by people with superior mental and physical abilities conquering by force those less well endowed by nature. It was the natural law of the survival of the fittest, which has no regard for the fairness of life nor for the doctrine that citizens have a responsibility to the State and the State to its citizens. With sufficient money and wits and the right personality it was never particularly difficult to rise in the social scale, provided one had the ability to assimilate and ape the behaviour of one's betters. This was never more true than during the nineteenth century, when large fortunes were being made very quickly. It was always easier to lose one's money and sink, of course, but once one had attained a certain level in the hierarchy one did one's best not only to stay there but to rise, if possible, even higher; and though the movement from class to class was possible, the classes themselves remained as clearly discernible strata.

At the top of the social scale were the nobility and great landowners, for ownership of land on a large scale remained the highest social distinction. These were the families who, during the eighteenth century, before the country became a democracy, had, with the guidance of Parliament, ruled Britain.

WANT OF FINISH.

"I SHALL REALLY HAVE TO PART WITH YOU, SUSAN. YOU'RE SO SKETCHY IN YOUR DUSTING!"

© *Punch*

The Servant problem in Victorian times

15

It has been estimated that in 1900 one in ten of the population were domestic servants and of the two million women between 15 and 25 who were in employment more than a third were in service. For girls of the labouring classes born in the country, or in towns where there were no factories or industries to give them work, there were few other ways of earning a living. Their wages were low and for their employers income tax was only a shilling in the pound. The moneyed classes of England were therefore able to live in a high degree of comfort. In the great houses of the aristocracy, most of which are today in the care of the National Trust, it was not unusual for forty or more indoor servants to be employed, as well as an army of gardeners and labourers for the adjoining estates, and the owners were able to maintain their households in much the same feudal splendour as their ancestors had enjoyed.

Below the nobility were the rich upper classes of Britain. These were the lesser landowners, the squires and members of the county families, and ranking equally with them were the members of some of the professions; and most of these people were able to run their smaller establishments at the same high level of comfort. The sons of this upper crust of British society were sent to the public schools and afterwards to the university, for they usually entered one of the accepted professions. The daughters, more often than not, were taught at home by governesses, learning a little French and music and a certain amount of housekeeping. They were also trained to administer to the poor, as part of their social duty, so that by the time they left the schoolroom they were ready to become the wives of neighbouring squires, of officers in the army or navy, of Indian or Colonial civil servants, of university professors or teachers in public schools, of clergymen, barristers or doctors.

It was from this class that the civil servants and administrators who served Britain so well during the days of her Empire were drawn. Though there are back-sliders in every section of the community, on the whole they created and maintained a tradition of personal integrity which won them universal respect. The best of them were incorruptible. They showed remarkable self-control in time of personal danger, had a keen sense of justice and acted with responsibility and humanity to those whose government and well-being had been assigned to them. Combined with these qualities which distinguished them as a class there was about most of them an arresting individualism. Some were to ridicule this tradition, or to become enraged by it, but it could not be ignored, and later generations, bewildered by contemporary examples of human behaviour, have come to realize that the capacity for disciplined, selfless service, arising from something more spiritual than logic, the rules of a trade union and the basic instinct for self-preservation, has about it an enviable quality of simple faith and goodness which has nothing to do with self-righteousness.

A solid Victorian villa with attic and basement accommodation for the servants.

The middle classes had their own subdivisions. The upper strata were usually wealthier but less well educated than those above them, having made their money in the mills and mines and speculation of industry. Their newly built houses were often as large as, if not larger than, those of the upper classes, and they employed as many servants. Their children developed according to their mental abilities and personalities. Some, taking advantage of the education they were now able to receive, moved without any trouble into the upper classes— sometimes by marriage, sometimes by entering one of the professions, sometimes merely by living on first-generation inherited wealth.

Others followed their fathers into the family industries and businesses and created their own middle-class social world.

The women of all these social classes, living in large houses, supplied with competent housekeepers who allotted the lesser servants their duties, with lady's maids for their personal needs and a nursery staff to care for their children, had no household duties at all. It was a point of correct social behaviour to attend Sunday morning service regularly and extend patronage to the vicar. For the rest of the week the greater part of their time was occupied in entertaining and being entertained in return.

The older-established county families still took a genuine interest in their estate employees and the villagers, maintaining something of the eighteenth-century comradeship which had existed so strongly; and the villagers in return regarded the people of the big house as real friends and counsellors. However, as the rich grew richer and people with a town tradition moved into the rural areas, to establish themselves as the new gentry—the poor meanwhile remaining as poor as they had ever been—the gap between them widened, and by 1900 had become a gulf which no amount of dutiful dispensation of charity from the gentry could bridge. The contrast in their fortunes was too sharp for any points of contact or common interest to survive.

The London summer season, which has been described as an "orgy of human intercourse", was usually part of the social programme of these upper classes, the majority following as closely as possible the pattern set by the elect few who actually visited the Court. The season consisted of a round of sociability and gaiety, of luncheon parties, the morning and late afternoon parades in Hyde Park, either riding or driving in an open carriage, dinner parties, balls and receptions, visits to the Royal Academy, to Epsom and the summer race meetings, to the opera at Covent Garden and the theatres. With the end of summer there were visits to Scotland and to Europe, till it was time to return to the country for the opening of the hunting season, with its attendant hunt balls and parties.

It was a good life while it lasted, a survival of the days of leisured elegance enjoyed by the favoured few at Bath during the eighteenth century and in the days of the Regency at Brighton, till its exclusiveness was ruined by the vulgarity of the railway. These people of fashion at the turn of the twentieth century did not glance backwards, however, to appreciate that a way of existence such as theirs, based on the labours of the unconsidered lower orders and financed by money which they had not themselves earned, has never, in the whole of human history, survived for more than a few generations; and few of them cared to look ahead, where they would have seen every reason why it was shortly to change.

The heavily furnished Victorian parlour.

The core of the middle classes—merchants, owners of small but prospering businesses and shops, members of some of the less socially acceptable professions and lower-grade civil servants, living on perhaps a tenth or less of the incomes of the rich—strove to achieve the same pattern of security, formality and comfort. The Victorian villas built for these people in the suburbs of London, in Pimlico, Kensington, Bayswater and Hampstead, as well as the outskirts of all the big towns and cities throughout the country, were solid and pretentious, with pillared porticoes and spacious rooms on the ground and first floors —though the basement kitchens and attic bedrooms between which the three or four servants, the cook, the parlourmaid, the tweeny and the nursemaid divided their time were dark, cheerless and barely furnished. At all costs a semblance of prosperity and decorum must be maintained, and here again the mistress of the household had little occasion to soil her hands with household duties, for the servants cleaned the house, the cook prepared the meals and the nursemaid took charge of the children, while tradesmen always called for orders and delivered them.

It was a comfortable way of life for those born "above stairs" and the social round of calls, the tea parties, dinner parties, visits to the theatre and occasional seaside holidays, with all their attendant etiquette, made up an existence which, if dulled by its very security, was nevertheless untroubled, so far as any human being can ever achieve that rare state. For people of this social stratum living in the country, life was even more spacious, for servants were as easy to come by and living and amusements simpler and cheaper. Even in the humbler households of the lower middle classes, which comprised the clerks, the lower-grade civil servants, the teachers, the shopkeepers and the black-coated proletariat, there was nearly always a resident servant, a cook-general, who, though grossly overworked and underpaid, served to elevate her mistress to the dignity of an employer and made her a faint image of her more prosperous sisters.

All these sections of the community, from the lowest of the middle classes upwards, strove to copy, to the best of their ability, the manners and customs, the dress and household furnishings of the class immediately above them, for "keeping up with the Joneses" was a national pastime. At the bottom of this social structure, however, well below any real human contact and understanding, existed the bulk of England's population. They were the untouchables, the unconsidered poor, whose numbers were so vast that some foretold that, if they were not kept in their place, they might one day threaten the financial security of the entire country.

These lowest classes were the artisans, the factory workers, the miners and industrial workers, the fishermen, the farm hands, the dockers, the sempstresses and domestic servants, the shop assistants and a large and murky residue of casual labourers and vagrants. They worked incredibly long hours for starvation wages, they had little or no education and were appallingly badly housed. When they fell out of work there was no unemployment pay. They had little money for medical attention and there were no pensions for old age.

The consciences of many Victorians had been roused by the terrible inequalities in the distribution of wealth, and throughout the nineteenth century reforms had been made, not only by philanthropic individuals and societies, but also by succeeding governments, both Conservative and Liberal, which were to lead in time to the establishment of the Welfare State of today. Nevertheless, there were many from

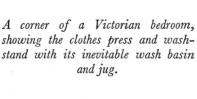

A corner of a Victorian bedroom, showing the clothes press and washstand with its inevitable wash basin and jug.

all walks of life, from the rich to the working classes themselves, who accepted the state of the poor unquestioningly, believing that the position in life to which one was born was part of the plan of an all-wise God, whose ways should not be questioned. Wealth was regarded as almost a divine right and poverty and misfortune a burden to be borne without demur, tempered by the debatable solace that things might be better in the next world. There had been a strong religious revival in the mid-nineteenth century and people were still singing with fervent conviction:

> The rich man in his castle,
> The poor man at his gate,
> God made them high and lowly,
> And ordered their estate.

21

This last line was an unwarrantable assumption on the part of the hymn-writer but a highly convenient argument for those who disliked the implications involved in the newer conception of the human race that

> ... the Colonel's Lady and Judy O'Grady
> Are sisters under their skins!

In the life of the people there was no obviously sudden and revolutionary change on the death of Queen Victoria and the accession of Edward VII. The social reforms of the twentieth century had had their beginnings quite early in the nineteenth century, for the new spirit of freedom was rustling through all sections of the community, as one by one the new scientific inventions became accepted and wrought their change in the pace of life, widening horizons and stimulating the imagination, dreams and ambitions of the people. The trouble was that while the equilibrium of society seemed to be superficially maintained many people deliberately turned a blind eye to the signs of any break in the smooth surface of life, caused by the seething resentment of the oppressed workers from below, and preferred to push the trouble out of sight rather than give it an honest examination.

The two pieces of legislation which legally transformed Britain into a democracy were the Parliamentary Reform Bills of 1832 and 1867. At the time of the passing of the earlier bill less than half a million people were entitled to vote out of a population of fourteen million, and none of the newly developed industrial regions had any parliamentary representation at all. After bitter argument and many postponements the 1832 Reform Bill was passed, but it proved a sore disappointment, for although 143 new seats were created in Parliament for the boroughs which hitherto had had no representation, people still were not allowed to vote unless they possessed a certain minimum of property. As the bulk of the population possessed nothing but their weekly wage, which was spent to the last halfpenny by the time the next pay day came round, the Bill brought in less than a quarter of a million new voters and those who most needed help from the Government still had no means of making themselves heard by constitutional means.

The appalling sufferings of the unemployed in England after the Napoleonic wars, when at one time one person in eleven was receiving Poor Relief, led to the Chartist riots of the 1840's, which many feared would end in civil war. The riots were suppressed before this happened and the poor continued to suffer and starve. During the middle years of the nineteenth century, when for the upper and middle classes life was so pleasant and prosperous and the new scientific inventions and improved social amenities so diverting and enjoyable, the bulk of the population was crying out for enough money for the bare necessities of survival, food, fuel and clothing. Their living conditions remained a disgrace until well into the twentieth century and in some parts of the country have still a very long way to go before they can compare favourably with modern standards.

The first move to improve matters came after the publication of the report of the Children's Employment Commission in 1842. It described how married women worked for twelve hours or more of the day down in the mines and then spent half the night washing and cooking and trying to clean their pathetically sordid little homes. Children were taken down the mines to work, usually at the age of eight or nine, but sometimes when they were only four or five, and both women and small children were employed to carry heavy baskets of coal on their backs. The mining children usually worked twelve to sixteen hours a day below ground, but when cases were found of children who had remained in the pits for thirty-six hours at a stretch and of girls of six years old who had been ordered to carry half-hundredweights of coal, Victorian consciences were startled and shocked into action. The Mines Bill made it illegal for boys under ten years of age to work in the pits or for women and girls to be employed underground at all, but the lot of the miners as a whole remained soul-destroying and hopeless; with no amenities or medical attention, they worked below ground for twelve to fourteen hours a day, and the majority contracted silicosis or tuberculosis and died before they were forty-five.

Factory conditions were no better. At the stocking-weaving factory at Hinckley, for example, where both parents and their children were employed, the average earnings for the entire family were 11s. 4d. a week. They lived on nothing but bread and porridge and were forced to work for seven days a week to avoid actual starvation; and in the sheds and cellars where they slept they could afford no beds. The nail workers of Sedgeley, who were paid at the rate of $5\frac{3}{4}$d. for the manufacture of 1,200 nails, each of which required twelve blows from a heavy hammer, were found living on the meat of diseased animals

23

which had been discarded for normal human consumption. The knife-grinders of Sheffield, working continuously in a bent position and inhaling metal dust particles, died in their late twenties or early thirties. Men, women and children in the potteries spent long hours dipping finished pots into fluids containing lead and arsenic. Their hands and clothing were always wet and their skin became softened and sore. Into the wounds the lead and arsenic gradually penetrated and within a few years they became victims of paralysis, epilepsy and tuberculosis or died of poisoning. The lace-making industry of Nottingham employed children of seven or even younger as runners, their work being to follow the threads in the elaborate patterns of lace, destined to adorn some Victorian drawing room, and withdraw them with a needle. The work was so detailed and fine that after a few years many of the children became incurably blind. The bobbin lacemakers were usually very young girls. They had to sit for hours bent almost double over their cushions, and as they wore stays with wooden busks, their ribs became displaced and they usually died early of consumption.

The makers of neckties contracted to work sixteen hours a day for 4s. 6d. a week, and shirtmakers, working from four or five in the morning till midnight, received 2s. 6d. to 3s a week. Dressmakers worked in similar intolerable conditions, in workrooms which were ill-lit and cold. In 1843 there were fifteen thousand dressmakers working at their employers' places of business in London alone. If they lived in, they had to pay a premium of £50 to £60 and were lodged and fed by their employers. Otherwise they paid no premium but had to keep themselves. In the best establishments the hours of work were half past eight in the morning till eleven o'clock at night in the winter, and eight in the morning till midnight or one o'clock the following morning in the summer, with an hour or two's overtime on Saturdays. The meal breaks were ten minutes for breakfast, fifteen to twenty minutes for dinner and fifteen minutes for tea. Supper, if they were lucky enough to have any, was served in the workroom. The girls never stood the strain for long. Those who did not marry, or find other work, broke down in health, usually dying of consumption, and the system was maintained only by a constant supply of fresh girls from the country.

> With fingers weary and worn,
> With eyelids heavy and red,

A woman sat, in unwomanly rags,
    Plying her needle and thread—
        Stitch! stitch! stitch!
In poverty, hunger, and dirt,
    And still with a voice of dolorous pitch
She sang the "Song of the Shirt"!

So wrote Tom Hood in 1843, pleading the cause of the dressmakers, as Elizabeth Barrett Browning did the cause of the child industrial workers in her poem "The Cry of the Children", while in the novels of Dickens are described the plight of nearly all the members of the labouring classes in the mid-nineteenth century.

Their housing was disgraceful, most of the industrial workers of the North and the Midlands living in the squalid little back-to-back cottages, devoid of the simplest amenities, which had been thrown up quickly by speculative builders about the time of the Napoleonic wars. In Glasgow, Edinburgh and Manchester the slums were appalling and Engels in his account of *The Conditions Of The Working Classes In England In 1844* wrote that "in London fifty thousand persons get up every morning not knowing where to lay their heads at night." Few Londoners who were not forced there by grim necessity had ever visited the Refuge for the Homeless in Upper Ogle Street, behind the Euston Road, which had been intended to accommodate three hundred people and where nearly three thousand flocked each night, or the Rookery around St. Giles's Church, where people could hire in one of the lodging houses a whole bed for sixpence a night, a half-bed for fourpence or a pile of straw for twopence.

After the Poor Law Act of 1834 many more workhouses were built and these were the only alternative for the destitute, but they were hated and dreaded. Families were separated and it was not till 1847 that husbands and wives of over sixty years of age were allowed to live together under the same roof.

It was in protest at these conditions that the trade union movement came into being. It was sternly repressed at every stage, as being dangerously Jacobin, but it gained strength through its persecution. In 1833, when six farm labourers from Tolpuddle in Dorsetshire met to plan an appeal to their employer for an increase in wages from 9s. to 10s. a week, they were arrested, brought to trial, found guilty of forming an illegal union and sentenced to deportation, but public outcry was so strong that within two years they were pardoned and brought back to England.

No government pressure could now stop the formation of unions and with their increasing strength came fresh demands for parliamentary representation. At the same time, all sections of the community were realizing the necessity for better education. Unions were at last recognized as legal bodies and in 1861 the first Trades Union Congress was held, but the method of "collective bargaining" supported by strikes was still illegal and punishable by imprisonment. In 1867 the Second Parliamentary Reform Bill gave workers in industrial areas the long-awaited right to vote, irrespective of any property qualification, and in 1875 the trade unions were further strengthened by being given a legal right to strike, it being laid down that "no act committed by a group of workers in furtherance of a trade dispute should be punishable unless it was a criminal act committed by an individual". In 1884 agricultural workers were given the vote, though all representations by women for a similar privilege were sternly rejected as being foolish, presumptuous and unwomanly.

Early in the century, though the number of public, grammar and private schools for boys was steadily increasing, there were few schools for girls, and the only chance for the poor to receive any education was offered by independent philanthropic and religious bodies, the British and Foreign School Society, the National Society for Promoting the Education of the Poor in the Principles of the Church of England, the Voluntary School Society, the Congregational Board of Education and the Ragged School Union. They obtained their funds from charity and charged the pupils a few coppers each week to help cover expenses.

The first indication that the Government was prepared to assume responsibility for education came with an education grant to these societies in 1833, but not till 1870 was the decisive step of the Elementary Education Act taken, which provided for the elementary education of every child in the country, with possibilities of secondary education for those with sufficient ability to profit by it. That year the Metropolitan School Board was set up and three years later the first elementary school was opened in Whitechapel. By 1900 an adequate supply of these schools had been built throughout the country and in London alone there were 481. In 1899 a Board of Education was created and by the Education Act of 1902 the control of elementary schools was given to the county, borough and urban district councils. During these years of increasing interest in education, the curricula of the public and private schools were overhauled and the teaching of mathematics, the natural sciences and modern languages introduced, to bring the education more into line with modern living.

A musical "At Home" in the 1890's.

And at last, though it was to be many years before they received the vote, something was done about the position of women in society. Working-class women in England invariably had to work for their livings, both before and after marriage, in order to obtain the bare necessities of life, but in the other social spheres girls and young women remained at home, waiting for a husband to appear. In the upper classes they were prepared for the marriage market by being "brought out" during the London season. Lower down the social scale matters were left more to chance, but it was usually a great relief to the parents when the girls were comfortably settled in life. They had little educa-

3

tion or training for outside employment and in any case there were hardly any openings for them, for it was ungenteel for a girl to earn her living and her whole life was directed to the one end of marriage.

"Women's most charming study is the modest, the winning display of those accomplishments that increase the magic of their charms, their dearest employment is gracefully to flit through all the mazes of the labyrinth of love; and the noblest aim of their existence is to generate beings who, as women, may tread in the footsteps of their mothers, or, as men, may excel in the higher virtues which . . . it is impossible that they themselves should attain," wrote one Victorian.

Some women accepted the indignity of this position with unthinking docility but an increasing number came to resent it bitterly. "Whenever I have seen, not merely in humble, but in affluent homes, families of daughters sitting waiting to be married," said Charlotte Brontë, "I have pitied them from my heart."

Throughout the nineteenth century the number of women in excess of men gradually increased and by 1900 there were thirty-six extra women in every thousand of the population, so it was obvious they could not all marry. In 1881, amongst women over twenty, 602 in every thousand were married. In 1891 the figure was down to 584 and by the beginning of the twentieth century it was 576. For girls seeking work because they had become orphaned or because, through some financial disaster, their parents could no longer afford to keep them at home, the prospects were bleak. They were still told that woman's place was in the home, but dogmatic statements of this kind were of no help to women faced with the problem of keeping alive. Some went as companions to wealthier relations or became governesses, where life was divided between a bleak back bedroom and the schoolroom, to which "her meals are brought to her by the servants who despise her for not being one of them and yet not being of the Family. At the very best she is paid £30 a year; at the worst she may have had to advance £50 for the privilege of having a 'comfortable home', which will be repaid in instalments as a salary."[1]

In 1869 this advertisement appeared in the *Daily Telegraph*. "Wanted. Daily Governess. Hours ten to six. For three children aged eight, ten and eleven. Requirements English, French, Music and

[1] Alison Adburgham, *A Punch History of Manners and Modes* (Hutchinson, 1961).

Needlework (and perhaps Drawing). Salary to commence at seven shillings per week." And as late as 1900 the *Irish Times* carried an advertisement for a "Distressed Lady, to mind and attend Elderly Lady and make herself generally useful about house: salary £7 to £8 a year to suitable person."

These were the conditions that gave rise to the feminist movement. It began slowly and painfully, enduring ridicule from the press, from most men and also from many women whose economic security seemed assured. Its aims were to provide proper education for girls, to open avenues of employment for them and to win them the right to a parliamentary vote.

The Society for Promoting the Employment of Women came into being. Queen's College, Harley Street, was founded in 1843 and a few years later the Ladies' College in Bedford Square. Miss Buss opened the North London Collegiate School for Girls and in 1858 Miss Beale was appointed headmistress of the new Ladies' College at Cheltenham. By 1872 the Girls' Public Day School Trust had been founded. Girton College was established at Cambridge and soon afterwards Newnham and the London School of Medicine for Women, as well as the women's colleges at Oxford. The prejudice that girls did not have the same mental capacity as boys died hard and anxious parents frequently argued that as men did not like clever women, girls with the new education would find it difficult to acquire husbands. Nevertheless the demand for education grew. An increasing number of women found themselves obliged to earn their own livings and others, not driven entirely by economic necessity, became eager to break away from the monotony of a spinster's sheltered life, in the home of her parents, and enter some form of employment. With the economic privations of spinsterhood alleviated, more women came to regard marriage, in the words of Miss Beale, "not as an object to be striven for, but to be received as the supreme grace of fate when the right time and the right person came".

In 1886, at the Oxford Conference of the Headmistresses' Association, a report was read on Occupations of Women, Other Than Teaching. By this time forty women had qualified and registered as medical practitioners and 170 had become dispensers. Some had trained as dental mechanics and masseuses, and 318 were employed as prison officers, though "gentlewomen did not often apply for these posts".

There was little scope in literary work, but the London, Edinburgh and Dublin post offices between them now employed 1,677 women clerks. Business houses were employing women book-keepers and the demand for them was increasing. They were employed by the Prudential Assurance Company, and bankers, accountants and stockbrokers were beginning to show a preference for women clerks. There was a demand for trained hospital nurses as well as private nurses and also for matrons and housekeepers, and women were increasingly employed as shop assistants.

A few years later, with the introduction of the telephone and the typewriter, the opportunity for women's employment quickly widened, but the idea of giving them the vote was still rejected. In 1870 Queen Victoria had written to Mr. Theodore Martin:

> The Queen is most anxious to enlist everyone who can speak or write in checking this mad, wicked folly of "Women's Rights", with all its attendant horrors, on which her poor, feeble sex is bent forgetting every sense of womanly feeling and propriety. Lady —— ought to get a good whipping.

However, the movement slowly gathered strength, and though women's suffrage was not to be won till well into the twentieth century, the Married Women's Property Act gave her at least the right to her own money, whether earned or inherited, which hitherto had belonged, like her person, to her husband. She was well advanced on the path to social freedom.

CHAPTER THREE

The Opening of the Twentieth Century

Of the amenities of scientific invention which we now use every day gas has probably the oldest history, for gas lighting was demonstrated in England as early as 1805, though there were many difficulties to be overcome before it was generally introduced into people's homes. However, by 1840 the Gas Light and Coke Company had been formed and was prepared to carry gas wherever its pipes would reach. Some country houses installed their own gas plants and at the Great Exhibition of 1851 the earliest gas cookers were on display.

The first railways were built in England early in the nineteenth century. Even before Waterloo a steam engine, the Puffing Billy, had been invented and used successfully at one of the collieries near Newcastle-upon-Tyne to carry coal from the pithead. In 1825 the first goods railway was opened, to make the short run from Stockton to Darlington, at a speed of sixteen miles an hour, and in 1830 Stephenson's Rocket was used to inaugurate the first passenger service between Liverpool and Manchester. Then Liverpool was joined to Birmingham by rail. Gradually, throughout the 1830's, a network of railways spread over the north of England, linking the most important industrial centres and proving a boon for the transport of coal and the other equipment of heavy industry, as well as a much appreciated convenience for passengers, despite the fact that the early railway carriages were open-sided, with only a canopy to protect them from the weather.

The canals were still busy but their decline in importance was inevitable, and horse transport was also doomed. After the railways reached London and the South, the mail coaches made gallant efforts, in speed and efficiency, to compete with them, but it was a losing battle from the outset and they did not survive for long. In 1841 the railway between Victoria and Brighton was opened, the journey taking at first from two to two-and-a-half hours. The first class fare was 14s. 6d., the second class fare 9s. 6d. and the third class 3s. 6d. It was expensive but well worth the novelty and adventure, and many people now saw the sea for the first time. The craze for sea-bathing had begun in the days of the Regency, amongst the élite of Brighton visitors, but now it was available to everybody. The towns of the south coast became extremely popular and it was at this period that many of them were developed and rebuilt.

Almost at the same time as the building of the first railways the first electric telegraph service was set up, in 1838, by Wheatstone and Cooke, and it proved almost essential in the efficient working of the new railway systems. By the end of the 1840's three thousand miles of railway had telegraph wires running alongside them and soon practically all the railways were equipped with telegraph wires.

In America, Morse and his friend Vail were working on their own electro-magnetic telegraph at this time and devising the Morse code. Morse had a hard struggle and many disappointments before the value of his work was recognized, but gradually the new telegraph wires spread over America, and in 1845 the various small companies which had come into being for the promotion of the telegraph were amalgamated in the Western Union. In Britain the Morse telegraph superseded the older and clumsier Wheatstone system. Telegraph lines now united whole continents and in 1858 the first Atlantic cable was laid.

With the appearance of the first railways England was seized by the great railway mania. Innumerable small railway companies were floated, some for the financing of such short lengths of line that they could never have become profitable concerns. By the autumn of 1845 no less than 357 new schemes were being advertised in the newspapers, inviting new shareholders for £332 million of investment. Nearly everyone with a few pounds to spare bought railway shares. Some lost everything. Others made fortunes, and outstanding amongst them was George Hudson, the Railway King, who by investing a legacy in North Midland Railways became so rich that he was able to buy a London mansion and gain entry into the exclusive circle of London society for a while.

The boom did not last. Many companies failed and their shareholders were ruined, amongst the casualties being George Hudson himself. However, some of the more stable companies survived and by the middle of the century there were some five thousand miles of railroad across Britain. The train had become the normal way of travel for long distances. In country districts, which the railways had not yet reached, ponies and traps, gigs, wagonettes, pony carts and landaus were to survive for many years to come, and in the big cities hansoms, growlers and horse omnibuses were the accepted method of transport, while horses were still used for carts and drays, ploughs and barges.

In 1863 London's Metropolitan underground steam-driven railway came into service, but by 1891 there was an even more startling innovation, the electric motor. That year the City and South London railway was opened, the first electric tube railway in the world, for England was still ahead in mechanical invention as well as industry.

As steam engines became more efficient, at the end of the eighteenth century, inventors set about trying to adapt them to the propelling of ships as well as locomotives. The American inventor Robert Fulton was first in the field with his North River steam boat. By 1825 the General Steam Navigation Company of Britain had fifteen small steamers trading between London and Europe and in 1840 the Cunarder *Britannia* was making the Atlantic crossing in fourteen days and iron ships were being built; but the great tea and wool clippers—the windjammers—were still in service on the high seas, the days of their decline beginning with the opening of the Suez Canal in 1869. For another twenty years these lovely ships continued their long journeys to the East, gallantly defying the competition of steam, but by 1890 the battle was over and the windjammers were seen no more.

During the Napoleonic wars and before the invention of his steam boat, Fulton had been in France, where he invented a submarine for the French government. The idea of an underwater vessel was not new but it had never before become so practical. Fulton's *Nautilus* comprised a watertight hull some twenty feet long and six feet wide, with a rounded, glass-sided conning tower. The keel was a large tank with water ballast which could be varied to make her submerge or surface. It was manned by a crew of three and the weapon was a looped metal spike protruding vertically from the conning tower. In action the submarine would steer beneath the keel of the enemy ship and the spike would be driven into it. A rope attached to the spike was towed away and at a safe distance a mine consisting of a copper barrel containing a hundred pounds of gunpowder was hauled back to the keel and fired.

Fulton demonstrated this device to the French government and they were suitably impressed, but in the end they rejected it, for some members condemned it as being too barbarous. Whether this was out of consideration for their enemies, the British, or whether they felt that the British, having once suffered from it, would quickly retaliate, history does not relate.

The fascination of being airborne had long occupied men's minds. Leonardo da Vinci made some of the earliest experiments with balloons and flying machines, during the fifteenth and early sixteenth centuries, but the first recorded successful invention of a balloon was at the end of the eighteenth century. John Sackville, the Duke of Dorset, who was the British ambassador to Paris, wrote to London in one of his dispatches of a "very extraordinary proposal" made to the French government by a Monsieur Montgolfier to construct a balloon to carry sixteen persons. "The project is to carry on a trade between this part and the south of France; Paris and Marseilles are the two places named. The balloon is to be freighted with plate glass, and the return to be made with reams of paper."

Later the duke wrote that "Great credit is given to Monsieur Montgolfier's superior skill in these matters and that gentleman's friends are sanguine in their expectations of his success. The weight he proposes to carry *exceeds that of a waggon-load*!" In further letters he declares that Monsieur Montgolfier "pretends to have at last discovered the means of directing the course of balloons" and that he "engages to depart from a town in Auvergne, distant from Paris 150 miles, and to descend at or near the City in the space of seven hours."

Montgolfier obtained money for his experiment from an unwilling French government only on a threat, according to the duke, that he would offer his invention to England if they failed him, but Louis XVI showed great interest in his work and came to see it, thereby starting a brief craze in France for the art of ballooning.

The early experiments which Montgolfier had made with his younger brother were highly ingenious but fraught with the most frightful hazards. Working on the principle that hot air expands and rises, they had constructed a large, spherical bag, thirty-five feet in diameter, of silk-covered paper. Attached below was a basket for a fire, the fuel for which was straw and rags, and also some four hundred pounds of ballast. When the fire was lit, the hot air caused the bag to inflate, and when the mooring ropes were released the balloon soared into the air, belching forth flames and smoke. At the first experiment the balloon was carried by the wind for over a mile before it came to earth again. When the first intrepid human passenger, de Rozier, ventured up he was able to control the height of the balloon by regulating the fuel supply and adjusting the ballast. In a journey of some five miles he achieved a height of 1,500 feet, but with this type of

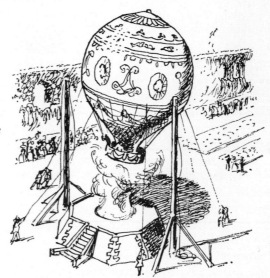

The hazardous ascent of the Montgolfier balloon.

balloon, the journey, even if it were not ended prematurely by the whole contraption catching fire, was obviously limited because of the bulky nature of the fuel it carried.

Other French scientists made experiments with hydrogen-filled balloons, thus dispensing with the dangerous fire, but once the ballast had been thrown out and the hydrogen released, in the process of controlling its height, the journey was inevitably over. The trouble with both these types of balloon was that they could not be navigated, so Montgolfier's plan to introduce a freight service never materialized and the Duke of Dorset's scepticism was not unjustified. However, captive balloons were used during the Napoleonic wars, and towards the end of the nineteenth century guided balloons were devised. Experiments continued and in 1875 a voyage of five hundred miles was made in a balloon which reached a height of 26,000 feet.

35

The first bicycle was also invented by a Frenchman, as long ago as 1867. It was a cumbersome affair of wood and iron and though a few reached England little interest was shown in them at first. Some twenty years later, however, a new design was manufactured in Coventry. The new models were made of steel, with at first solid rubber and later pneumatic tyres. They were far easier to ride than

Ethel: "I hope Bicycling will go out of fashion before next Season. I do hate Bicycling so!"
Maud: "So do I! But one *must*, you know!"

© *Punch*

When cycling was High Fashion.

the old bone-shakers and penny-farthings and a good deal safer and more comfortable.

The fashion for cycling caught on, but at first only amongst the rich and leisured. "When the vogue began", writes Ralph Dutton, "bicycles were treated much as if they had been horses. The machine was sent in the charge of a footman to Battersea Park or Regent's Park, whither the owner would drive in her carriage. Arrived at her destination she would leave her victoria and with a good deal of ceremony mount her machine, and ride gracefully round and round on the broad, smooth roads. The exercise over, the bicycle was handed back to the keeping of the footman, and the lady would return home as she had come. The simple pleasure of bicycling entailed at that time a good deal of work on the part of a devotee's staff."[1]

This was in the 1890's, when women were just beginning to gain their freedom. The crinolines had disappeared twenty years earlier and now the bustles which had followed them, though women were still tightly corseted and their skirts still swept the ground. The rational dress which Mrs. Bloomer had advocated in America as early as 1849 had never caught on.

Bloomerism was described as "A sort of shemale dress . . . : trousers tight at ankles and for most part frilled; tunic descending with some degree of brevity, perhaps to the knees, ascending to throat and open at chemisette front, or buttoned there. Collar down-turned over neckerchief; and, crowning all, broad-brimmed hat, feathered, trimmed, ribboned, variegated, according to the fancies and vanities."[2] With the bicycling craze an attempt was made to revive Bloomerism and some women appeared in knickerbockers and Norfolk jackets, shirts and ties, flat straw hats or trilbys, black stockings and flat-heeled shoes; but by far the greater number cycled in their tight-waisted, long, full skirts, tightly fitting bodices with full sleeves and much betrimmed hats.

Interest in bicycling quickly spread to the less exclusive members of society. With wages rising, under pressure from the trade unions, more and more people could afford the new freewheel model which now appeared on the market. Cycling became an accepted form of transport and the Cyclists Touring Club was formed, affording infinite pleasure to thousands who now had the opportunity to explore the English countryside for the first time.

For the rich there was a new diversion—the motor car. With the invention of steam-driven locomotives early in the nineteenth century steam-driven carriages had been devised, which had attained a speed of thirty miles an hour along level roads, and by the 1830's a steam

[1] Ralph Dutton, *The Victorian Home* (Batsford, 1954).
[2] Alison Adburgham, *A Punch History of Manners and Modes* (Hutchinson, 1961).

omnibus was running from London to Birmingham. However, the railway magnates had at once seen the possibility of dangerous competition with their new railways and had pressed for the Locomotive Act which forbade them and turned them off the roads; this Act remained in force in Britain throughout almost the whole of the nineteenth century. A few steam-driven "horseless carriages" appeared but there

An early woman cyclist in sporting, yet dignified habit.

was little motoring in Britain till the Act was repealed in 1896 and the import of cars from France and America began. By this time the internal combustion engine had been invented. Daimler had adapted one to a horseless carriage in place of the old steam engine and Henry Ford was making his Tin Lizzies. These petrol-driven motor cars were now allowed on English highways at a maximum speed of fourteen miles an hour. They were all roofless at first and very high, for the engine was under the driving seat, and they had large wooden wheels. They were usually made for four passengers, two sitting on the front seat and two behind, the driver steering with a vertical wheel, but in some models the passengers sat in front of the driver and facing him. By the turn of the century motoring was still a hobby for the rich, but as rapid improvements were made in comfort, design and speed it quickly became recognized as a pleasant and convenient method of transport.

In America, the Scottish-born Graham Bell had invented the telephone in 1876. The National Telephone Company had been formed

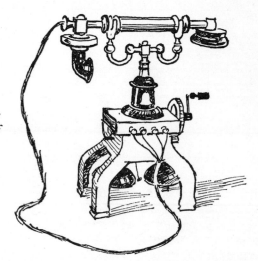

One of the ten thousand telephones in the country at the beginning of this century.

to commercialize the invention in Britain, and shortly afterwards this company, together with the Electric Telegraph Company, which had been founded in 1846, were both taken over by the Post Office, the first public telephone exchange being opened in London in 1878. By 1900, however, there were still only ten thousand telephones in the whole of the country.

Born in the same year as Graham Bell was the American inventor Thomas Edison, who when very young became interested in telegraphy. He had an astonishing ingenuity, inventing multiplex telegraph systems, automatic printers and a mimeograph and developing the efficiency of the typewriter. He made considerable improvements to the Bell telephone and invented the phonograph, first with cylindrical records turned by hand and then with circular discs driven by clockwork. Then came his most important contribution of

39

all. He devised the means by which electricity could be used for lighting and in 1879 produced the first electric light bulb. It was to be many years before electric light superseded gas but its ultimate arrival was inevitable.

The processes of photography were discovered by the Frenchman Daguerre as early as 1835, when he invented a method of taking photographs on paper coated with silver iodide. A few years later William Fox Talbot in England was perfecting many of the early processes and Octavius Hill and Mrs. Cameron were taking remarkably successful portrait photographs. In 1854 the Royal Photographic Society was formed, making the processes developed by Fox Talbot and others available to enthusiastic amateurs, though the apparatus was expensive and the complicated process of developing the plates needed time, the roll film not being devised till the turn of the century.

A favourite diversion of the Victorians was the magic lantern. An even earlier amusement was the "flicker book", which consisted of a number of pictures illustrating a simple story, each picture drawn with the characters in a different stage of a single movement; by flicking the pages of the book quickly one gained the impression that the characters were actually moving. This was brought about by the optical illusion created by persistence of vision, the eye retaining the image of a picture for a fraction of a second after it has been removed from the field of vision. It was Friese-Greene who, using this phenomenon, allied with photography and the principle of the projection of the magic lantern, produced the first Magic Box, to show moving pictures. The first public showing of moving pictures of boxing matches and short comic scenes took place in 1897. It was the beginning of the film industry, which was to affect manners and morals throughout the entire world so markedly. It was to prove not only a source of entertainment but a powerful propaganda weapon and a medium for mass indoctrination. In the same year, Marconi and Oliver Lodge were experimenting with wireless and in 1901 Marconi received the first transatlantic wireless signal.

The basic inventions of modern science were already in British hands, therefore, when the twentieth century opened, and Britain possessed a navy which was the envy of the entire world. At the beginning of Victoria's reign the navy possessed a few steam warships but otherwise life on board and at sea had been little changed since Nelson's time. There was no regular uniform for ordinary seamen, no long-term service, the press gangs were still operating and floggings were a daily occurrence. The Lords of the Admiralty were averse to the use of steam and our biggest ship, carrying 110 smooth-bore, muzzle-loading guns, was entirely under sail, shorter and less than eight feet wider than Nelson's *Victory*, which had been in service for seventy years.

The *Warrior*, launched in 1860, was the first of the ironclads, a warship with iron armour plates, four or five feet thick, protecting more than two hundred feet of her length and carrying rifled guns, but she still had sail. It was not till 1871 that the first British warship entirely without sail, the *Devastation*, was launched, and, in fact, for several years after this heavily rigged battleships, capable of proceeding under sail alone, were still being built.

During the seventies, however, steel plates took the place of iron, and steel was used in construction. The speed was greatly increased and torpedo boats were developed. After that progress came quickly, with breech-loading guns, improved powders, better armour, boilers and engines and the introduction of searchlights. Steam, hydraulic and electrical machinery was substituted for manpower in work such as loading, training and elevating guns, and the machine-gun was developed.

By 1900 British naval forces were 145,532, including reserves. The cost of a battleship was £1 million and the Navy Estimate was £27,522,600. Britain had 45 battleships, with another 16 being built, 126 cruisers, with 22 under construction, 91 gunboats or torpedo gun-boats, with 17 under construction, and 99 torpedoes. The navy of the Kaiser, who was so envious of British naval power, consisted at this time of 12 battleships, with 9 being built, 9 cruisers and 1 torpedo boat, with 9 being built.

The British army was by no means in such good shape, though great advances had been made in the last two or three decades before 1900. In 1837 our soldiers, in stiff stocks and tight scarlet coats, were using flintlock muskets. They enlisted for twenty-five years and most of their service was spent abroad. Flogging was as frequent as in the navy and a thousand lashes are known to have been imposed for comparatively trivial offences. Men were given only one solid meal a day and there were no social amenities such as married quarters or military savings banks. There was no centralized War Office but half a dozen different departments to be consulted in time of emergency, each shifting responsibility on to the other, and when the Crimean War broke out in 1856 there were not fifty guns available which were fit for active service.

Despite the numerous small wars Britain had fought throughout the century, mainly on the fringes of the Empire, the country had been lulled into a false feeling of security, but the early disasters of the Crimea came as a sharp awakening, and from then on a War Office was established and the army directed with more cohesion. By 1900 Britain had 70,000 men in the Indian army and the 30,000 troops who had been sent in the first place to South Africa, when the Boer War broke out, had been increased to 250,000.

Education at all levels of society was increasing and a plea was already being made for a Ministry of Education. With the exception of the vexed problem of franchise for women, the country could now call itself a democracy, and though the condition of many of the working classes was little improved from mid-Victorian times their demands for better living were being met with increasing success.

The writings of Darwin, Wallace, Herbert Spencer and Huxley were to bring about profound changes in people's thinking and their attitude to religion, and the new scientific rationalism resulted in a marked decline in church attendance. The Evangelical movement of the Wesleys and John Whitfield at the end of the eighteenth century had done much to reform a society which had become morally debased; but with the advance of the nineteenth century the movement had lost much of its early saintliness and its members had become narrow-minded and rigidly unyielding to the changing standards of behaviour in the new world. As a challenge to the Evangelists, the Oxford High Church party of Newman, Keble and Pusey had come into existence during the middle years of the nineteenth century, setting itself to combat the new spirit of rationalism and free thought by infusing a fresh spirit into the Christian Church. However, the party's method was to lay stress on the objective aspect of Christian worship and they based the power of the Church on the apostolic succession. They revived obsolete ritual which many members of the Church of England had come to regard as mere superstition, and the members of the Oxford Movement had no hope of becoming the leaders of religious thought throughout the country. The Church of England developed and pursued its own policy, maintaining that no amount of rationalism could explain the mystery of life itself or its Creator, and Dean Farrar, writing in 1901, said: "The future of the Church of England in the new century must depend on the extent to which her ministers show themselves capable of study and open-mindedness; and on the candour which does not try to rear insuperable barriers in the path of progressive truth; and on the manliness which scorns the petty spite of party calumnies; and on the capacity to distinguish between essential truths and effeminate nullities; and on the strenuous determination to press forward every movement which adds to the enlightenment and the amelioration of all mankind."

During these years of religious and philosophical discussion many of the writers, artists, architects and actors associated with the Edwardian years were already at work, and others, who died before the end of the century, were to leave a deep influence on the work of those who survived. The two great nineteenth-century poets who lived long enough to influence the writing of the twentieth century were Tennyson and Browning. Alfred, Lord Tennyson, born in 1809, died in 1892; his most important works were *In Memoriam*, which appeared in 1850, and *The Idylls of the King*, which appeared in twelve parts between 1859 and 1885. In the rare beauty of thought and language of these poems lay much of that struggle between the senses and the soul which harried so many Victorians, increasingly beset by rationalistic doubts and problems of ethics and religion. Robert Browning, Tennyson's friend and husband of Elizabeth Barrett Browning, born in 1812 and dying in 1889, was a dramatic poet with a deep understanding and sympathy for his characters, but to many his writing was obscure, and Tennyson himself, while profoundly respecting his intellect, remarked that "he seldom attempts the marriage of sense with sound".

The English novel came into its own during these years. Charles Dickens (1812–1870) gave us the most vivid descriptions of English labouring and middle-class life that yet exist in the language. Most of his novels had an underlying social purpose. *Bleak House*, for example, exposed and satirized the evil practices of the Court of

Chancery, and in *Nicholas Nickleby* the picture of Dotheboys Hall was an attack on conditions in some of the mid-century boarding schools; but Dickens was such a supremely good story-teller that these secondary motives in no way detract from their artistic value, as might well have happened with a lesser writer.

William Makepeace Thackeray (1811–1863) was another writer with a motive, who was also a fine story-teller. He wrote of upper-class English society, much of which he satirized with humour, but without mercy, for its snobbishness, and throughout much of his work he reveals his impatience with sham of all kinds. He was a great debunker and made fun not only of other people but of himself as well. The three Brontë sisters, Charlotte, Emily and Anne, were all born early in the century and died young, Emily in 1848, Anne in 1849 and Charlotte in 1855; but Charlotte's and Emily's novels—good stories, with conflicts arising from the social conditions of the times in which they lived—are read as much today as they ever were.

Anthony Trollope, born in the year of Waterloo and living on till 1882, though not so great an artist as Dickens, Thackeray and the Brontës, was a thoroughly entertaining writer, describing the life of the Victorian middle class to which he himself belonged. The plots of his Barsetshire novels were fairly complicated but the stories always ended tidily, with every problem solved and every wrong righted. Of one of his own books Trollope said: "The story was thoroughly English. There was a little fox-hunting and a little tuft-hunting, some Christian virtue and some Christian cant. There was no heroism and no villainy. There was much Church, but more love-making. And it was downright honest love."

George Eliot, Robert Louis Stevenson and George Meredith were all writing late into the century, Meredith living on till 1909. The historians were Macaulay, Carlyle and Froude, while the writings of Ruskin and Matthew Arnold exerted as strong an influence on British thought as those of Darwin, Huxley and Cardinal Newman.

Little literature was written especially for children before the nineteenth century, but now there came a spate of books, many inspired by the adventures of the Empire pioneers. Amongst them were the adventure stories of G. A. Henty, Captain Marryat, R. M. Ballantyne and George Manville Fenn, the school stories of Thomas Hughes and Talbot Baines Reed, the fairy stories of Andrew Lang, the works of

Charles Kingsley, the romances of Mrs. Ewing, Mrs. Molesworth and Miss Yonge and Edward Lear's nonsense rhymes.

In the early years of Queen Victoria's reign the school of English water-colour painting was at its finest and Turner, Cotman, De Wint and David Cox were still alive and working. However, the typically Victorian artists belong to the later years, the most notable being Landseer, Leighton, Poynter, Alma-Tadema, Alfred Stevens, Albert Moore, Orchardson and G. F. Watts.

British painting at this time was, in the words of Sir William Orpen, "a homely, easily understandable art, appealing to the people by clear representation of simple themes often founded on everyday life, and almost always tinged by a sentiment perceptible and congenial to the humblest intelligence. Subject was of paramount importance, every picture told a story, and the story was usually of a simple nature that required no erudition for its comprehension."

Landseer, who was said to be Queen Victoria's favourite painter, achieved his greatest success with his paintings of animals, moving, sentimental, sometimes humorous and always appealing. He was also a portrait painter and sculptor, his best known work in this field being the lions in Trafalgar Square.

Leighton painted classical subjects. Fifty years earlier the interest in classical Greece and Rome had revived in France after the Revolution. Now, with an increasing interest in archaeology and ancient history, Leighton introduced the classical movement into British painting. Poynter too was best known for his painting of Greek, Roman and Egyptian subjects, though he was also a successful portrait and landscape artist. Sir Lawrence Alma-Tadema and Albert Moore also painted classical subjects. Alfred Stevens, less well known than other Victorian artists, was a magnificent sculptor, his most important surviving work being the Wellington monument in St. Paul's Cathedral and the mosaics under the dome.

G. F. Watts was a sculptor and painter of portraits and allegorical subjects. "My intention", he said, "has not been so much to paint pictures that charm the eye as to suggest great thoughts that will appeal to the imagination and the heart, and kindle all that is best and noblest in humanity." Sir William Orchardson was the most important of the Scottish artists, a popular academician who was above all a distinguished portrait painter.

Working apart from the main school of British artists were the Pre-Raphaelites. Dante Gabriel Rossetti, son of an Italian patriot living in exile in London, had been a pupil of Cotman. Like his friends Millais and Holman Hunt, he found his inspiration in the Italian primitives and early Renaissance artists, whose work culminated in the genius of Raphael, and because of their love for these

Sir Edward Burne-Jones.

William Morris, poet, craftsman and socialist.

early painters they called themselves the Pre-Raphaelite Brotherhood. Ford Madox Brown was also in sympathy with their interests, though he never considered himself a member of the group.

With the rapidly increasing population of the nineteenth century there was inevitably a great demand for the cheap, machine-made furniture which was coming into production in Britain, but very soon came a reactionary movement for better design and hand craftsmanship once more. It could not check the main flood of production but it made its mark. William Morris and his friend Burne-Jones were growing up during the middle years of the century, when fashion in furniture and interior decoration was greatly influenced by Prince Albert's Great Exhibition of 1851. These young men did not like what they saw, for, influenced by the writings of Ruskin, they had developed a love of Gothic art and medieval romanticism. They too became associated with the Pre-Raphaelite movement, Burne-Jones as an artist and William Morris as a designer of furniture, fabrics, wallpaper, metalwork and pottery. The products of the firm Morris founded, "Fine Art Workings in Painting, Carving, Furniture and the Metals", were soon selling well. For many years the firm supplied Liberty's and it was only in 1940 that it was finally closed.

The Gothic revival spread to architecture in late Victorian times, the principal architects being George Street, who built the Law Courts, and Gilbert Scott, who designed the Albert Memorial and St. Pancras station. The early domestic architecture of Norman Shaw was also in the Gothic tradition and he revived the fashion for gables, Tudor timbering and lattice windows; but his later work was Renaissance, deriving from the architecture of ancient Greece and Rome, as had many of the eighteenth-century houses and buildings of England. Now more buildings were erected in this style, elegant and beautifully proportioned, a welcome relief from the fussy imitation Gothic style of some of the late Victorian and early Edwardian buildings.

In the world of the theatre, the nineteenth century had been the era of actor-managers and at the turn of the century the greatest of them all was Sir Henry Irving. Though there were still moralists in England who objected to the theatre, because it showed people behaving wrongly, theatregoing had never been more popular, and with increasing facilities for travel and more money to spend there came a demand for stage entertainment of all kinds—comic opera, farce, musical comedies, comedies of living manners, melodramas and spectaculars. There was the usual difficulty of gauging the public taste and managers sometimes lost their money. On the other hand, a success meant a long run, for the numbers of the public anxious to see a successful show were increasing. Long runs were not good for young actors needing experience in a variety of acting parts but they were highly remunerative to the managements.

With the fashion for realism in painting came realism on the stage. It was Madame Vestris who first brought realism into the theatre with a box set, a ceiling which would hold a chandelier and doors and windows which functioned. Tom Robertson firmly established the production of realistic dramas of contemporary life with his production of *Caste*, and it continued with the Pinero plays.

47

Melodrama which did not tax the intellect and spectacular shows made the most money, as well as the Christmas pantomimes, which borrowed talent from the increasingly popular music halls. Generally speaking, the commercial drama of the nineteenth century was poor stuff and few authors of distinction bothered to write for the stage. Then Ibsen's plays reached England, shocking some with their uninhibited observation of modern life and delighting many. Ibsen's work influenced British playwrights and Bernard Shaw began to attract the attention of the public. "George Bernard Shaw was the most important British exponent of social realism and it was largely through his work that drama was again raised to the heights of literature. In these circumstances, acting naturally lost its flourish and exaggeration and became restrained, natural, even casual, as it mirrored contemporary manners. To some extent, actors lost their independence, as they had to submit to the wishes of living authors who knew the interpretation they wanted and gave their directions to the cast."[1]

Throughout all the vagaries of public taste, there was always an audience for Shakespeare. Charles Kean produced nineteen of his plays and Phelps nearly all of them. In 1900 Ellen Terry and Henry Irving were attracting enthusiastic audiences to the Lyceum and other theatres throughout the country and there was already a demand for a subsidized English theatre solely for the production of Shakespeare.

The provincial theatres of England were changing in character, for the old stock companies, with their resident band of players, including the star, heavy lead, lead, heavy, juvenile and first and second low comedians, were giving way to the new touring companies which were now beginning their progress throughout the country, complete with their own casts and scenery.

Another change was in the social position of the actor himself. No longer was he a rogue and a vagabond. His social standing was vastly improved. "Today," wrote Henry Irving, "we find the stage recruited by a constant influx from the educated classes." Sir Henry Irving was, in fact, the first actor to receive a knighthood, and he was also invited to dine at Marlborough House with the Prince and Princess of Wales, but the social acceptability of actresses was still a little doubtful until Lily Langtry, herself a member of society, went on the stage to pay her husband's debts.

[1] Clifford Turner, *The Stage as a Career* (Museum Press, 1964).

CHAPTER FOUR

The Edwardians

The coronation of King Edward VII had been fixed for 26th June 1902. London was in festive mood, for the plump, shrewd and kindly sixty-year-old King was popular with everyone, rich and poor. They did not hold the gaieties of his youth against him, for most of them felt that they would have behaved in just the same way if they had been given the chance. Now he was their King he behaved with dignity and consideration, and already he had established friendly relations with France, our centuries-old European rival, which were to earn him the title of Edward the Peacemaker. His beautiful Queen Alexandra was as much loved as Edward. Decorations were run up everywhere and flags and bunting fluttered gaily in the midsummer sunshine, as the first of the distinguished foreign visitors began to arrive and the people of Britain made ready for a day or two's junketing. Two days before the ceremony was due to take place, however, Londoners were disconcerted by the cries of the newsboys. "King seriously ill. Coronation postponed."

The King's physicians, Sir Francis Laking and Sir Frederick Treves, had diagnosed appendicitis. It was a condition which in those days usually proved fatal. The King's only chance lay in an immediate operation, but an appendectomy had hardly ever been performed before. Twenty-eight years earlier, Sir John Erichson had said that surgery was "rapidly approaching finality of perfection" and predicted that "the abdomen, the chest and the brain would be for ever shut from the intrusion of the wise and humane surgeon." It was the work of his brilliant pupil, Joseph Lister, during the succeeding quarter of a century, which made possible the King's operation. As a student at University College Hospital, Lister had been present at the first operation ever to be performed under anaesthesia in Great Britain. After he entered practice he developed his technique of antiseptic surgery, using the results of Pasteur's researches into the activity of micro-organisms, and in the face of ridicule and opposition from many of his fellow surgeons, as well as from that arch-enemy of all dust and dirt, Florence Nightingale, had reduced the deaths in the surgical wards of British hospitals from the appalling rate of two in every three patients to a figure comparable with that of today.

Lord Lister, now an old man and a widower, living out his last, lonely years in retirement, was called to the King's bedside for consultation. The operation was performed and was successful. Lister, grave and gentle and infinitely wise, who had once said that "worldly

The romantic hansom cab which would soon have to share the London streets with the motor taxi.

distinctions are as nothing in comparison with the hope that I may have been a means of reducing, in some degree, the sum of human misery", was awarded the newly founded Order of Merit and made a member of the Privy Council; and Edward VII was duly crowned on 9th August.

London in 1902 was still a city of hansoms, growlers and horse buses, though the twopenny tube was running between Shepherds Bush and the Bank. In winter there were terrible fogs, thick yellow pea-soupers, which swirled up from the river and brought the traffic to a standstill, blotting out the yellow gas lamps and the flickering, flaring jets over the stalls in the street markets; but it was a busy, vigorous, prosperous city for the middle classes and the rich. Servants

(*above*) Road works in White-hall in 1900: people taking away the old wooden road blocks for fire wood.

PLATE I

(*right*) Horse-drawn buses at the corner of Tottenham Court Road, London, early in the twentieth century.

PLATE 2

(*right*) Learning to lay a fire. A housewifery lesson in an L.C.C. elementary school in 1900.

PLATE 2

(*below*) The parlour of a working-class Cockney household in 1911.

(*above*) A street market in the East End of London, 1912.

PLATE 3

(*below*) 1911: a London slum. It was in poverty-stricken conditions such as these that millions had to live.

(*above*) The first flight of the Wright brothers' plane at Kitty Hawk.

PLATE 4

(*below*) King George V, the Kaiser and the Duke of Connaught at the funeral of King Edward VII. " . . . the greatest assemblage of royalty and rank ever gathered in one place and, of its kind, the last." (*Barbara Tuchman*)

(*above*) Suffragettes demonstrating in London about 1912. Mrs. Emmeline Pankhurst is the third from the left.

PLATE 5

(*below*) The 5th Standard Science class, Friern School in 1907.

PLATE 6

(*left*) 1914: a woman recruiter persuading a young man to volunteer for the army.

(*above*) Ypres in 1914: British soldiers going to the Front.

(*right*) Women munition workers making cartridges in the First World War.

(*above*) David Lloyd George with Marshal Foch and M. Briand at Chequers in 1917.

(*below*) Mr. Edward Leer broadcasting from Savoy Hill, 2 LO. Notice the thick curtains that were used to sound-proof the studio walls in the 1920's.

PLATE 7

(*above*) The General Strike, 1926. A bus which has been wrecked by irate strikers is being towed away.

PLATE 8

(*below*) The March of the unemployed from Jarrow to London in 1936. Miss Ellen Wilkinson who organized it is in the second row.

were still plentiful, there was an increasing number of diversions, business was booming, there was a certain 5 per cent on your money and nothing much to worry about.

It was the London of lamplighters, walking at dusk through the streets with their long poles and pausing at each lamp-post to leave a twinkle of yellow gaslight; the London of German bands and Italian organ grinders, with their patient monkeys dressed up in scarlet jackets and feathered caps; of Punch and Judy shows and one-man bands and Frenchmen with performing bears, of lavender sellers and men selling hot chestnuts and roast potatoes. The bell of the muffin man, miraculously balancing on his head his tray of muffins covered with a green baize cloth, brought white-capped servants darting up the area steps to the pavement from basement kitchens, to buy hot muffins for tea on winter afternoons. It was all very cosy and comfortable and secure, with a plentiful supply of workers to keep the wheels turning.

The first motor taxi arrived in London in 1903, but hansoms and growlers remained till 1914, when the horses were needed for active service. Motor buses came in 1904 and did not take so long to oust the old horse buses, which were nearly all off the road by 1911.

The people of Britain were still sharply divided by money and speech. The life of the rich was never more pleasant and for all ranges of the middle classes it was extremely good, for a great many of the pleasures that the rich were now enjoying were also becoming accessible to those who were less well off, and it was only the very poor whose plight was little altered from Victorian times, though there were signs that their day was coming before very long. The rich set the pace and the rest followed, to the best of their means and abilities.

In 1902 the shops, hotels, restaurants and theatres of London were at their most gay and glittering. Swan and Edgar's, Whiteley's, Harrod's and Marshall and Snelgrove's had all been established for some years and now Mr. Gordon Selfridge opened his great store in Oxford Street, the first of its kind to offer to an admiring public such a bewildering variety of merchandise all under one roof. Everyone paid a visit to Selfridge's, though many considered it vulgar, and it was far smarter to shop in the small establishments of Bond Street, St. James's Street and Piccadilly, Regent Street and the Burlington

Arcade, which were equipped with all the luxury and elegance befitting the imperial city of a great empire.

Large hotels were built in London at the turn of the century, on the lines of those which had been appearing in Europe, particularly in Austria. Blocks of large flats were built too, also on European lines, as for example in Kensington, Victoria and Bloomsbury. They were roomy and comfortable, with the servants' quarters discreetly hidden at the end of the kitchen corridors.

The Savoy had been built by D'Oyly Carte in 1889, Claridges in 1897 and the Carlton in 1899, but now appeared the Ritz, the Piccadilly and the Waldorf, all of which still retain their Edwardian standards of comfort and good service. Dining out became the new, popular diversion. It was not for young girls, of course, who still were accompanied by chaperones when they ventured abroad, but older, married women were beginning to taste a new freedom. The Savoy, the first restaurant to have an orchestra in its dining room, was in particular the fashionable place to be seen on a Sunday evening, and it is recorded that as early as 1896 the Duchess de Clermont Tonnerre actually smoked a cigarette in public at her dinner table at the Savoy.

At the same time there were opened in London a number of smaller, cheaper and more intimate restaurants, all with European chefs. At the Florence, Pinoli's, the Cavour, Gatti's in the Strand, the Café Marguerite in Oxford Street and a score of similar restaurants you could eat a six-course dinner for three shillings or less, excellently cooked and served. The thick Turkey carpets, so beloved of the Edwardians, the pink-shaded new electric light of the table lamps, the linen and silver, the flowers and the service all gave a good imitation of the discreet luxury of the more expensive and exclusive restaurants, while in Soho there appeared dozens of little Italian, French, Swiss and German restaurants where you could dine for even less, the Boulogne, for example, offering in 1906 a six-course meal for 1s. 2d.

For those who wanted to see for themselves the famous Bohemians of the world of art and letters—William Orpen, Augustus John and George Moore were all regulars—there was always the main dining hall of the Café Royal, with its crimson banquettes, gilded pillars, mirrored walls and magnificently painted ceiling, for people from every walk of life frequented it from time to time, though the private dining rooms, where the waiters always discreetly knocked before entering, were too expensive for most pockets.

The first tea shop had been opened in the Strand as early as 1861, by the Aerated Bread Company, and it had proved a boon to the young women who were just entering the business world as clerks. Now, with the stream of typists steadily increasing each year, more

MODERN SOCIETY

"Oh, how is Mrs. Jones today?"

"I don't know, Madam. Shall I ask?"

"Oh, never mind. Only tell Mrs. Jones I inquired
   after her."

© *Punch*

Etiquette in 1907.

53

and more tea shops were opened throughout the City and other parts of London, where they could take their midday meal in seclusion, while the men continued to frequent the taverns and chop houses.

In King Edward's London the theatres were in their heyday. We still sing the songs which were first heard in Edwardian musical comedies: *The Merry Widow*, in which the lovely Lily Elsie won fame with Joe Coyne, *The Chocolate Soldier*, *The Arcadians*, *The Dollar Princess* and *The Belle of Mayfair*. At the Savoy Theatre the Gilbert and Sullivan operas, which had been such a success a generation earlier, were still drawing the crowds, for Gilbert and Sullivan had come together again, after the quarrel which had broken their partnership for several years. At Covent Garden London was hearing for the first time the lush melodies of Puccini, in addition to Wagner and Verdi. Bernard Shaw's *Pygmalion*, introducing for the first time on the stage the expletive which has now become part of everyday language, proved delightfully shocking and amusing, as well as Sir Arthur Pinero's *The Second Mrs. Tanqueray*, first produced in the nineties—for divorce, though still only for the advanced, was no longer the shocking and unmentionable occurrence that it had once been; while the dramas of Henry Arthur Jones, in particular *The Silver King*, were as popular as ever. For those with more exuberant tastes there were the music halls, the stages of which were thronged with names which are still famous, such as Little Tich, George Robey, Harry Lauder, Marie Lloyd and Albert Chevalier. Their songs, some sentimental, some gay, some full of that audacious Cockney humour which is fast vanishing, were revived in the thirties at one or two of the theatre clubs, and proved so refreshing that they have remained with us ever since.

In 1908 Maud Allan startled Londoners with her new Greek dancing at the Palace Theatre, for never before had they seen anyone appear on the stage wearing so little. The following year they were to see for the first time Diaghilev's Russian Ballet, after its outstanding success in Paris. The brilliant colours, the magnificent staging, the Oriental splendour of Leon Bakst's décor for *Scheherazade*, and its sensuous beauty, had a profound effect on fashionable London and created a new taste for the art of the East.

Travel, restaurants and theatres were all cheap in those days, so that it was well within the reach of all sections of the middle classes to savour the delights of high life, even though for some it could happen only very occasionally.

The new rich, who were making their money in trade and industry, were mingling more and more with the aristocracy—not yet socially accepted by all, perhaps, though the King himself enjoyed the company of many of them, but fast winning the battle. At the same time

Late Victorian fashions called for respectability rather than comfort.

a few of the hereditarily rich, their wealth beginning to diminish with increasing income tax and the death duties which were now being levied—to help pay for the social services which were coming into existence, and the great battleships which were being built for the navy—were now turning their hand to trade and business themselves, venturing at first into the more genteel pursuits, such as antique shops, millinery, dress and flower shops.

At the opening of the century, tailor-made costumes first appeared for women, but though the jackets were masculine skirts still reached the ground, and some day dresses still had trains. Dresses and skirts fitted tightly over the hips and were worn over high, stiffened corsets which pushed women up in the front and out at the back, so that the overall silhouette was an S-shape. Hats were very large and as heavily trimmed with feathers, flowers and ribbon as they had been during the eighteenth-century craze for elaborate head-dresses. With the popularity of Léhar's *The Merry Widow*, however, many women copied Lily Elsie, and hats, though still very large, acquired a more elegant, sweeping line. Bodices tended to pouch over the waist and this line was accentuated by hanging flounces, long, flowing sleeves, wide at the wrist, and fur stoles. Though evening dresses were cut so low that their method of suspension remained something of an enigma, daytime clothes—and we must remember that the majority of English women wore nothing else—covered the body as closely as they had during Queen Victoria's time. There was a brief fashion for low-cut "pneumonia" blouses, but after a few months women of fashion resumed their high-cut bodices, decorated with jabots and collars of lace or net, which were often cut high up under the chin, and kept in position with small, uncomfortable-looking whalebones on either side of the neck.

The famous Camille Clifford, the model for Dana Gibson's Gibson girl, was the fashionable type until about 1908, and then curves gave way to a simpler shape for the female human form, the "long languid lines" of the Directoire style. Dresses became simple, uncluttered sheaths, devoid of extraneous trimmings and extremely becoming to those slim enough to wear them easily, but difficult for those who found themselves unable to lose their curves overnight. By 1909 fuller, fussier dresses were in again, with panniers and waists. Hats were as large as ever and with them went enormous handbags and very tall, slim umbrellas and parasols. The influence of the Russian ballet inspired Parisians to design the harem skirt for evening wear, but it did not catch on in London to any great extent. The following year, however, though the large hats remained, tight-laced corsets were gone for ever, as well as the high-boned collar; but now arrived the most extraordinary of all women's fashions, the hobble skirt. Skirts were so tight that it was difficult enough to walk, let alone climb upstairs. In the daytime close-fitting long tunics were worn over these skirts, high-waisted and giving something of the effect of the early nineteenth-century Empire style. Evening dresses, in which one was expected to dance, had to be slit at the side seam, thereby revealing, for the first time, a substantial length of a woman's leg.

This style of dress, beginning about 1910, with gradual modifications in cut and the figure becoming more drooping as waists disappeared, continued till 1914, but hats, because they could not reasonably become any larger, grew smaller instead, developing into the enveloping cloche. This was the standard of dress maintained by Edwardian women of society, despite the growing trend to simpler, less restricting clothes which were also coming into fashion, with the

Early motoring was, of necessity, a leisurely pleasure.

advent of the motor car and the increasing interest and participation in outdoor sports.

Cars remained for some years the prerogative of the rich, for they were expensive. The first British car was the Lanchester. Then Daimlers were made at Coventry and at the 1909 Motor Show at Olympia the Rolls-Royce "Silver Cloud" was exhibited, other British makes being the Riley, Lagonda, Sunbeam, Singer, Napier and Swift. As early as 1901 cars had assumed their modern shape, with the engine in front of the driver, but they were high and roofless. Motoring on country roads which had not been macadamized caused clouds of dust, and both men and women took to motoring goggles and long, enveloping coats. Women at first wore their large hats, anchored by motoring veils, but soon some were taking to cloth caps like their menfolk. In 1904 there were eight thousand cars in Great Britain and by 1908 the speed limit was twenty miles an hour.

The advent of the motor car made the country week-end a popular feature of society life, but it remained for several years a very formal business. Anthony Glyn, in his biography of Elinor Glyn,[1] says: "It was not correct to lunch in tweeds and ladies were expected to change into a frock. After lunch they changed back again to tweeds if it was a shooting party, or put on a full length sealskin coat if they were to go motoring. For tea they changed back again into tea-gowns, seductive, diaphanous affairs with low-cut bodices, while the men wore brightly coloured velvet smoking suits: sapphire blue, emerald green, crimson. For dinner they wore full evening dress, the men in white ties and tails and the women in dresses with trains, carrying ostrich feather fans."

Women were now driving their own cars and each year securing more freedom, but the richest were slow to give up their elaborate and restricting clothing, clinging to their femininity as other women began to take their place in the world of business and the professions and demanded ever more insistently the right to vote. They were making a last stand against dressing in a manner which would make them indistinguishable from the middle classes.

Men's clothes had been almost as uncomfortable as women's during the nineteenth century, but as they spent more time on sport their costume gradually became less formal, and their womenfolk followed the trend. Riding and shooting were the only fashionable pastimes for men until the Crimean War. In the 1860's they began to play cricket, in the 1870's lawn tennis and by the 1890's they were playing golf and riding bicycles. The Norfolk jacket and knickerbockers became the correct male costume for these pastimes. Before women took to the Norfolk jacket over a long skirt for these activities their clothes remained formal. A suggestion for a tennis dress, for example, was "a cream merino bodice with long sleeves edged with embroidery; a skirt with deep kilting reaching to the ground; over it an old-gold silk blouse-tunic with wide sleeves and square neck. The tunic looped up at one side with a ball pocket sewn to it. Large coal-scuttle straw hat."[2]

[1] Hutchinson, 1955.
[2] Willett Cunnington, *The Art of English Costume* (Collins, 1948).

Dr. Willett Cunnington says that "When, in the nineties, the bicycle brought with it the need for still greater mobility, the skirt would be weighted with lead 'so that no possible peep at the knickerbockers can be obtained.'"

Men still wore their restricting clothes for formal occasions. Variations of the modern lounge suit had appeared in the mid-nineteenth century. During the first decade of the twentieth century it had a long jacket, high-buttoned waistcoat and narrow trousers. The Victorian bowler was now seen as often as the top hat, which men had been wearing since the days of Waterloo, but on Sundays men of the upper classes continued to wear a top hat and frock coat, and this was the accepted costume for business in the City for most of the middle

"Look, Ethel, look—there goes Sir Beerbohm Alexander."
"So it is; but how unlike!"

© *Punch*

The fashions and humour of 1914.

classes as well, up till 1914. The dinner jacket came into fashion during the Boer War. The tailed evening coat was still worn for formal evening occasions, sometimes with the romantic, scarlet silk-lined cloak, but the simpler dinner jacket steadily gained favour.

Ballooning became a craze with the rich during the opening years of the century and the Aero Club was formed in 1901. In 1906 it was reported that "Certain aristocratic adventurers are taking up the idea with eagerness. It is elegant and exclusive, necessarily confined to the rich, but full of mild excitement and beyond doubt health-inspiring to a degree." That was the year that the *Daily Mail*, "the busy man's daily journal", the "penny newspaper for one halfpenny", which had been founded in 1896, offered a £1,000 prize for the first person to fly from London to Manchester.

News of a more serious development of mechanical flight reached England from across the Atlantic when the Wright brothers succeeded in flying half a mile in a flying machine at Kitty Hawk, thereby solving the problem of heavier-than-air flight. Few people, apart from the scientists, seemed to realize the implications of the new invention and ballooning remained the fashionable pastime. However, the success of the Wrights set the inventors working, improving both the design of the flying machine and its engine. Blériot, Farman and Voisin were experimenting in France, Hawker, Moore-Brabazon, Sopwith and Rowe in England. The idea of flying the Channel seemed as fantastic as any piece of Jules Verne science fiction till Blériot actually did it, landing in England in 1909. He achieved fame for his skill and courage, but people now came to see that air travel was an accomplished fact and that it carried with it, as well as potential pleasure, potential danger. Britain was no longer an island. There was a feeling of vague apprehension along with the excitement. Ursula Bloom, in her book *The Elegant Edwardians*,[1] quotes her mother's feelings at the news. "I wish I could think all this was nonsense or a passing fashion," said Polly, "but the trouble is that I can't. I know that flying will be our future, and I can't believe that I am going to live happily in a world which is in such a hurry."

"The world is progressing very fast; it has got a spurt on," replied her husband. "I don't suppose all of us are going to like the new

[1] Hutchinson, 1957.

world which is now on our threshold, but whatever we do or say, it is bound to come."

On another occasion Harvey said: "The trouble with inventions is that people are quite happy without them, then when they come along everybody wants them. This is, I suppose, the age of science. I wonder if it is really going to be a good thing?"

For better or worse, the Hendon Flying Club was formed and Mr. Grahame-Wright began giving two-guinea aeroplane trips, both at Hendon and Brooklands.

For the gay Edwardians there were still more diversions. While the Royal Navy was building its Dreadnoughts, equipped with armour plate, explosive shells, wireless and torpedoes, as well as destroyers, submarines and cruisers, the *Mauretania* was launched, a great passenger liner of 32,000 tons, which held the Blue Ribbon of the Atlantic from 1907 till 1929. Foreign travel was becoming extremely comfortable. The King set the fashion for taking the waters at the European spas, particularly Marienbad, at the end of the summer season, which closed after Cowes week at the beginning of August; and in winter people began to visit Switzerland, to try their skill at ski-ing. The Ski Club of Great Britain was founded in 1906 and the first Englishwomen members somehow managed to ski in their long skirts and tight corsets.

The middle classes of England amused themselves in a more modest fashion, with their own diversity of entertainments and pastimes. Cricket was the national summer game and the county championships were followed with keen interest. There were cross-country running clubs and amateur and professional cycling races. Croquet, which had suffered an eclipse with the rising popularity of tennis, made a return to favour, but it became less of a leisurely pastime to be accompanied by pleasurable dalliance and philandering and more of a purposeful, scientific game. London croquet championships were held at the Queen's Club and also at Wimbledon. Golf was increasingly popular, played by both men and women, and new clubs came quickly into existence. St. Andrews drew up a new code of play and standards of performance soon improved. Rackets and tennis were as popular as ever and the annual amateur rackets championship was held at the Queen's Club. Nearly everyone played what was first known as ping-pong; when the vellum bats were replaced by wooden ones it was called table-tennis.

The Oxford and Cambridge boat race attracted large crowds and rowing became a favourite summer sport wherever there was a river and a boat at hand. Hockey was the Edwardian craze, played by both men and women. There were international and county matches and hockey was introduced for the first time into schools' sports programmes. Association football was becoming more popular than Rugby and the mania for the league tournament and Football Association cup ties began, though the Rugby International matches still attracted large gates. Lady beaglers appeared on the scene, wearing "Norfolk jackets, long skirts, cloth caps, thick stockings and boots". The diehards deplored such unfeminine goings-on, but Swedish drill was generally acceptable after the Lord Chief Justice himself had said that "if systematic physical training for girls was more widely adopted, we should see far fewer young ladies with bent-over ankles and turned-over feet walking along the street."

A few women studied ju-jitsu and fencing and the aristocratic habit of winter sports began to reach down to the next strata of society. Women soon took to riding breeches for ski-ing. At first the Swiss hoteliers were outraged, but since the British had good money to spend they soon learnt to countenance such immodesty, and within a few years the modern ski-trousers were designed.

By 1906 men were wearing knitted pullovers or waistcoats with their golfing knickerbockers, woollen stockings and Norfolk jackets, and women were appearing in knitted jumpers, with their long skirts, cloth caps and tailored jackets. The fashion for knitted garments spread. Men often wore knitted pullovers under their Norfolk jackets for country house week-ends, and though they still clung to their stiff collars, the lounge suit, worn with a knotted or bow tie, was ousting the formal frock coat. The trilby hat arrived, to vie with the bowler and the top hat, and even the aristocracy began to show a preference for comfort and utility in their dress.

Amongst the entertainments offered by the rich "musical evenings" had been popular, hostesses inviting some eminent artist to entertain their guests. In middle-class homes, few of which did not possess a piano, guests provided the entertainment themselves, singing, reciting, or playing the piano or some other instrument. The new craze for bridge altered all that and bridge parties became so fashionable that the "musical evening", much ridiculed but often highly enjoyable, and encouraging amateur talent which was sometimes of a high order, gradually died.

Auction bridge developed from whist. It was played in the West End clubs in the first place, the Portland and Bath clubs establishing the rules, but very quickly small bridge clubs came into existence where women in particular flocked during the afternoons, when they were not giving bridge parties in their own homes. The bridge clubs introduced a mild form of gambling and games were taken very seriously.

The invention of the pianola and the increased popularity of the gramophone were further discouragements to the amateur musicians, but choral societies were immensely popular, the most famous being the Royal Choral Society, and magnificent choir festivals were held at the Crystal Palace. For music lovers there were also ballad concerts, smoking concerts, the Promenade concerts at the Queen's Hall and a diversity of concerts at the Albert Hall, while in the ballrooms people were dancing the two-step, the Boston and the ever-popular waltz.

Sir Edward Elgar was the greatest British musician of Edwardian times. His *Enigma* Variations, completed and performed in 1899, had first brought him fame, and the following year his great oratorio *The Dream of Gerontius* was first performed. During the next ten years his most important works were his Symphony in A Flat and his Violin Concerto; his Symphony No. 2 in E Flat was completed in 1911 and dedicated to the memory of Edward VII.

In London, church attendance showed a marked decline during these years. Father Bernard Vaughan thundered forth from his pulpit at the Farm Street Jesuit church about the flagrant sins of a godless society; the Salvation Army, which William Booth had founded in the 1860's, rattled their tambourines and preached and prayed at the street corners; and Gipsy Smith, the evangelist, called people to a better life by way of the Crystal Palace.

London set the fashion and the country people, the solid core of gentry and middle classes, followed, but at a slower, sedater pace, shedding their Victorian etiquette and courtesy, their integrity and friendliness, more gradually. The larger country houses nearly all possessed a car of sorts, but the smaller houses still retained their ponies and traps, or even horses and carriages. In the remoter districts few had electric light or gas and most were still using lamps and candles. Few houses had indoor sanitation and fewer still had baths. There were plenty of servants to carry cans of hot water up to the bedrooms, where those who felt inclined could bath in large tin hip baths, but frequent bathing was not encouraged, for it was said to be enervating and seldom took place more than once a week.

It was still usual for girls to be taught at home by governesses, despite the new schools that were now available. The idea of girls working for a living was all very well in the towns, but the prejudice against career women died hard in the country and the old order of careful training in order to make a good match still persisted.

It was very important to maintain the outward signs of dignified living, and poverty, except amongst the very poor, was something one did not discuss. Professional incomes were low but living was cheap, with milk a penny a pint, bread a penny a loaf, sugar a penny a pound. Even the smaller country houses had plenty of land and room for a vegetable garden and an orchard; and most families kept a pig, which they killed and cured themselves, and a few chickens. Material for clothes was cheap, the popular voile for summer garden party frocks costing 2½d. a yard. Men could buy a ready-made suit for £2 and a good tailor charged only £4. Servant girls from the village lived in for their keep and wages of three or four shillings a week.

It was a gay, sociable few years. Everyone knew one another and entertained freely. In summer there were tennis and croquet parties, garden parties and cricket matches on the village green. In the autumn there were shooting parties and picnics, in winter skating parties and dinner parties, with charades or bridge to follow.

When new neighbours arrived in the district, one called within the first month. Calling hours were between 3.45 and 4.30 in the afternoons, though never on Saturdays or Sundays. The correct length for the visit was twenty minutes and on leaving one left cards on the hall table. A married woman calling on another married woman left her own card, with the top left hand corner turned down to show that she had left it in person, and two of her husband's, one for her hostess and the second for her hostess's husband. The call was invariably returned and visits repeated on "At Home" days, when tea was served. Church attendance, particularly at morning service, remained steady in the country for several years to come and the vicar was a frequent guest at dinner and garden parties.

Though the richer people went to Europe or Scotland every summer, ordinary middle-class families did not take a summer holiday each year as a matter of course. The habit developed gradually. When they did decide on a change of air they usually took apartments

An Edwardian villa.

at one of the seaside towns, where they bought their own food, which the landlady undertook to cook. Boarding houses had not yet been established in any great numbers and hotels were too expensive. Bathing costumes had been cumbersome affairs of navy blue serge, high-necked and long-sleeved, with skirts over baggy, calf-length legs, all befrilled and trimmed with white braid and highly unsuitable for their basic intention; but they slowly gave way, under much protest, to one-piece stockinette costumes, which were more practical though hardly more becoming.

There was a good deal of house-building on the south and south-east coasts during the Edwardian years, mostly of gay, fussy little places, with white-painted balconies, pepper-pot turrets and sharply pointed gables. In the suburbs of London and the big towns larger

65

versions of this type of house were built, easier to run than the Victorian villas and with no basements. Smaller, plainer and much duller versions were also built in the less fashionable suburbs, in new developments of long, depressing streets, creeping ever more relentlessly into the countryside, to house the steadily increasing population of the lower middle classes and artisans.

In London itself few large buildings survive which were built in King Edward's reign, apart from the hotels and Selfridge's. Perhaps the best known are the post office in Newgate Street, built on the site of the old Christ's Hospital, and the offices of the Church Commissioners on the Victoria Embankment. Australia House was not built till the reign had ended but it is Edwardian in style and atmosphere.

Women in London were beginning to use make-up but in the country a surreptitious recourse to the discreet little packets of papier poudré which were just appearing was the absolute limit to which ladies might go. Scent was in doubtful taste but coming into fashion, though no servant was allowed to use it.

The art of conversation was still cultivated. It was considered unmannerly to talk about oneself. Discourse was of events, social trends, current fashions, new books and new plays; and the subjects which were coming more and more under discussion were the activities of the Suffragettes and the Socialists.

Intelligent middle-class women all over the country were becoming increasingly indignant at the Government's refusal to give them the vote. Emmeline Pankhurst and her daughter Christabel, with a group of loyal followers and friends, had founded the Women's Social and Political Union to further their aims. They tried every peaceful means of persuasion but with no result. In 1904, at a Liberal meeting in the Manchester Free Trade Hall, the W.S.P.U. first resorted to militant methods when Christabel stepped forward on to the platform, in front of Mr. Winston Churchill, and made the first public appeal for the woman's vote. The Suffragettes, as they were nicknamed by the Press, continued to further their claim at all political meetings. They organized processions in London and chained themselves to the railings of the Houses of Parliament, so that, during the time it took the police to release them, they could proclaim their demands, loud and clear, to the watching public. They suffered imprisonment for disturbing the peace and when they went on hunger-strike suffered the indignity and pain of forcible feeding. Undaunted, they renewed their efforts once they were released, knowing full well that more prison sentences were in store for them. Opposition to the Suffragettes was bitter, adamant and completely illogical.

"Them were the sort that went on the ducking stool," said the country folk, and the rest of the opposition was at the same level of

H. G. Wells.

unreasoning prejudice. All through the Edwardian years the Suffragette campaign grew in intensity and desperation, suffering one disappointment after another, and achieving little but a growing sympathy from some and a more resolute opposition from others.

Socialism was an uncomfortable doctrine which was beginning to cast a shadow on the bright day of Edwardian middle- and upper-class society. It was a plea for the workers, the submerged four-fifths of the population, made by a small group of middle-class intellectuals who talked a great deal and appeared to be joining forces with the leaders of the trade unions. The novels of H. G. Wells and Arnold Bennett were uncovering social evils which had far better not be discussed. The poor were unfortunate but they were thriftless and lazy. Give them money and what did they do with it but spend it.

"Socialism is only another name for unselfishness. Socialists are the true Christians," argued their supporters, but the opposition declared that "Socialists believe in splitting everything everyone has with everybody else, and then finding, in six months' time, that the poor are still poor and the rich are still rich."

John Galsworthy's first novel of the Forsyte Saga, *The Man of Property*, published in 1906, gave an excellent picture of Edwardian upper middle-class life, but his plays, *The Silver Box*, *Strife* and *Justice*, which examined the inequalities of class and sex and the social injustices of the times, were too disturbing to be completely enjoyed. It was more comfortable to read the romantic adventures of Rider Haggard, the gentle, escapist stories of J. M. Barrie or even the romances of the lady novelists who were now publishing regularly —Marie Corelli, Elinor Glyn, Ruby M. Ayres, Berta Ruck, Christine Jope-Slade and Ethel M. Dell.

In the spring of 1910, after a short illness, King Edward died. At his funeral there rode behind his coffin nine crowned heads of Europe. "In scarlet and blue and green and purple, three by three the sovereigns rode, with plumed helmets, gold braid, crimson sashes and jewelled orders flashing in the sun. After them came five heirs apparent, forty more imperial or royal highnesses, seven queens—four dowager and three regnant—and a scattering of special ambassadors from uncrowned countries. Together they represented seventy nations in the greatest assemblage of royalty and rank ever gathered in one place, and, of its kind, the last."[1] The chief mourner was King Edward's son, the more serious-minded and less exuberant George V, and beside him rode his cousin, Emperor William II of Germany, Victoria's favourite grandson, whom King Edward had always disliked and mistrusted. "Dear Pussy made a mistake when she had that infernal son of hers," he had once remarked.

Londoners paused to mourn their King and marvel at the glittering scenes of pomp and majesty at his funeral. Then they began the preparations for the coronation of King George V and Queen Mary and resumed the gay life with an ever-increasing momentum. Jazz and cocktails had arrived from America. Isadora Duncan appeared on the stage to outrival Maud Allan in her dancing and shock those who were still shockable. The tango arrived and with it the mania for tea dances.

[1] Barbara Tuchman, *August 1914* (Constable, 1962).

Smart young men about town took to monocles, tightly rolled umbrellas and spats, and women were seen, for the first time, at boxing matches.

This was the face that Britain showed to the world, in particular to the American millionaires who were now to be seen staying at the Ritz, the Savoy and Claridges, a Britain with a still mighty empire, an invincible navy, a flourishing trade and industry and a brilliant, gay capital. In the heart of the country, in its ancient universities, in country rectories and the public schools, in quiet towns and villages in the shires and marches, young men and women were growing up, dreaming as young people do of an idyllic, effortless future of peace and happiness for all mankind, both rich and poor, little knowing that in four short years the life they had known and loved would be shattered in the catastrophe of the First World War. These were the last years of that peaceful, happy England that the young Rupert Brooke loved so well, as he wrote:

> God! I will pack, and take a train,
> And get me to England once again!
> For England's the one land, I know,
> Where men with Splendid Hearts may go;

And Laurence Binyon was writing:

> O summer sun, O moving trees!
> O cheerful human noise, O busy glittering street!
> What hour shall Fate in all the future find,
> Or what delights, ever to equal these:
> Only to taste the warmth, the light, the wind,
> Only to be alive, and feel that life is sweet?

It was a gay, rapturous time for so many, but unfortunately it was by no means the whole of Britain's story. How were the workers of Britain faring, the miners and factory workers, the clerks and shop assistants, the millions who as yet had no share in the good things that the opening years of the twentieth century had to offer, and how did we stand in relation to the other countries of Europe, who were engaged in the same race as ourselves for wealth and world trade?

CHAPTER FIVE

The Other Half

Lord Salisbury, Queen Victoria's last Prime Minister, died shortly after the old queen herself and during the opening years of Edward VII's reign the Conservative government was under the leadership of Arthur Balfour, with Joseph Chamberlain as Colonial Secretary. One of the first pieces of legislation of the new government was the Education Act of 1902, whereby control of elementary and secondary schools passed from the old School Board to the County Councils, which became the local education authorities, their Education Committees being responsible for the financing of the schools, with money from the local rates, supplemented by grants from the Government. With the new arrangement many more secondary schools came into existence, as well as technical schools and training colleges for teachers. The old Church voluntary schools also came under the authority of the new Council Education Committees, supported by the rates. The Liberals, many of whom were Nonconformists, resented this concession to Church of England schools, and during the bitter controversy which followed they gained many supporters.

The next storm was roused by Chamberlain's policy of tariff reform. His object was to protect British industries from foreign competition and give preference to the import of Empire food by taxing all other imported foodstuffs. Half the population, remembering the sufferings caused during the previous century by the Corn Laws, which had kept the price of bread artificially high during years of unemployment and terrible distress, were against any form of import duties and agitated for free trade. The Conservatives themselves split on the issue and the Government fell. At the next general election the Liberals, under Campbell-Bannerman, were returned to power with a large majority. In this election the Independent Labour Party, which had been launched in 1893 and had won East Ham for Keir Hardie, the first Labour Member of Parliament, now entered the political scene as a strongly organized force; and of the fifty candidates they put in the field, twenty-nine were returned to the Commons.

After the Boer War, Britain had relaxed her policy of standing alone, without allies, in international affairs. Despite Edward VII's dislike of the Kaiser, the nation and the Government had strong sympathies with Germany, the members of the Labour Party in particular expressing friendship with their fellow workers in Germany. Chamberlain had suggested an alliance between Great Britain, the United States and Germany, and discussions between Great Britain and Germany were held in regard to colonial arrangements, particularly in Africa, where the short-lived European land grab was in full swing, and also in New Guinea. Germany, however, was wary. She disliked Chamberlain's policy of tariff reform, seeing in it a threat to her own economic prosperity. She rejected the alliance and began to expand her navy till she became third in the world race for carrying power, America running second and Great Britain still in the lead. Japan's navy was supreme in the Pacific and Britain made an alliance with her, in order to safeguard Australia and deter Russian activity in China.

France and Great Britain had come near to the brink of war a few years earlier, during a quarrel over African territories. General Gordon, during his service as Governor of Equatoria, had established a fort at Fashoda, but when Kitchener reached it, in 1897, he found that the French had incorporated the town into an easterly outpost of the French Congo. Tempers ran high but the Fashoda incident was solved diplomatically, mutual concessions being granted elsewhere in the continent.

King Edward had always hoped for an alliance with France. He had been a frequent visitor there and was immensely popular. Now, under his benign influence, much of the old antagonism was smoothed away and Great Britain and France declared an alliance to restore the balance of power in Europe. France was already established in Algiers. In 1903, with a view to ultimate colonization, she began to turn her attention to Morocco. The following year France and Great Britain came to an agreement whereby, in return for Britain's occupation of Egypt, which the French had long resented, France should have a free hand in Morocco. However, the Kaiser, watching jealously, raised a strong objection to France's activities, not only posing as the protector of the Moslems, but alleging that Germany was being encircled.

Once more the threat of war was averted by diplomacy, and

Campbell-Bannerman's new Liberal government, with Sir Edward Grey as foreign secretary, was determined on a policy of peace. Germany was pleased with its free trade policy. The British workers, with their German brethren, dreamed of an international "brotherhood of labour" and were convinced that democracy would cleanse foreign politics of intrigue and secret diplomacy. For Britain the time appeared to be ripe for disarmament and a programme of social reform at home. Campbell-Bannerman was dying, but during his last months of office he pleaded for world disarmament, in the interests of humanity and civilization, and gave a lead by reducing Britain's own shipbuilding programme. On his death, in 1908, Mr. Asquith took his place, and with Sir Edward Grey, still Foreign Secretary, they laboured for conciliation and peace, despite the warnings of Lord Roberts, the hero of the Boer War, and set about the long overdue social reforms at home.

The trade union movement was growing steadily in Great Britain, and by the Trade Disputes Act of 1906 "peaceful picketing" and "collective bargaining" on the part of trade unions were made completely legal. The Amalgamated Society of Engineers, which had been formed in 1851, had restricted its membership to skilled men who had served their full apprenticeship, for the scientific methods of industry had called for a revival of the old apprenticeship system in certain trades. Most of the earliest unions were, in fact, of men skilled and trained in crafts or industries, and they were, of course, amongst the highest paid manual workers, paying relatively high dues and receiving in return substantial benefits. Now came unions of unskilled workers, both men and women, and the labourers. The Gas Workers' and General Labourers' Union was formed in 1889, later to develop into the National Union of General and Municipal Workers, and also the Dock, Wharf, Riverside and General Workers' Union, which in the years to come was to amalgamate with thirty other unions to become the Transport and General Workers' Union. This was the year of the great dock strike, when John Burns called a strike of casual workers for a minimum rate of sixpence an hour, and Ben Tillett brought out his Stevedores' Union in support.

Two more legal battles were fought by the unions before 1914. In 1900, when the Amalgamated Society of Railway Servants took strike action on the Taff Vale Railway in South Wales, the railway company took legal action against the society and won substantial damages. By thus proving that strikes could be liable to civil actions, the case robbed the trade unions of much of their power, but strength was restored to them by the Trade Disputes Act, which provided that "the Courts should not entertain actions against trade unions in respect of tortious acts alleged to have been committed by or on behalf of a union". The second clash was in regard to the political activities of the unions. When members were asked to pay a subscription towards the expenses of the Parliamentary Labour Party it was deemed illegal and the unions were said to be exceeding their rights. The Labour Party campaigned against this ruling and in 1913 the Trade Union Act allowed political activity "provided it was paid for out of a special fund and administered under conditions laid down by the Act".

Trade unions now had all the power they needed, and their leaders became people of importance, sometimes, it was alleged by their supporters, separating themselves, by higher incomes and a resultant social superiority, from real contact and sympathy with the people they were representing.

Between 1906 and 1914, despite the gathering clouds over the international situation, many important social reforms were carried through in Great Britain by the Liberal government, under pressure from the Socialists, a group of people who in the first place were drawn mainly from the intellectual middle classes and were in deep sympathy with the trade union movement. The Socialists demanded the end of sweated labour and pleaded for humane working hours and better working conditions.

The Factory Act had fixed the number of hours that a worker might be employed. The first Trade Board Act of 1909 fixed a legal minimum wage for factory workers, though it did not have the power to fix overtime rates, and in 1912 the legal minimum wage for coal-miners was fixed. For many the greatest blessing of all was the granting, in 1909, of the first Old Age Pensions, which saved many old people from the shame and desolation of the workhouse. The first scale was five shillings a week to people over seventy and seven shillings and sixpence for two old people living together; and with the years it has steadily increased. In 1911 came the National Insurance Act, whereby people paying a small weekly sum could register with a

73

doctor and obtain free medical and hospital treatment and also insure against loss of wages during sickness or unemployment. The Workmen's Compensation Act, the Sweated Industries Act and the Town Planning Act were all passed during these years and arrangements made for the regular medical inspection of schoolchildren.

This may sound as though England were rapidly turning into a Utopia which was inexplicably destroyed by the First World War. Conditions, however, were far too grim amongst the poor, evasion of the law too frequent and the number of inspectors too inadequate for the amelioration to come about in so short a span of years.

In his book *The Condition of England*, published in 1909, C. F. G. Masterman wrote of Britain's labouring population: "They work in unventilated rooms. They are stinted of holidays. They are compelled to work overtime. They endure accident and disease. They are fined and cheated in innumerable ways. Their life is often confined to a mere routine of work and sleep. Yet they endure; and even at the heart of foul and impossible conditions retain always some rags of decency and honour."

In the pottery towns people were still suffering as they had from the beginning. A Medical Officer of Health reported that infant mortality was quite one in five because of the diseases suffered by married women employed in the earthenware and china works, and of those who survived many were themselves sick and ailing for all their short lives. "Stunted, inefficient, overworked, underfed, they struggled towards maturity." He found "forty little girls, twenty-one of whom were half-timers [spending part of their day at school and the rest at the factory], licking adhesive labels by the mouth at the rate of thirty gross a day. Their tongues had the polished tip characteristic of label lickers, and the rest of the tongue coated with brown gum." In the Nottingham lace trade children were still being blinded by the double work of school and the terrible eye-strain of their employment in the lace industry.

In the big drapery stores it was customary for the shop assistants to live in, and some twenty thousand of them at last combined in a trade union, demanding a minimum wage of £1 a week, which would enable them to sleep out in lodgings of their own choosing. Meetings of shop assistants were held after working hours in all the big cities throughout the country. A government commission was appointed to inquire into the matter but found it difficult to collect evidence, as many shop assistants were so terrified of losing their jobs. "If my name is published I get the swap," said one witness, "and I have to go at a minute's notice; and my employer would not mind spoiling my reference. He does not know that I have come here today."

The overall picture was a consistent one of unappetizing food, monotonous and badly served, bad sleeping accommodation, with often five beds in a room, and a cheerless sitting-room, like a waiting-room at a railway station. Assistants worked seventy hours a week and at the end of the day were usually too tired for anything but bed. One report, which told that "washing accommodation was inadequate, food badly cooked, table service not clean, men's sitting room, three chairs and a broken table for the use of twenty men", also stated that "every apprentice is required to attend a place of worship at least once on a Sunday".

More sinister still, because less easily cured, was the report that there was coming into the business a kind of immorality of the mind. One witness said that "the old system of trying to build up an establishment on the value of your goods, and on giving real worth for money, has been steadily changing, and the assistant now who is considered the smartest assistant is the one who can sell to customers worthless goods, goods that yield a very large profit, goods that look showy on the surface but are not really wearable, and are not satisfactory in other ways".

Men and women assistants could not marry, of course, and wages were too low for them to save and escape from their servitude. "We're in a blessed drainpipe," said Mr. Minton to Kipps, in H. G. Wells's novel,[1] "and we've got to crawl along it till we die." Kipps at last realized that "the great stupid machine of retail trade had caught his life into its wheels, a vast, irresistible force which he had neither strength of will nor knowledge to escape." "Night after night he would resolve to enlist, to run away to sea, to set fire to the warehouse, or drown himself, and morning after morning he rose up and hurried downstairs in fear of a sixpenny fine."

When the shop assistants grew too old for the strain of work in the big stores they disappeared into even less rewarding jobs. Some became cab drivers, others insurance agents. From the big stores of

[1] H. G. Wells, *Kipps*.

South Wales some went down into the pits. Mr. Debenham, of Debenham and Freebody's, and Mr. Derry, of Derry and Toms, were the first two drapers to change the system, giving their assistants wages which would enable them to live in places of their own choosing, in freedom and some measure of dignity.

Another scandal which persisted well into the thirties was the pay of the women outworkers, particularly in the tailoring and dress-making businesses but also in a score of other trades involving hand work. They worked in their own homes, collecting the work from the factories and business houses and returning it when finished. Neither their hours of work nor their rates of pay could be supervised, and they were shamefully exploited. By working fifteen or sixteen hours a day the best and quickest of them might earn ten shillings a week. Pett Ridge[1] quotes a woman and her daughter, living at Islington, costume machinists who bought their own thread and used their own sewing machine, who earned 1s. 10d. each, in a day of fourteen hours, and counted themselves fortunate. A woman in Bethnal Green making artificial flowers for sixteen hours a day earned 1¾d. an hour.

These women, widows and spinsters, or married women with too many mouths to feed, lived out their lives in an unending drudgery, in squalid little rooms in the slums of east and north-east London, making an infinite variety of garments which would eventually end up for sale in the luxury stores—embroidered underclothes and blouses, coats and skirts, babies' bonnets, ostrich feather trimming, millinery, men's ties and waistcoats, as well as boxes and toys, toothbrushes and motoring gloves, artificial flowers and paper bags, by the unending score.

A toothbrush maker, a spinster of fifty-nine, living alone in one room for which she paid 5s. a week rent, was able to earn 16s. to £1 a week when trade was brisk, but complained that recently work had been slack. A maker of men's ties and bows was paid 10d. to 1s. 6d. a dozen and the most she could ever hope to earn was 15s. to 16s. a week, out of which 6s. 6d. went on rent. Ordinary waistcoats were made for 6d. to 9d. each, including the pockets, but better class ones might bring in 3s. to 4s., although they took hours to make, so were not any more profitable in the long run. Embroideresses of silk blouses and jumpers, sometimes designing their own patterns, could, if in regular work,

[1] W. Pett Ridge, *The Home Worker* (Home Workers' Aid Association).

make 16s. to £1 a week, but making lined motoring gloves, at 3s. 6d. a dozen pairs, brought in a weekly wage of only 8s. a week. Payment for the outworkers was actually on the decline, because "women are always applying for work, and they have no work to give them; and therefore they cut the prices down, because the women go and beg for work".

A home sempstress had a struggle to exist on her meagre earnings.

The long monotonous hours, the drudgery and hopelessness of it all dulled them into apathy. "Can you suggest anything that anybody could do for you which would induce your master or perhaps compel him to give you a fairer or a larger wage?" one woman was asked. "If he would only time an article," she replied, "and state how long the article would take to make, and give you a certain rate of so much an hour, it would be fair, if it was only a living wage. We only want to live."

They only wanted to live! That is what so many people forgot. They did not want charity. Large, organized charities certainly existed. They were a feature of Victorian and Edwardian times. But charities are little more than a sign of indifference to the fundamental problem, an effortless palliative to quieten the stirrings of conscience. The brief moment of compassion passes and is usually forgotten as quickly as the cause which aroused it.

In 1906 the average earnings for women of the labouring class were 15s. 5d. a week and for men about £1. They lived a life apart from the rest of the population, with their own codes of behaviour. Married women did not go out to work except through sheer necessity, their philosophy being that when they did the husbands tended to leave the wage-earning solely to them. "I've never known a man to work once his wife has begun to keep him," they said. The women, however, always had the spending of the money, the men invariably handing over the whole of their wages each week. Women who had been in factories before their marriage were usually very ignorant of the problems of housekeeping but those who had been in service were usually quicker-witted than their husbands and very skilful at planning the spending and making the money go a long way. Husbands and wives were much nearer an age than in the upper classes, where the husband was usually several years older than the wife. Amongst the poor the wife was not infrequently older than the husband, having deliberately chosen a younger man, who would be able to keep her in her old age.

There was hard drinking, when they could spare the money for it, especially amongst the men, but more often than not they were good husbands, devoted to their families. Though the labouring classes hardly ever went to church themselves, considering churchgoing a pleasure for the well-to-do, they sent their children to Sunday school. Sometimes it was to the Nonconformist school in the morning and the Church of England school in the afternoon, but they saw nothing incongruous in that. In the early 1900's there was a tendency to persecute the Jews living amongst them, and there was a fear and suspicion, especially in London, of Roman Catholics, but most of them had a personal religious belief in a vaguely conceived Supreme Being, who was intimately concerned with the course of their lives; and though they had little knowledge of the tenets of orthodox Christianity, they believed in the power of prayer. They had no fear of death and often welcomed it. Neither did they cherish any memories of happier days in the past, for they had none. All they could remember was a time when highly skilled artisans were forced to work as labourers, ten hours a day, for a wage of twelve shillings a week. Their present condition, with a general tendency for wages to increase and working hours to be shorter, was a slight improvement on the bitter past, deplorable as it still was. "Father feels a new man, now he doesn't have to go out, not before five in the morning," a girl remarked with simple pleasure.

On the whole they were delighted that their children were now given some education. There were some who still wondered whether it were not a waste of time, as the woman who remarked: "Here's John-Henry nine years old and never earned a farthing yet", and her neighbour who said: "I don't mind their learning Emma jography; but hist'ry, I don't call it according to her station". But most of them were immensely proud of their children's scholastic attainments. Despite the disabilities under which the early elementary schools had to function, teachers struggling with classes of fifty or sixty young children, poorly clad and often hungry, and sometimes accused of giving an education which was an "irreducible minimum" and destroying all the poetry and enchantment of a child's mind, they did excellent pioneer work. The children enjoyed their lessons, the stories they were told, the games they played, and the years of their childhood were doubled.

Below this stratum of the very poor were the tramps, the beggars and the floating prison population, but the poor had their own castes, and those who retained the strength to cling to their pride and respectability had no dealings with the lowest orders of all, who had failed to conform in any way to the rules of society.

The rural life of England had been disrupted, as we have seen, with the decline of British farming which followed the import of cheap food from the Empire during the nineteenth century. As prices collapsed many farmers faced ruin, and where there was little capital to weather the storm, productive land went to waste and reverted to scrub; farm buildings and houses fell into disrepair; land drainage systems were neglected and no longer functioned properly; farm roads became overgrown; livestock broke through damaged fences and overran neglected pastures; hedges were no longer trimmed; obsolete machinery was not replaced. Thousands of farmers gave up their farms and half a million people left the land, but the farming community as a whole kept going, mainly by turning to dairy farming, feeding their cattle on imported cake and corn, which were cheaper to buy than to grow. Acres of arable land had reverted to permanent grass, but with over-use, forced on the farmers through economic necessity, much of it had developed into poor grazing of very low productivity. Cheese-makers and butter-makers had to face the competition of New Zealand, Canada and Holland, but liquid milk was always needed, and of all the stock farmers the milk producers suffered the least and the size of the national herd increased. Pig and poultry keepers benefited from cheap imported corn but prices were subject to sharp fluctuations.

Prices improved a little during the Boer War and this improvement was maintained till 1914, so as rent and wages did not change, the lot of the farmer was somewhat better, though agriculture as a whole was regarded as a "depressed" industry. A farm labourer's wages at this time were, on an average, 12s. a week, which with summer overtime could rise to £1. The rent of a cottage was usually 1s. a week and it included a garden large enough for him to be able to grow his own vegetables, apart from potatoes, which he was usually allowed to grow on the farm. Labourers had free wood for fuel, often free milk, and rabbits were to be had for the shooting. Stockmen, carters, shepherds and dairymen earned 13s. to 14s. a week, with a free cottage. Cottage accommodation was primitive but agricultural workers did not go hungry or cold. In fact they were well fed and had an advantage over the town labourers, with a rent of 4s. to 5s. a week to be paid and no garden. Their horizon was narrower but their needs were fewer, and for the most part they were content.

As Trade Board Acts and legislation gradually improved the wages, hours and working conditions in the factories, many girls who would normally have gone into domestic service began to have second thoughts. With the alternative employment in the factories now available, they could dictate their own terms and parlourmaids were demanding, in addition to their keep, £20 a year, cooks £22 a year and tweenies £15. It still did not occur to them to ask for a weekly day off or for holidays, but employers who could not afford to pay these wages had to do without the servants. Even those who could pay found that the supply of girls willing to go into service was growing smaller. The ways of life were changing and for those who had been used to servants it was growing uncomfortable.

As the upper ranks of the working classes gradually organized themselves into trade unions, subsidized the Parliamentary Labour Party and made themselves at last a force to be given serious consideration, it was not the moneyed and upper classes who feared them so much as the class immediately above them, the lower middle classes of inner suburbia. They were a new breed of Britisher which had come into existence half a century earlier, with the development of the country's trade and industry. They were the black-coated workers, who spent most of their lives in offices. Nearly half a million of them worked in the City of London alone, streaming in at early morning and scattering again in the evenings to their comfortable little homes in the long silent streets of the suburbs. Their lives were secure. Their wives usually kept a servant, if they could find one. They usually sent their children to the nearby secondary school. Each August they flocked to the seaside.

Their grandfathers and great-grandfathers had probably been artisans or shopkeepers, small farmers or craftsmen, and they had no roots in the straggling, impersonal suburbs, no tradition of public service or civic responsibility. They were kindly and good-natured within their limits, and unostentatious, but utterly absorbed in their own affairs and their own families. Their outside interests were few. They patronized football and cricket matches, which they preferred to watch rather than play. They were avid readers of the new popular magazines, *Answers*, the *Royal* and *London Opinion*, which were just introducing the picture puzzle and competition craze. Their children grew up to be office workers like themselves, minor civil servants or schoolteachers in the elementary schools. A few won scholarships to the universities and moved to a wider world, but mostly they stayed in their own safe but desolate sphere. They took little interest in organized religion and seldom went to church. They had no real conception of the wider aspects of politics, substituting for them a social convention; and always they voted against the working classes, resenting them because they had to pay taxes to help educate their children and keep them in old age, and fearing them lest before long they should invade their own suburbs and bring down the tone of the neighbourhood.

As the years of the first decade of the twentieth century passed, they and their growing children became increasingly absorbed in the vicarious pleasure of watching sport, while avid reading in the newspapers of the activities of the gay set amongst the rich gave them false values, which some dreamed of emulating one day. They did little to create a culture of their own. Intellectually they were passive, artistically they were imitative. Many were content enough, and even smug, but some were beginning to grow restive and yearn for wider horizons.

The practical Socialists had been working both in Britain and on the Continent since the beginning of the nineteenth century; after them came the theorists, both Germans, Karl Marx and Friedrich Engels. Marx organized the first international association of working men in 1864, and three years later published the first volume of his book *Das Kapital*, in which he urged the workers in all countries to unite for political and economic redress. Marxism was a rationalization of the Socialist doctrine and another attempt to save the world from the disastrous results of the all too sudden introduction of machinery.

Machinery, argued Marx, had created a new class of society, the capitalists, who used their surplus wealth to buy more equipment, by means of which their labour force could produce for them more wealth. As the process was repeated, the capitalists grew richer and the labourers ever poorer. He explained the mechanism of capital and the necessity for Socialism. Karl Marx was the first Communist, advocating that a country's wealth and sources of production should be owned by the State and that individuals should be regarded as servants of the State, their lives so controlled that they worked for the good of the community and in return received a fair share of the nation's wealth.

There were not many in Great Britain at the beginning of the century who were prepared to go as far as this, for as Ramsay Macdonald says, in his book *The Socialist Movement*, "Socialism is a tendency, not a revealed dogma, and therefore it is modified in its form of expression from generation to generation. The goal remains the same, but the path twists and twines like any other human path."

However, the Social Democratic Federation was launched in Britain in 1884, by followers of Marx, changing its name in 1906 to the Social Democratic Party. In 1885, after many arguments, a group broke away to form the Socialist League, with William Morris as one of its strongest supporters. In 1884 the Fabian Society had also come into existence, a group of middle-class intellectuals led by Beatrice and Sidney Webb, with whom Bernard Shaw was in close sympathy, to spread the gospel of its own particular brand of Socialism. The Socialist League gradually disappeared and the Social Democratic Party made little headway, sometimes coming into open conflict with the trade unions, but the Fabians made their mark, converting more and more leaders of the trade unions to Socialism. The Independent Labour Party, which was the result of these activities, was a union of Socialists

Karl Marx, the founder of Communist doctrine.

and trade union leaders. At first the Communist Social Democratic Party also joined forces with the I.L.P., but later withdrew and continued in isolation, attracting only a straggling band of followers, including extremists and cranks. Describing one of their meetings, H. G. Wells wrote of the "dusky largeness of ... the Queen's Hall ... thick but by no means overcrowded with dingy, earnest people." In the chair was "Lady Warwick, the remarkable intruder into the class conflict, a blonde lady, rather expensively dressed, so far as I could judge, about whom the atmosphere of class consciousness seemed to thicken." It gave the impression of a "gathering of village tradespeople about the lady patroness. And at the end of the proceedings, after the red flag had been waved, after the 'Red Flag' had been sung by the choir and damply echoed by the audience, someone moved a vote of thanks to the countess, in terms of familiar respect that completed the illusion." Writing of the Fabians, Wells described Sidney Webb as a "small, active, unpretending figure with the finely shaped head, the little

83

imperial under the lip, the glasses, the slightly lisping, insinuating voice", his followers having "excessive bureaucratic notions, and a belief that everything can be done without anyone wishing to do it."

Small wonder that at this stage the struggling poor, often driven to the limit of human endurance, "sunk below the level of consciousness which can respond to any hope of change", had little interest in the new doctrine of Socialism. Paradoxically, even amongst the skilled artisans it tended to triumph during times of prosperity and lose its interest in periods of depression, for then all they needed was security and the means to maintain life for the next few days, with little energy or spirit left to plan for a hypothetical future.

However, the change was slowly coming. The Government was well aware of the growing problem and knew that charity, however well organized, far from being really helpful, was aggravating the position by creating a race of paupers. The only solution was to give people higher wages and a measure of security, so that they could become responsible citizens, not only receiving the benefits of citizenship but also performing the duties which citizenship must also carry. When Labour made its demands, therefore, they were met with sympathy and understanding. "Not even the brainiest of them (such men as Shaw and Wells, for example) could realize that they were bringing up battering rams to knock down an open door."[1]

Some now feared that the country was approaching a stage when all wrongs would be righted and her people, robbed of all incentive to strive, which is the stuff of true living, would face a life of infinite boredom; but their fears were groundless, for that time never came. Instead Britain was suddenly plunged into the carnage of the First World War and the wheels of social progress went into reverse.

[1] Michael Harrison, *London by Gaslight* (Peter Davies, 1963).

CHAPTER SIX

The First World War (1914–1918)

Historians are still examining the events which led to the outbreak of the First World War and the reasons for the sudden, devastating conflagration in Europe. Was it the result of a series of calamitous misunderstandings, of diplomatic messages delivered too late, perhaps having been deliberately delayed, of bluff called against all expectations, of muddle-headedness and a few false moves which once made could not be retracted? Such conjectures have a tantalizing interest, fifty years after the event, but they are rather like regretting one had not remembered to lock the door after the burglars have called. The war happened, and with it came an appalling destruction of human life and a revolution in the social order throughout the whole of Europe. An examination of events in Britain, France, Germany and Russia, the principal protagonists, during the preceding years shows a mounting expansion of power and population in all four countries, with their accompanying demands and needs, due to the nineteenth-century mechanical inventions, which must inevitably culminate in some great climax, resolving itself into either a union of interests or conflict.

Imperial Germany had been created less than fifty years earlier. Previously the German people had lived in a number of small, independent states, the most important of which was Prussia. These German states were loosely linked by the congress at Frankfurt, to which each state sent delegates. There were a few brief years when, influenced by the democratic parliament which had come into existence in Great Britain during the nineteenth century, the states might have united to become a similarly governed democratic country, for the German congress developed into a national assembly elected by the German people, and the King of Prussia, Frederick William IV, was invited to become king of a united Liberal Germany. The Prussians, however, had no liking for such democratic institutions, for Prussia, not yet industrialized, was still ruled by an autocratic land-owning aristocracy, the Junkers. On the advice of Count Bismarck, King Frederick William of Prussia declined the offer, refused to recognize the authority of the National Assembly and set about reinforcing the military strength of Prussia.

When Frederick William grew senile his brother, the Kaiser's grandfather, became regent, and on the old king's death was crowned King William I of Prussia, pursuing the same autocratic, militaristic policy of government, and in 1864, under Bismarck's direction, embarked on a series of wars in Europe. The first was against Denmark, from whom Prussia won the Duchies of Schleswig-Holstein. The second was against Austria, in order to prove the supremacy of Prussia amongst the lesser German states, and in seven short weeks Bismarck was again victorious. The third war, in 1870, was against France, to settle the problem of the frontier states of Alsace and Lorraine. Prussian armies invaded France in August, and by January 1871 the brave new capital of Paris was surrounded and besieged. It was another undisputed victory for Bismarck and Prussia, and by the terms of the peace treaty Alsace and Lorraine were duly handed over. William I, King of Prussia, emerged as Emperor William I of a united Germany, and for the next forty-three years Germany remained the leading power on the European continent. When William I died, in 1888, his son, the Crown Prince Frederick, who had married the English Princess Royal, Victoria's eldest daughter, was himself a dying man, so that within a few weeks it was his son, William II, who at the age of twenty-nine became the Kaiser of Imperial Germany.

Britain was climbing to the peak of her naval and imperial power and it was at this stage that the young Kaiser, watching her jealously, began the expansion of his own navy. Germany was still on friendly terms with Russia, though the German people disliked the Russians, and Austria, becoming apprehensive of Russia's activities in the Balkans, was urging Germany to help her in a military action to check Russia's encroachment on her south-western frontiers. Germany did not do this. On the other hand, her government did not support Russia in her occupation of Bulgaria. France, never forgetting 1870, remained in close alliance with Russia, and the Kaiser, in an attempt to maintain the balance of power, tried to draw Great Britain into the triple alliance of Germany, Austria-Hungary and Italy, but Great Britain retained her policy of isolationism for a few more years.

Austria-Hungary, which was responsible for the first aggressive moves in the 1914 war, was a relic of the old Hapsburg empire, in which lived a variety of races. The Empire, a union of Austria and Hungary, had been created in 1867, at the request of the two principal groups of inhabitants, the Germans and the Magyars. In Austria there were ten million Germans and eighteen million Czechs, Poles, Ruthenians, Croats, Serbs and Slovenes, but parliamentary power was in the hands of the German minority. In Hungary there were ten million Magyars and eleven million Rumanians, Croats, Serbs, Germans and Slovaks, and here again power was held by the minority group, the Magyars. The Germans were tied to Germany by bonds of race and the Magyars were loyal to Germany through fear of the Slav states which had been coming into being across the Danube to the east and also of the Russians themselves. Moreover, Germany needed a friendly Austria-Hungary to protect her eastern frontiers, so the political and diplomatic links between Germany and Austria-Hungary were very strong. The Slavs in Austria-Hungary, however, numerically outnumbering the Germans and Magyars, but with little power and fewer privileges, were helplessly resentful of the corruption of the government and the numerous injustices from which they suffered. Some were for breaking away and forming themselves into an independent Slav state, and tension between the Austrians and the Slavs yearly grew greater.

On 28th June 1914, the Archduke Francis Ferdinand, heir to the Emperor Franz Joseph of Austria, was shot in the streets of Sarajevo, capital of the Slav province of Bosnia. The attack, it was later proved, had been organized by the head of a Serbian organization, the Black Hand, which had its headquarters in Belgrade. The antagonism between the Austrians and Slavs was thereby brought to a head. It was high summer and thousands in that gay pre-war world were on holiday, thronging the beaches and watering places of Europe. They waited with bated breath. After the first few days it seemed that nothing serious was going to develop. Another week or two passed and their thoughts turned once more to their holiday-making. But Austria was making a secret treaty with the Kaiser that Germany would support her in all her demands for redress from Serbia, and then, towards the end of July, she presented her ultimatum, giving only forty-eight hours for a reply. Acceptance of Austria's demands would have reduced Serbia to a vassal state, for the Austrian Government proposed nothing less than the annexation of the entire country as a protectorate.

Serbia appealed to Russia, while Germany, through her ambassadors, informed the foreign ministers of France, Great Britain and Russia that she approved Austria's demands to Serbia. To the relief and surprise of most people, Serbia's reply was so conciliatory that it seemed as though the quarrel would be solved diplomatically. She accepted practically all Austria's demands and asked for a discussion on minor points. Austria, however, bent on a quarrel, rejected the note and both Serbia and Austria began to mobilize.

The Kaiser, weak, emotional, but also arrogant and obsessed with the vision he had created of himself as a great emperor and military leader who could lead his empire to world domination, supported Austria enthusiastically during those early days of the crisis; but when he began to realize the implications of Austria's aggressive policy, the possibility that Russia would fight for Serbia's cause, that France would join with Russia and that Great Britain might support France, he began to have second thoughts and to panic. The Serbian answer, he frankly admitted, had removed every cause for war.

Sir Edward Grey approached Germany, France and Italy with a view to calling a conference in London to mediate in the Austro-Serbian quarrel. France and Italy were agreeable but Germany refused. The Russian foreign secretary also appealed for peace, but Austria refused to negotiate, and on that same day, 28th July, declared war on Serbia. Germany was now committed too, but still hoped that Russia and Britain would remain neutral. Russia, however, saw the necessity for protecting her western frontiers and began partial mobilization. Telegrams were exchanged between the Czar and the Kaiser in a last-minute effort on the part of the Czar to avoid the conflict. The hopes of Europe were centred on Germany, for it was the Kaiser alone who could now restrain the Austrians, irresponsibly rejoicing at the prospect of a quick conquest of Serbia; but the Kaiser, panic-stricken, with a weak chancellor, afraid of losing his only ally, Franz Joseph of Austria —for Italy had already declared her intention not to join them—hesitated, torn between fear of failure and exhilaration at the prospect of the power and glory which might be just within his grasp.

When the Russian generals urged the Czar to sign the order for total mobilization, which in that vast country was a slow and cumbersome process, he hesitated. "Think of the responsibility which you are asking me to take," he said. "Think of the thousands and thousands of men who will be sent to their deaths."[1] The Russian generals, however, argued that the safety of Imperial Russia itself was at stake and at last, unwillingly, the Czar signed the fateful order. The news reached Germany on 31st July, and the following day the Kaiser gave the order for mobilization in Germany and declared war on Russia. France began to mobilize. Between Germany and France lay the little neutral country of Belgium. Great Britain at once sent notes to Germany and France, reminding them of Belgium's neutrality, which must be observed. France agreed but the German reply was evasive. On 2nd August Germany sent an ultimatum to Belgium, asking for the free passage of German troops through her territory. Belgium refused and appealed to Great Britain for diplomatic intervention. On 4th August German troops crossed the Belgian frontier, planning a swift attack on France. Great Britain demanded their immediate withdrawal. The note was rejected and at midnight Great Britain declared war on behalf of herself and also the countries of the Empire, over whose foreign policies she still had control.

Japan joined the Allies. Turkey threw in her lot against Russia, and Egypt became a protectorate of Great Britain, Turkey's control of Egypt, which for years had been only nominal, at last ending. In 1915 Italy entered the war against Austria and Bulgaria joined with Germany and Austria. In 1916 Rumania joined the Allies against Germany, and in 1917 the United States of America and China. Thus the whole world became involved.

In 1914 men had in their hands the products of the new technical discoveries of the nineteenth and early twentieth centuries, to use for good or ill. The worst now happened. They used their newly acquired skills for a wholesale destruction of mankind, such as had never before been contemplated by the most savage and inhumane of aggressors. At the outset of the war artillery had not yet been mechanized and was still horse-drawn. The Royal Flying Corps consisted of a hundred men and sixty-six aeroplanes with open cockpits. The Royal Naval Air Service had sixty-four machines and eight hundred men, and the navy possessed seven small airships and no kite balloons. Aircraft had never been used in war. Neither had submarines, since the decision of Napoleon's generals that submarine warfare would be too diabolical. Poison gas had never been used and tanks had not yet been devised.

[1] Kautsky Documents. Quoted in Virginia Cowles, *The Kaiser* (Collins, 1963).

Four years later, air, submarine and tank warfare was an accepted part of the conflict and the manufacture of all types of guns, from machine-guns to the giant howitzers, with the accompanying iron, steel and engineering trades, was an industry which employed three million workers in Great Britain alone.

British soldiers were to fight in the Dardanelles, Gallipoli, Mesopotamia, Syria and East Africa, but the heaviest casualties were on the Western Front, in the fighting against the Germans. Germany's plan was to make a rush through Belgium for Paris, hoping for the speedy collapse of France, so that Great Britain would be forced to withdraw. In the first few weeks the plan seemed to be working successfully, for German troops pressed quickly through Belgium into France. To the surprise of the Allies, Germany revealed an air force vastly superior to Britain's and each column of advancing Germans was led and directed by aeroplanes. At the same time, however, the Russians on Germany's eastern flank were overrunning East Prussia.

The young men of Britain and the Empire—the labourers and clerks, the costermongers and shop assistants, the civil servants and the professional men, the poets and writers and students, the young men about town, the squires' sons and the farmers' sons—were soon joining the ranks of the regular army. Quickly they were trained and drilled and sent over to France. In the county regiments, farm workers and estate workers sometimes found themselves batmen to young officers who had been their peace-time employers. It was the last remaining vestige of Britain's days of feudalism.

The first great clash on the Western Front came between the German and French soldiers near Metz; two million Germans met 1,300,000 Frenchmen, and 300,000 Frenchmen were killed, wounded or taken prisoner. Namur was abandoned and the British, who had taken up their positions at Mons, joined the great retreat which reached almost to the gates of Paris. In the East, Hindenburg checked the Russian advance into Prussia with a resounding victory at Tannenberg, in which a million Russian soldiers were killed, wounded or taken prisoner.

The French halted their retreat on the Marne and, with the British, checked the German advance into France. The Germans retreated and then rallied for an attack on the Channel ports. Antwerp fell but thereafter British and Belgians held firm, at the first battle of

Ypres. By November of 1914 the first battle of the Marne was over and France was still unconquered. Germany's first manœuvre had failed and nothing had been achieved, but on this Western Front alone the toll of German, French and British soldiers, dead, wounded or taken prisoner, was more than a million and a half.

For the next three years the war in Europe was largely defensive. Trench warfare developed, and at one time there were long lines of trenches right across Europe, from which neither side could emerge without an appalling loss of life. Throughout 1915 Germany remained mostly on the defensive on the Western Front, while the Allies launched costly but abortive attacks, which lost France another 1,500,000 men, Great Britain 400,000 and Germany 600,000. This was the year that the Germans first used poison gas, on the French, Canadian and British troops entrenched along the Yser, for the defence of Ypres. Unprepared for the green clouds of chlorine gas which came billowing towards them, the first casualties were terrible, and even after the first crude respirators had been issued to the troops, hundreds of men suffered and ultimately died, even though years later, from the effects of the gas attacks. On her Eastern Front, Germany drove the Russians from Poland and Lithuania and the Bulgarians turned them from Serbia and Montenegro. Germany thereby achieved control of the Balkans and was able to make contact with Turkey.

At the beginning of the war, in addition to their aeroplanes, the Germans had ready a large fleet of zeppelins, and on 14th April 1915 the first bombing raid by zeppelin took place over southern England. It was the first time Britain had been attacked on her own ground since 1066. Between 1915 and 1917 there were forty-nine zeppelin raids on south-eastern England and London, but Britain's output of airships and aeroplanes proceeded rapidly, as well as her technique in the use of anti-aircraft artillery, and by 1917 so many zeppelins had been shot down that the Germans abandoned this method of attack. They continued their raids with aeroplanes, and Britain retaliated with her own rapidly growing air force. The air war intensified and by 1918 the command of the air had passed to the Allies, who had accounted for four hundred enemy machines during the previous twelve months.

In 1916, in an attempt to break the deadlock on the Western Front, the Germans launched an attack on the French at Verdun and the

British on the Somme. Six months later, by which time the fighting had taken a further toll of more than two and a half million men, almost a million of them Germans, they knew they had failed.

During these years Great Britain had virtual command of the seas, for the Kaiser had forbidden von Tirpitz to use the German fleet for a major naval engagement, anxious to preserve it for the days of vic-

A zeppelin raid on London in the 1914–18 war.

tory. The battle of Jutland, in 1916, was, in fact, the only important naval engagement of the entire war, and through a misjudgment of Admiral Jellicoe it was a victory for the Germans, though the British lost no dreadnoughts, and the overall strength of the British Navy was unimpaired.

Each month the British blockade of Germany grew more severe. The German people were strictly rationed and beginning to have serious doubts of the much vaunted invincibility of their armies. The slaughter went on and by the summer of 1916 Germany alone had lost two and a half million men. Both in Austria and in Germany there were rebellions, food riots and protest strikes. The people were hungry, sickened by the casualty lists, utterly broken and weary. In Russia matters were even worse. The armies were ill-equipped and thousands of lives had been thrown away through lack of organization and inefficiency. The peasant soldiers bore it stoically for the first two years. Then their resentment became active. Throughout 1916 Russia had been mainly on the defensive, but food was desperately short and many soldiers had neither guns nor ammunition. Feeling against the Czar, the court circle and the landed aristocracy hardened. Early in 1917, food riots in St. Petersburg turned to open revolution. The Czar abdicated and a Socialist republic was established under Kerensky which continued fighting with the Allies against Germany; but the Russians could suffer no more. A few months later mutinies broke out in the army and then revolution throughout the whole country. The Kerensky government was overthrown and power seized by more extreme Socialists, a union of workers and soldiers under the leadership of Lenin.

It was also in 1917 that the Germans launched an intensive U-boat campaign against Atlantic shipping. President Wilson broke off diplomatic relations with Germany and two months later America declared war. The U-boat campaign took severe toll of British food supplies, and food, already very short, had to be rationed. Margarine was manufactured in increasing quantities to take the place of butter. In February 1918 fat and meat cards were issued and in July the first National Ration Books.

The war at sea accelerated and gradually, with the expenditure of ever more loss of life, the submarine menace was partially overcome. By August 1918 the British Navy had sunk 150 German submarines and the rate of destruction had increased so steadily that more were being destroyed than Germany could build. At the same time the output of merchant shipping from British and American shipyards exceeded the rate of loss.

In October 1917, when the U-boat campaign was at its most dangerous, the Italians suffered a crushing defeat at Caporetto and took no further effective part in the war. The next month Lenin's government sued for a separate peace with Germany. Negotiations opened in December 1917 and the peace was signed at Brest Litovsk on 2nd March 1918.

On the Western Front, 1917 had been a terrible year for the Allies and they had suffered enormous casualties. In the spring there had been the British offensive at Arras, the French attack between Soissons and Champagne and the Canadian capture of Vimy Ridge. Later had come the slaughter at Passchendaele and then at Cambrai, still with no decisive result. Both in Great Britain and in America came the realization that no side was ever going to win the war; but Germany was having it all her own way during the peace negotiations with Russia and already considered herself the victor.

In the spring of 1918, Hindenburg and Ludendorff, with men and guns freed from the Eastern Front, put a million men and 3,000 guns on to the Western Front, in the hope of one last, smashing victory. At first they were successful, but when the Germans appeared to be on the verge of victory, the drive against the British line at St. Quentin was halted. A second German attack on the British front at Armentières was also thrown back. In May the third German offensive was launched against the French at Soissons. Five British divisions went to their help and the attack was repulsed.

Conditions in Germany grew worse and food ever shorter. Ludendorff concentrated on one more tremendous attack on the Western Front, a last bid to bring the Allies to their knees. In July 1918 he concentrated on the region of Rheims with a barrage of 8,000 guns. He was three months too late, for from April onwards half a million Americans had been arriving in France. Within a week Ludendorff had to admit that his giant offensive had been a total failure and it was in this month that the Czar and all his family were murdered by the Communist secret police in their home at Ekaterinburg.

Under General Foch, the Allies launched a counter-offensive against Ludendorff, and accompanying their armies they launched weapons never before seen in any numbers on a battlefield—mobile forts known as tanks. For the German armies, already exhausted, they proved the last straw. They were unable to fight back at them and withdrew. The Allied armies marched eastwards, and by September 1918 the Kaiser and the German High Command, knowing that all hope of victory was gone, set about ending it all and asking for peace.

Few people in England, on that June day of 1914 when the Archduke Franz Ferdinand was murdered, could have had any idea of what lay in store for them. None could have dreamt that four years later the "carnage incomparable and human squander"[1] would have

[1] Wilfred Owen.

mounted to eight and a half million dead, a million of them young men of Britain, with a score of million hurt and wounded.

During the first week of August they could laugh with *Punch*:

> Well, if I must, I shall have to fight
> For the love of a bounding Balkanite;
> But O what a tactless choice of time,
> When the bathing season is at its prime!
> And *how* I should hate to miss my chance
> Of wallowing off the coast of France!

When the Germans invaded Belgium, however, and the possibility of Germany holding the Channel ports and the whole of Europe became all too clear, the mood of the nation quickly sobered. Anger at the machinations of the Kaiser and the Emperor Franz Joseph fanned the flames of a fierce patriotism. This was a fight for life and men flocked to the recruitment centres to join Kitchener's army and depart for France, confidently assuring their families that they would be home by Christmas; but Christmas 1914 brought nothing but the casualty lists and the grim realization that, with a million and a half French and British soldiers already lost, the struggle had only just begun. More men were poured across the Channel to fill the gaps in the ranks. They went singing bravely, but with grief in their hearts, for there was little glory in the fighting now, despite all the fine speeches and gallant sentiments. In the trenches of France and Flanders the struggle had become a war of attrition, offering nothing but mud and blood, indignity, squalor, death and destruction. This is where the youth of England—a whole generation—met their end, praying that they might die as well as they had lived.

> I, that on my familiar hill
>   Saw with uncomprehending eyes
> A hundred of Thy sunsets spill
>   Their fresh and sanguine sacrifice,
> Ere the sun swings his noonday sword
>   Must say goodbye to all of this;
>   By all delights that I shall miss,
> Help me to die, O Lord

wrote W. N. Hodgson, just before he was killed, at the age of twenty-three, in the battle of the Somme.

The trainloads of wounded arrived back in England, some to be patched up and sent back to the fighting, some so frightfully mutilated that they lived out the remaining years of their lives as grim human shells, never mixing again with the rest of humanity, but confined behind hospital walls, too grotesque to be shown to the world. The war went on, however, and on the home front it had to be organized and paid for. Factories for munitions and aircraft were hastily brought into being. Shipyards and mines worked at full pressure. Farmers cultivated their neglected fields, to produce more food and ease the strain on shipping. Hospitals were prepared for the steadily increasing flow of wounded, and doctors and nurses worked as they had never worked before.

Ever more money was needed to pay for it all and in 1915 income tax rose to the unprecedented figure of 3s. in the £. Railways and mines were taken over and administered by the State for the duration of the war and there was an increasing amount of State control in the farming industry.

There was very soon an acute labour shortage. The Suffragettes had called off their fight with the Government over the vote at the outbreak of war and Mrs. Pankhurst had offered her services in whatever capacity the country could best use them. Mr. Lloyd George now sent for her and asked if she would organize a great recruiting campaign amongst women for work in munition factories, where hitherto they had never been allowed even to enter, on the land, as farm workers, as bus conductresses in the transport services, and in any other ways that presented themselves. It was a triumph for the Suffragettes and Mrs. Pankhurst responded gladly. She organized the campaign and women rallied by the thousand. Soon women were working at all manner of employments in which a year or two earlier their presence would have been deplored. They eased the labour problem and it was a foregone conclusion that the vote was as good as theirs. It became legal with the Fourth Franchise Bill of 1918, in which the vote was given to all women over thirty.

Civilian life continued as best it could. Shops kept open, with dwindling supplies of goods for sale. Children had to be cared for and educated and homes kept going for husbands and sons away at the fighting. Though taxes were rising and the Government was for ever urging economy, there was plenty of money about amongst the wage-earners, though the rich suffered increasingly from death duties and income tax, which by 1918 had risen to 6s. in the £. The cost of food and all other commodities rose sharply, but so did wages, and many manufacturers, working on Government contracts for armaments, uniforms, manufactured food and all the paraphernalia of war, made enormous profits, became the new rich and moved up into higher social spheres.

Amongst all the bereavement and sorrow of the war, there was an ephemeral gaiety about life in London and the other big cities of England, and the uncertainty of existence made for a fatalism which became almost pagan. Men on embarkation leave or home from the trenches for a few days' respite wanted two or three hours when they could laugh and be merry and forget that tomorrow the chance of dying was high and that each month the odds grew heavier.

In London there were the theatres. No longer did they provide glittering displays of clothes and jewels. Most of the men were in uniform and if the women still wore evening dress it was plain and restrained. This was no time for serious drama. The wartime taste was for revues and escapist musicals, the two most popular being *The Maid of the Mountains* and *Chu Chin Chow*, which opened in 1916 and ran for just on five years. The restaurants were crowded, though the standard of food steadily declined, and during the last year of the war fat and meat cards had to be produced at each meal and clipped by the waiter. Dancing was as popular as ever, both in private houses and in the new night clubs which were springing up in the West End of London, and where smoking and drinking amongst women increased rapidly. Ragtime was being played for the first time in England and people were learning to accustom themselves to syncopation. There was also a great vogue for fortune telling and crystal gazing.

The fashion in women's clothes gradually adapted itself to the new ways of life and the last vestiges of Edwardian elegance disappeared. In 1914 skirts had been ankle length and very tight. Now women had become more active. Most servants had departed into war work. There were no chauffeurs and many people had handed their cars over to the Government. Women had to do their own housework and many did war work as well. They had to walk, to climb on to buses, even to run. Skirts became shorter, to six or eight inches from the ground, and they also became fuller. The large hats disappeared, replaced at first by small, high hats with tall feathers in front, rather like military shakos, and with them were worn long fur stoles and large fur muffs. Blouses were high-necked, with a modesty vest or a high frill, up to the chin in front and reaching to the ear lobes at the sides.

By 1915 fashions were becoming more practical for the energetic lives that women were beginning to lead.

By the summer of 1915 skirts were quite full and tending to grow even shorter. Clothes generally became more casual and in the country women took to wearing tweed skirts, loose blouses and knitted cardigans which were little different from the uniform of the average countrywoman today. It was a long time before they took to trousers, however, and until 1918 they were worn only by munition workers employed in processes which made skirts impractical or even dangerous. Late in 1916 the tailored coat-frock made its appearance, a practical and economical dress which served for most formal occasions.

Everyone was being entreated to save, for the war was costing Britain £7 million a day and by 1918 the national debt had reached nearly eight thousand million pounds. Moreover, the City of London was still floating loans to help the economies of the Allied countries.

War Loans and Savings Certificates were issued and ever more stringent economies were made.

The war dragged on and with it the killing and the bereavement. There was hardly a family in the country which did not suffer some grievous loss, and though the outward forms of social life continued there was everywhere a consciousness of "the heartbreak in the heart of things".

All scientific inventions during these years were directed towards the war effort and methods of destruction. It was Lieutenant-Colonel E. D. Swinton who first suggested the use of caterpillar tractors, later known as tanks, to cross the trenches. This idea interested Winston Churchill who did much to encourage the development of this weapon. By the end of 1916 tanks were being used in France and eventually broke down the last German resistance. Ships, armaments, airships, aeroplanes, automobiles and motor cycles were all developed as instruments of war and field telephones and radio were in constant use.

Most of the London hansoms and growlers had disappeared early in the war, when the horses were commandeered for service in France or the Middle East with the artillery. By the end of the war, though they were still being used in the Middle East campaigns, horses were little used in France. Nevertheless they did not return in great numbers to the streets of London, where the taxis and motor buses had come to stay.

Education during the war years proceeded under great difficulties. The elementary schools carried on with women teachers taking the place of the men who had gone into the services. Boys from the secondary, grammar and public schools, some of whom in normal times might have gone on to the universities, usually went straight into the army on leaving school at seventeen or eighteen. The universities themselves were understaffed, though they were able to carry on as the numbers of students were so reduced.

In the treatment of the sick and wounded, great advances were made in medicine and surgery. The deaths amongst the troops from diseases such as malaria and dysentery were far fewer than during the Boer War, but it was in surgery that the most spectacular advances were made, and the plastic surgeons, inspired by the skill of Sir Harold Gillies, performed miracles of muscle, bone and skin grafting to patch up shattered limbs and faces, even creating new chins, noses, eyelids and foreheads for some victims, who otherwise would have been too disfigured ever to move about in society freely and without self-consciousness.

The psychologists and psycho-analysts, influenced by the work of Adler, Freud and Jung, had been making themselves noticed before 1914, and now psychotherapy was included in the treatment of shell-shock victims. In the hands of skilled and responsible practitioners, psychotherapy proved of immense value to many war sufferers, but the later craze for psycho-analysis, the principles of which were often ill-assimilated, was to have far-reaching, harmful effects in the years to come.

There was little domestic or public building during the war, and experiments in modern functional architecture, as opposed to building which was in some traditional or revived style, did not begin on any large scale till the twenties. Film making, too, came almost to a standstill in England. There had been a few small film companies before the war, making mostly newsreels and short comedies. Film shows were given as short music-hall turns or as peep-shows on circus grounds, but were not yet considered seriously as part of the entertainment industry.

The first story film, *The Great Train Robbery*, had been made in America in 1903. It was eight hundred feet long and played for about ten minutes. By 1918 the United States had become the greatest film-producing country of the world, the industry being centred on Hollywood, in California, because of its clear, sunny and reliable climate for the shooting of exteriors. In England there was so little production during the war that the industry almost collapsed, and in the new Electric Palaces and Picturedromes which were built throughout the country early in the 1920's, and which became so popular, the films shown were almost all American till as late as 1926.

The outstanding creators of the war period were the poets and painters. The shock and misery of life on the battlefields was something which the average man could not convey to those at home, even if he had wanted to. It was indescribable. It had robbed him of his youth and the memory remained with him always, forming a barrier, sometimes barely perceptible, sometimes almost insurmountable, between those who had shared it with him and those who had not.

The young poets, many of whom died in their early twenties, were able to express some of these common sufferings in poetry, which helped those who had been at home to understand a little of what their husbands, brothers and lovers had endured. The outstanding theme of this poetry is a sense of fellowship with their companions and a love of life itself, of nature and of animals.

> The kestrel hovering by day,
>   And the little owls that call by night,
> Bid him be swift and keen as they,
>   As keen of ear, as swift of sight.
>
> The blackbird sings to him, "Brother, brother,
>   If this be the last song you shall sing,
> Sing well, for you may not sing another;
>   Brother, sing."
>
> In dreary, doubtful, waiting hours,
>   Before the brazen frenzy starts,
> The horses show him nobler powers;
>   O patient eyes, courageous hearts![1]

These youths and young men had looked back to their school and college days, to the English countryside and their English homes. There was little dreaming of the love between man and woman and little hope for the future, for death was always present.

> The thundering line of battle stands,
>   And in the air death moans and sings;
>
> If I should die, think only this of me:
>   That there's some corner of a foreign field
> That is for ever England

wrote Rupert Brooke, and the foreign field where he was buried, at the age of twenty-eight, was the Greek Island of Skyros.

Robert Nichols and W. N. Hodgson both wrote of the love they bore for their comrades, who suffered with them.

> Was there love once? I have forgotten her.
> Was there grief once? Grief yet is mine.

[1] From "Into Battle" by Julian Grenfell (born 1888, killed in action 1915).

> O loved, living, dying, heroic soldier,
> All, all my joy, my grief, my love are thine!

wrote Robert Nichols, and W. N. Hodgson, too young to have lost his **faith** or grown cynical, wrote almost in triumph:

> We that have seen the strongest
> Cry like a beaten child,
> The sanest eyes unholy,
> The cleanest hands defiled,
> We that have known the heart-blood
> Less than the lees of wine,
> We that have seen men broken,
> We know man is divine.

Robert Nichols's description of trench warfare, the waiting for the signal to rush an advance, in an attempt to capture a few feet of Flanders mud, in that interminable, futile deadlock, reveals something of the tense, agonized terror that gripped them all.

> Time. Time!
>
> I hear my whistle shriek,
> Between teeth set;
> I fling an arm up,
> Scramble up the grime
> Over the parapet!
>
> I'm up. Go on.
> Something meets us.
> Head down into the storm that greets us.
>
> A wail.
> Lights. Blurr.
> Gone.
> On, on. Lead. Lead. Hail.
> Spatter. Whirr! Whirr!
> . . . . .
> Men crumpled, going down. . . .
> Go on. Go.
> Deafness. Numbness. The loudening tornado.
> Bullets. Mud. Stumbling and skating.

These poets spoke for all that lost generation of Britain's youth

They went with songs to the battle, they were young,
Straight of limb, true of eye, steady and aglow.
They were staunch to the end against odds uncounted.
They fell with their faces to the foe.[1]

The war artists of the 1914–1918 war also played an important part in bringing home the stark tragedy of the struggle. Moreover, the war itself had a deep effect on British art, bringing realism back in place of the experimental painting of the Cubists and Futurists of the immediate pre-war years, whose work, often incomprehensible to the uninitiated, had emerged from the Post-Impressionists, developing after the popularity of photography and the realization that the artist's task entailed more than mere faithful representation.

Early in the war, artists were commissioned by the Parliamentary Recruiting Committee to paint posters for the recruiting campaign. It was a challenge to present to the world, through the medium of art, an idea of the urgency of the situation and the poignancy of the suffering in Europe. Frank Brangwyn's "Remember Belgium" and G. Spencer Pryse's "The Only Road for an Englishman" appeared in London's Underground railways. Not only were they successful in their main intention of propaganda but they stimulated a new public interest in the significance of art.

C. R. W. Nevinson was one of the first artists exhibiting in London after actual war experience. His pre-war painting had been influenced by the Futurists and Cubists and he used some of their technique, particularly in conveying movement, to paint war pictures which were dramatically and profoundly realistic. He also used the straight lines of Cubism which, as Clutton Brock said, "express, in the most direct way, the sense that in war man behaves like a machine or part of a machine, that war is a process in which man is not treated as a human being but as an item in a great instrument of destruction, in which he ceases to be a person and is lost in a process. The Cubist method, with its repetition and sharp distinction of planes, expresses this sense of a mechanical process better than any other way of representation."[2]

Eric Kennington was another painter who had experienced active service and conveyed in his work the true nature of the conflict men

[1] Laurence Binyon, "For the Fallen".
[2] Quoted in *The Outline of Art*, edited by Sir William Orpen (Newnes).

were enduring, stripped of the false romanticism which some of the older-established artists were exhibiting at the Royal Academy, without having experienced the actuality of the fighting. The poster painters and cartoonists did such valuable work that in 1916 the Government decided to appoint official war artists to make permanent records of the war scenes. These included Muirhead Bone, James McBey, Sir William Orpen, Paul Nash, C. R. W. Nevinson, Eric Kennington and Sir John Lavery.

Other important artists of these years painting war pictures were P. Wyndham Lewis and William Roberts, both using some of the Cubist technique, and Stanley and Gilbert Spencer, John Nash and Henry Lamb, all of whom successfully conveyed ideas and emotions which captured the imagination and sympathy of the public, using techniques which were to influence the development of painting in the years to come.

And then, at eleven o'clock on 11th November 1918, the war ended. One by one the lights went on again in Europe, and people had time to pause, to reflect on the carnage and desolate waste that had been wrought and the millions of lives which had been sacrificed in achieving nothing; to survey the damage, and to realize how deep it had gone.

CHAPTER SEVEN

Great Britain after the First World War

At the news of the armistice, the people of Britain, apart from those too numbed with grief and bereavement for any rejoicing, went wild with thankfulness and merrymaking. King George V and Queen Mary drove to a service of thanksgiving at St. Paul's Cathedral and Lloyd George, the Prime Minister, attended St. Margaret's, Westminster. The Kaiser escaped into exile in Holland, and Germany, starving and shattered, declared herself a republic, under the presidency of Friedrich Ebert, who had been the leader of the pre-war German Social Democrat party. The Allies were to occupy the Rhineland, declared the newspapers, and the entire German fleet, including all the U-boats, together with all German aeroplanes and guns, were to be surrendered; all Allied prisoners were to be returned immediately, and the question of reparations was to be considered at the forthcoming peace conference.

As the troops and freed prisoners of war flocked back to England, families were joyfully reunited; and after the first weeks of happiness together they planned to rebuild their lives on the pattern of 1914, but this was not to be. The war had changed the world too much; and after the wanton destruction of men and material came the day of reckoning.

Lloyd George first called for a general election, and on 14th December 1918 he and his coalition government were returned to power with a strong majority. The Peace Conference of the Allies, France, Italy, Great Britain and America, was held in Paris early in 1919. Monsieur Clemenceau, the aged President of France, was elected President of the Conference, Signor Orlando represented Italy, President Wilson led the American delegation, Lloyd George, Arthur Balfour and Bonar Law the British, and amongst the Empire statesmen attending were General Botha and General Smuts from South Africa. No representatives from Germany, Austria, Bulgaria or Turkey were invited, for this was to be a dictated peace; and Russia was still torn by civil war and succumbing to the power of the Bolshevik Communist party.

The published peace aims of Great Britain were to "make the world safe for democracy". Small nations, such as Belgium, Holland, Switzerland, Poland, the Scandinavian countries, Greece and the Balkan states, must be recognized "as having exactly as good a title as their more powerful neighbours ... to a place in the sun". Britain wanted the "substitution for force and for the clash of competing ambition, for groupings and alliances, and a precarious equipoise, of a real European partnership based on the recognition of equal rights, and established and enforced by a common will".[1]

President Wilson, the idealist who believed in the fundamental goodness of mankind, had already suggested the formation of a League of Nations, which the Allies, early in 1917, had approved in general principle, saying: "In a general way they [the Allied Governments] desire to declare ... their whole-hearted agreement with the proposal to create a League of Nations which shall assure peace and justice throughout the world. They recognize all the benefit which will accrue to the cause of humanity and civilization from the institution of international arrangements designed to prevent violent conflicts between nations, and so framed as to provide the sanctions necessary to their enforcement, lest an illusory security should serve merely to facilitate fresh acts of aggression."[1]

America's four peace aims, announced by President Wilson early in 1918, were:[1]

First, that each part of the final settlement must be based upon the essential justice of that particular case and upon such alignments as are most likely to bring a peace that will be permanent.
Second, that peoples and provinces are not to be bartered about from sovereignty to sovereignty as if they were mere chattels and pawns in a game, even the great game, now for ever discredited, of the balance of power; but that
Third, every territorial settlement involved in this war must be made in the interest and for the benefit of the populations concerned, and not as a part of any mere adjustment or compromise of claims amongst the rival states; and
Fourth, that all well-defined national aspirations shall be accorded the utmost satisfaction that can be accorded them without introducing new or perpetuating old elements of discord and antagonism that would be

[1] National War Aims Committee, *Aims and Efforts of the War* (1918).

likely in time to break the peace of Europe and consequently of the world.

Italy had only a minor role in the peace talks, and before the end Signor Orlando had walked out of the conference room. France, having suffered so grievously and lost nearly a million and a half men fighting to defend her own soil, was determined on the severest measures against Germany and the German people.

From the outset the Peace Conference was an unhappy one. Fundamentally, the problem which caused the dissension was whether the Germans themselves could be held responsible for the war and should be punished as guilty people, or whether the war had been an inevitable result of the long years of competition between the nations of Europe, in which case blame could not be laid at the doors of any one group of people but could be assigned to the bad system, which must be abolished.

The Americans took the view that the German people were blameless and had been helpless in the hands of their leaders. "We are not enemies of the German people," said President Wilson, "and they are not our enemies. They did not originate or desire this hideous war, and we are vaguely conscious that we are fighting their cause, as they will some day see it themselves." The British, now that the fighting was over, were also inclined to be lenient to the German people themselves, though the Press was clamouring for enormous reparations, with little thought as to how the money was to be forthcoming.

The French were more realistic. They had been invaded and overrun by Germany three times in a century, in 1815, 1870 and 1914. Though the Germans were now starving and broken, the French distrusted the new German Republic which had been created from the ruins of the old militaristic empire. They wanted not only reparations but a concrete safeguard against further invasion. "A German republic based on the same principles of centralization and militarism as the old empire will still present great dangers and will still be a redoubtable menace to peace," they declared. The Rhine itself was the only safe frontier for France against such a threat, they considered, and they demanded that their territory be extended to its western bank. The other Allies, however, rejected France's claim, on the grounds that the occupation of German-populated territory would be against the principles on which the peace treaty was to be based.

In regard to the formation of the League of Nations, France advocated that it should be supported by an international army of French, British and American soldiers, to keep Germany from any future aggression, but here again they were defeated, for President Wilson would not countenance any such arrangement.

At last the territorial problems were settled by the conference. Alsace and Lorraine were restored to France. Belgium received a small extension to her territory. The people of Schleswig were given the right to vote whether they preferred to be included in Danish or German territory. Germany's Polish territory was taken from her and formed into a republic. All German colonies in South-west, West and East Africa and in the Pacific were entrusted to one or other of the Allies, under a mandate of the newly formed League of Nations. The Rhineland was to be occupied by Allied troops.

German territory thereby remained practically intact. The French signed with great unwillingness, giving up their claim to the Rhineland only on Great Britain and America guaranteeing the defence of France in the event of any future German attack. Even so, when Marshal Foch heard the details of the terms of the treaty he exclaimed: "This is not Peace. It is an Armistice for twenty years."

Nevertheless, Germany had been left temporarily powerless. Two days after the signing of the treaty her navy surrendered—five battle cruisers, ten battleships, five light cruisers and twenty-eight destroyers arriving in solemn procession at Scapa Flow. The officers of the German navy, however, made a last defiant, despairing gesture, and once the surrender had been accepted they themselves, to the mortification of Great Britain, secretly scuttled the great armada of which the Kaiser had been so proud.

All German artillery and weapons were destroyed. Her army was disbanded and she was allowed only a regular force of 100,000 men for the maintenance of internal order. No military aeroplanes or submarines were allowed and her navy was limited to a few small vessels of under 10,000 tons. She had lost almost the whole of her property abroad. She had lost her supplies of iron ore. Her trade and industry had been crippled and in particular she had lost her world lead in the dye and chemical industries.

While Germany was pondering on her problematical future under the terms of the Versailles Treaty, Mr. Wilson returned to the United

States to present the Senate with the Covenant of the League of Nations and a copy of the treaty for ratification. He received a cool reception, a shock from which he never recovered. The Senate refused to ratify the guarantee to France for defence in case of any future aggression by Germany, which had already been signed by Clemenceau, Lloyd George and Wilson himself, and at the general election a few months later, in 1920, his party lost office. With Coolidge as President, the Republicans now held the field, pursuing a policy of isolationism. They were determined to have no more dealings in European affairs and withdrew from the League of Nations, leaving as the two principal partners Great Britain and France.

The greatest trouble arising from the Versailles Treaty, however, was in the fabulous demands for reparations made by the Allies. They were an attempt to make Germany pay for the actual cost of the war, regardless of the fact that in order to do so she must manufacture and export, at the expense of the Allies' own markets; and that in order to reorganize her industries and manufactures she must, in the first place, borrow heavily from the Allies themselves. The Allies seized £100 million worth of German assets, but within a few years Germany was borrowing back £50 million, mainly from the United States and Great Britain.

Great Britain had lent millions of pounds to the Allies during the war and had herself been borrowing heavily from America. Though Britain had already cancelled many of the Allies' debts, declaring that they had been incurred during the fighting for a common cause, America insisted on interest from Great Britain for her own debts.

In 1922 Great Britain sent a note of the situation to the French and Italian governments. "The food, the materials, the munitions, required for the immense naval and military efforts of Great Britain, and half the £2,000 million advanced to the Allies, were provided by internal borrowing and taxation. Unfortunately a similar policy was beyond the power of any other European nation. Appeal was therefore made to the United States; but it was only on our security that they were prepared to lend it."

It was in this year that the Conservatives in the coalition government, who held the majority of the seats, decided that it was time for another Conservative Prime Minister. They broke with Lloyd George, who resigned, and his deputy, Bonar Law, became head of the government, with Stanley Baldwin as his Chancellor of the Exchequer. Mr. Baldwin's first task was to visit the United States with Mr. Montagu Norman, the Governor of the Bank of England, to discuss the problem of the war debt. He hoped for a lessening of the burden but was told that the debt must be paid, with interest at $3\frac{1}{2}$ per cent, which meant that Great Britain must pay £35 million each year for sixty-two years.

A few months later Mr. Bonar Law had to resign through ill health, and shortly afterwards he died. His deputy, Mr. Stanley Baldwin, became Prime Minister and Winston Churchill the new Chancellor of the Exchequer. Mr. Churchill went once more to the United States to discuss the war debt, pointing out the economic chaos throughout the world which the payment of these enormous sums of money would cause; but the United States of America was adamant. "They hired the money, didn't they?" was President Coolidge's comment.

Great Britain had suggested an all-round cancellation of war debts, but after learning of the United States' insistence on payment she declared to the Allies, in the Balfour note, that "she would collect no more from her debtors, Ally or former enemy, than the United States collected from her". At the end of the war Britain owed the United States some 4,000 million dollars and the Allies, mainly Russia, owed us 7,000 million dollars and the United States 6,000 million dollars. "'The enforcement of the Baldwin-Coolidge debt settlement", said Mr. Winston Churchill, "is a recognizable factor in the economic collapse which was presently to overwhelm the world, to prevent its recovery and inflame its hatreds."[1]

America also insisted on settlements from Italy and France, though at a lower rate of interest, and in order to find the money Great Britain, France and Italy now began to press Germany, who made a first payment on 31st August 1921, but the immediate result was a decline in the value of the mark. The German economy almost collapsed and for a while French troops occupied the vast coal-mining and iron-smelting districts of the Ruhr, as a reprisal for the non-payment of further instalments. Germany was saved by a loan from America. French troops were withdrawn from the Ruhr and by 1925 Germany was well on the way to economic recovery, but it was at the expense of British trade and commerce.

[1] Winston Churchill, *The Second World War*. Vol. I, *The Gathering Storm* (Cassell, 1948).

Wilhelm Dibelius, a German writing for Germans about Britain, said a year or two later: "The Peace of Versailles injured Germany deeply; but was the war worth while? Its immediate reactions have been most unsatisfactory. France and the United States have been strengthened politically in a way that is by no means to Britain's interest. Versailles, the League of Nations and separate treaties have built up for France a position of power in Europe that is most un-welcome. . . . Economically, too, where Germany has been successfully competed with on the Continent, the profits have gone to France, not to British industry. Even more striking is the post-war ascendancy of the United States. It is the great gainer by the war, financially, indus-trially and politically. It has gathered in Europe's gold, in payment for war supplies; it is the creditor of the States of Europe and takes ruthless political advantage of its financial superiority. . . . Financial power has further immensely increased American commerce; while British exports to all parts of the world have fallen, American have gone up. Where Germany has been driven from the field it has been to the advantage, not of Britain, but of America—and Japan. While American industry expands, British industry, in its vital sections (coal, cotton), contracts. America has become the greatest financial magnate in the world."[1]

This gloomy picture of Great Britain's economic plight was all too true. As her people, recovering from the peace celebrations, tried to pick up the threads of the old pre-war life again, they gradually realized how broken and entangled they had become.

To quote Dibelius again: "The landlords were burdened by Lloyd Georgian death duties, which, though not in origin connected with the war, were aggravated during its course and subsequently, with the result that in England as elsewhere the older aristocracy of birth and education was replaced by war profiteers who had come up from below: the vulgar parvenu flourished like the green bay tree, while the finer culture of the older social order collapsed under the combined pressure of prices and taxes."[1]

The levelling process of the social classes throughout Great Britain, which had begun before the war, now developed rapidly. Those who had formerly been rich moved out of their big houses, which they

[1] Wilhelm Dibelius, *England,* translation M. A. Hamilton (Cape, 1930).

could no longer afford to maintain, and there was the first threat of inflation.

Industrial and commercial concerns struggled to reassert themselves in the world markets and found others there before them. They had established themselves in the old days by paying low wages and offering cheap goods. Now the trade unions refused to accept less pay. They were determined to maintain the workers' standard of living, which was higher than anywhere else in Europe. British goods thereby became expensive and the rest of the world could not afford to buy them when cheaper goods of the same quality were available from elsewhere. The result was that there were not enough jobs to go round in Britain and many men returning from the fighting could find no work at all.

By July 1921 there were more than two and a half million unemployed in Great Britain. The figure gradually fell during the next year or two to 1,200,000, where it remained till 1930, when it rose sharply again to well over two million.

In 1920 all workers, except those in agriculture or domestic service, had to be insured against unemployment, and the following year the unemployed were also given an allowance for their dependent relatives. The queues at the labour exchanges for work or for the dole grew steadily longer and the men more hopeless. Some, in desperation, joined one or other of the services again. Some emigrated. The rest —and for years this meant, at best, more than a million men—managed to eke out an existence on the dole money, and as the months passed by, bringing nothing but continued disappointment and frustration, their vitality was sapped and they acquired the patient, defeated look of utter hopelessness. Children were born into unemployed families and grew up knowing no other way of life but the weekly trudge to the labour exchange for the dole. It was enough to keep people alive but allowed nothing for the simplest amenities beyond food and rent.

In the early 1920's the British Medical Association estimated that to maintain reasonable health a family of a man, wife and three children should spend 22s. 6½d. a week on food. The maximum unemployment benefit the man could draw was 29s. 3d. and the rent of the worst slum tenements was an average of 6s. a week, leaving him practically nothing for fuel and clothing.

Unemployment was worse in the industrial North and the Midlands, in Lancashire, Yorkshire, Durham, Staffordshire and South Wales, but the whole country was affected. Ex-officers and men who had had public school educations were glad to become commercial travellers, hawking silk stockings, encyclopaedias and vacuum cleaners from house to house.

With the re-establishment of the import of cheap food from the Empire the price of food fell, though the cost of other commodities rose. Cheap food, however, spelt ruin to the farmers once more. On 5th July 1921, the Minister of Agriculture announced in Parliament that the Government intended to decontrol agriculture and that the guarantee of minimum prices for corn and minimum wages for farm workers would have to be abandoned after the harvest of that year. The Wages Board reduced the minimum agricultural wage by four shillings, to 42s. a week, and then the Board itself was dissolved.

These decisions came without warning, and disaster for the farmers followed as suddenly. The price of wheat fell from 84s. 7d. a quarter to 44s. 7d. within a year, and with it fell the price of oats and barley, meat and milk. There was a rush to abandon arable farming again. Fields that had been ploughed for wheat for the following year were sown with neither wheat nor grass, and the furrows were left to tumble back into the weeds.

By December of 1921 agricultural wages had fallen to 37s. a week and by the end of 1922 the average pay was down to 28s. a week. The farm workers pressed for the re-establishment of wage control and this was achieved for them by the Agricultural Wages Act of 1924. For those in work things were better, but as economic conditions for the farming community as a whole remained bad, farmers who could not pay the legal wage had to get rid of their men.

The only government help to the farmers during these years was the introduction of the subsidized sugar-beet industry in 1924. Sugar-beet is an expensive crop to transport and it was therefore grown as close as possible to the first sugar-beet factories, which were built near the arable areas of the eastern counties. It proved a great help to the farmers of East Anglia, but elsewhere farmers were in dire straits. It did not pay to plough and more land was put to pasture. Even so, by 1927 more farmers had gone bankrupt and retired from the struggle. The year 1928 was a fair one for weather but 1929 was a drought, and to make matters worse North America had a record wheat harvest that summer and created a surplus. English wheat fell to 20s. 9d. a quarter, the lowest it had been for a hundred years, and as farm wages were not allowed to fluctuate with the varying fortunes of the industry, each year saw more and more farm workers unemployed.

By the end of 1921 it was estimated that not only were there more than two million unemployed in Britain but seven million workers had received wage cuts. The following year, with unemployment and the trade depressions growing, the Geddes Economy Committee recommended further cuts in government expenditure, which affected the pay of the army, navy and air force and of the teachers, as well as war pensions, and represented a saving of £64 million.

In 1925 the Locarno Pact was signed between Germany, Italy, France, Poland, Czechoslovakia, Belgium and Britain. By this time Germany had sufficiently recovered to have signed commercial treaties with France, Britain, Belgium and Luxembourg. Now she sat at the table as an equal partner with the other European delegates. This was intended to be the final peace agreement. Germany became a member of the League of Nations and the Allies prepared to leave the Rhineland. Mr. Baldwin signed for Great Britain, Herr Streseman for Germany. The Western democracies thereby agreed to keep the peace and made mutual agreements whereby if one power attacked any of the others, all would combine against the aggressor. It was in this year that President Ebert died and the ageing Field-Marshal von Hindenburg was elected in his place as President of the German Republic.

The situation in Europe seemed happier and more settled than it had been for years. Germany was a member of the League of Nations and making good use of the loans she was receiving from the United States and also from Great Britain. Though some Frenchmen still distrusted the German Republic, most hoped that the new climate of peace and goodwill would continue. "Away with rifles, machine-guns, cannon!" exclaimed Monsieur Briand, the French Prime Minister. "Clear the way for conciliation, arbitration, peace!"

In the meantime, Britain still had the problem of her reduced markets, particularly in Europe, as well as her vast army of unemployed, and Mr. Baldwin was a worried man. In October 1923 Parliament had been dissolved and in the General Election the Labour Party obtained 191 seats, the Liberals 158 and the Conservatives 258. With

PLATE 9

(*above*) Amy Johnson, who in 1930 flew solo from England to Australia.

(*left*) Rochester, June 1926: Sir Alan Cobham climbing into his plane for his flight to Australia.

(*below*) An early Imperial Airways plane at Croydon Airport.

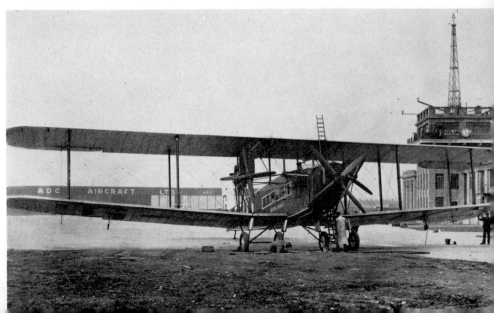

(*above*) Unemployed
dockers waiting at the
dock offices for casual
labour in March 1931.

PLATE 10

(*left*) Pontypridd, South
Wales, 1934:
unemployed miners
working on allotments
in order to feed their
families.

Contrasting housing conditions.

PLATE 11   (*above*) A Victorian street in Shoreditch.

(*below*) A "between wars" L.C.C. housing estate.

(*above*) A forlorn scene
in a Barcelona street on
28th August, 1936. In
the Spanish Civil War
women and children
fought side by side with
the men.

PLATE 12

(*right*) Spanish refugees,
fleeing from their
unhappy country, pour
over the border into
France, January 1939.

(*left*) Queen Mary being enthusiastically greeted by small patriots at Shorncliffe, Kent, July 1939.

PLATE 13

(*below*) The Oxford Street Sales in the 1930's. Even at slash prices goods often remained in the windows during these hard times.

(*above*) Mr. Neville Chamberlain meets Hitler at Berchtesgaden, September 1938, in one of three desperate attempts to preserve peace at any price.

PLATE 14

(*below, left*) Three soldiers in Whitehall reading the news of 3rd September, 1939.

(*below, right*) In 1939 all eyes were upon Neville Chamberlain, seen here with his parliamentary private secretary (now Sir Alec Douglas-Home).

PLATE 15

(*above*) May 1940: British soldiers on the beaches at Dunkirk, waiting for transport back to England.

(*below*) A German Dornier 17 burning on the beach, having been shot down while machine-gunning the streets of an English coastal town.

(right) Adolf Hitler, 1939.

PLATE 16

(below) 10th September, 1940: the beginning of the aerial attack on London. Mr. Winston Churchill is inspecting air-raid damage. (On his right is Mr. Duncan Sandys.)

the support of the Liberals the first British Labour government was formed, with Ramsay Macdonald as Prime Minister. Less than a year later, however, it was defeated and the Conservatives returned to power with Mr. Baldwin again Prime Minister.

The cost of living was rising and the trade unions were demanding higher wages. Mr. Baldwin felt that if wages could be reduced, more

Stanley Baldwin, three times Prime Minister.

people could be employed. A Royal Commission to inquire into conditions in the coal mining industry was set up. It found that three-quarters of the coal in the country was being produced at a loss, the mine owners were taking too much profit, the miners were being paid too highly and the industry was on the verge of bankruptcy; and it recommended nationalization.

The report confirmed Mr. Baldwin's belief that wages were too high and he selected this point alone to cure the trouble. He recommended a $13\frac{1}{2}$ per cent cut in wages and longer working hours, whereupon the Trades Union Congress threatened strike action. The Government stood firm and the strike began on 3rd May 1926. Socialists saw this as a clear-cut battle between capital and labour, with the capitalists cheating labour of the fruits of their work. The Trades Union Congress called for a general strike, which involved not only the miners but other industrial workers, railwaymen, transport workers and printers, amounting to nearly four million men. The Government refused to negotiate. It called on the army to keep power supplies and communications going, and citizens not involved in the dispute went about their daily work as best they could.

Nine days later the strike was called off, on the understanding that the Government would enter into negotiations to settle the dispute. Nothing was settled in the immediate future, however. The strike had been costly and proved another setback to industry. Unemployment figures rose and the queues for the dole grew longer. A year or two later the Prince of Wales (later to become Edward VIII and subsequently the Duke of Windsor) made an extensive tour of the areas which were suffering most extensively from the distress of unemployment, and afterwards he said: "Some of the things I see in these gloomy, poverty-stricken areas make me almost ashamed to be an Englishman. . . . Isn't it awful that I can do nothing for them but to make them smile?"[1]

It was in the same year as the General Strike, 1926, that a new constitution was drawn up for the countries of the British Empire. With complete freedom in their international relationships, they were now defined as ". . . autonomous communities within the British Empire, equal in status, in no way subordinate one to another in any aspect of their domestic or external affairs, though united by a common allegiance to the Crown, and freely associated as members of the British Commonwealth of Nations." The High Commissioners represented not the British Government but the Crown; and High Commissioners, acting as ambassadors, were exchanged between London and the countries of the Commonwealth as well as between the individual members themselves.

The next two or three years of the Baldwin administration brought little change in the country's economic troubles. In 1928 women at last won complete franchise, when they were given the vote at 21, just ten years after it had been given to women over 30, and the following year they had their opportunity to use it, in the General Election of 1929.

Labour was returned, with 289 seats. The Conservatives polled 259 and the Liberals 58, so that once again Labour depended on Liberal support. Ramsay Macdonald became Prime Minister, winning the election with his promise to nationalize coal, transport, the power in-

[1] Quoted in John Montgomery, *The Twenties* (Allen and Unwin, 1957).

dustries and life insurance, and to increase the taxation of the rich. Philip Snowden was his Chancellor of the Exchequer, Arthur Henderson the Foreign Secretary. Margaret Bondfield, the first woman cabinet minister and privy councillor, was Minister of Labour and Mr. J. H. Thomas was appointed to the newly created post of "Minister for Unemployment".

The depression in Britain was deepening. The markets for British manufactures were threatened by the expanding industries of America, Germany, Italy, Japan and the Dominions, and Britain's manufacturing costs were among the highest in the world, and still rising, for British working men were demanding higher wages than the economy of trade and industry could afford, as well as shorter working hours and the long week-end.

Mr. Macdonald's government had been in office for no more than a few months when the world slump came which the economists had been forecasting. It began in the United States, with the collapse of the money market on Wall Street. Too much credit had been given with too little security. Twenty thousand banks suspended payment in America and thousands of people were ruined and penniless. Trade and industry were thrown into confusion. Wages fell and unemployment quickly spread, till it reached the appalling figure of ten million.

The effect was quickly felt in Europe. In Germany, five million men were thrown out of work and in Britain the figure rose from just over a million to nearly three million.

The Macdonald government was in a desperate plight. It could not balance the Budget and found itself incapable of dealing with the situation. In 1931 Macdonald resigned and an emergency National government was formed, composed of ministers drawn from all three political parties, with a Cabinet of four Conservatives, four Socialists and two Liberals, to deal with the national crisis and find ways of meeting the Budget and restoring confidence abroad in British finances. Ramsay Macdonald was again Prime Minister, with Mr. Baldwin as second in command.

In September 1931, because there was not sufficient gold in the vaults of the Bank of England to back the numbers of pound notes that were being issued, the value of the pound had to be declared less. A pound would no longer buy so many goods nor so much foreign currency. The following month a new election was held and there was an overwhelming Conservative majority, but the new government was still an emergency National government with Ramsay Macdonald remaining as Prime Minister. He was not equal to the tremendous task entrusted to him. "His health and powers were failing fast, and he reigned in increasing decrepitude at the summit of the British system for nearly four fatal years," wrote Winston Churchill. "And very soon in these four years came Hitler."[1]

[1] Winston Churchill, *The Second World War.* Vol. I, *The Gathering Storm* (Cassell, 1948).

CHAPTER EIGHT

The 1920's

Though the background of the 1920's was one of increasing economic difficulties and the tragic, incurable core of the unemployed, the face Britain presented to the world was in some ways as gay as in the Edwardian days. It was a different, less elegant gaiety, noisy and brash, but now all those who were not immediately caught up in the deepening depression or the blight of unemployment had a chance to take part in it. The middle classes followed the rich and the proletariat the middle classes. Wages and salaries were not high, but they were adequate, and with the building of cinemas and dance halls, the popularity of radio, the increasing mania for watching sport, as opposed to taking part in it, and the opening of dozens of tea shops, cafés and restaurants, as well as roadhouses, which people could visit in their new, cheap motor cars, amusements were easily accessible.

Everyone wanted to forget. They wanted to forget the war years and the bereavement, the sight of the wounded and maimed, the unemployed and the dole queues, and the lurking suspicion that though the fighting had stopped for the time being, the world was fast descending into an even darker chaos. There were so many new and entertaining ways to divert oneself that for a few years life was one long party, and by the time people had wearied of it and paused to wonder where it was all leading they found themselves gadarening down into disaster at a speed which they were powerless to check.

During the first years of peace they danced. Jazz had arrived from America and dancing became a mania. There were tea dances at most of the hotels as well as dinner and supper dances. Society went to Mrs. Meyrick's night clubs, artists and writers to the Ham Bone, and in between these two types, the fashionable and the Bohemian, there were dozens of night clubs for dancing and drinking where, more often than not, the Negro music was played by Negro musicians imported from America.

Great dance halls were built for the proletariat and here they went with their partners to dance for hours. A girl or young man who had no partner would sometimes go alone, determined not to be left out of the current craze, and there were masters of ceremonies to introduce them to one another and keep everyone happily milling around the crowded floor.

It took some time for the older generation to grow accustomed to jazz after the honey-sweet melodies and simple rhythms of the pre-war waltzes and veletas.

> There was an exuberant coon
> Who invented a horrible tune
>   For a horrible dance
>   Which suggested the prance
> Of a half-epileptic baboon[1]

wrote one sufferer in *Punch*; but generally speaking familiarity wears down resistance, and few could help becoming familiar with jazz during the 1920's.

After jazz came the Hawaiian guitars and the hula-hula, and later the throbbing, melancholy beat of the Blues. In 1926 America introduced the most inelegant of all dances, the Charleston, the vogue for which spread from London to the provinces in a matter of weeks, till it seemed as though the whole of Britain was jerking, kicking and "twinkling".

Everyone danced, young and old. Except at the dance halls, one seldom went to a dance without a partner, and even at private dances guests were asked to bring their own partners or were provided with them and expected to dance with them for the whole evening. The days of the little white and silver, silk-tasselled dance programmes, when it would have been most indiscreet for a girl to allow the same partner to dance with her for more than two or three times in the course of the evening, had vanished, and so had the chaperones. In fact the chaperones were now dancing themselves, and those who were widows or spinsters often paid younger men to partner them. Sometimes they were unemployed ex-officers, only too glad to earn the money. More often they were impecunious but immaculately dressed young men who battened quite mercilessly on the older generation of lonely women. They were the "lounge lizards", who disappeared after the Second World War, never to return.

[1] Quoted in Alison Adburgham, *A Punch History of Manners and Modes* (Hutchinson, 1961).

Servants were still extremely difficult to come by, so that dancing and dining out increasingly took the place of entertaining at home. The old forms of etiquette and mannerliness, decorum and restraint, disappeared, and in their place came casualness, carelessness, freedom and a general laxity in standards of behaviour. Nothing much mattered in the end, so why worry!

Wages for servants were still low. A cook was paid about £60 a year, a parlourmaid £50 and a housemaid £40, and while there was alternative work to be had in factories, shops and offices young women preferred this to domestic service. Only during the worst period of the slump and the increased unemployment from 1929 onwards did some of them turn once more to domestic work, but by then many of the people who would otherwise have been glad to employ them were too hard pressed for money themselves. The rich, who had formerly kept large staffs, were now impoverished by estate and death duties and had abandoned their Mayfair mansions, many of which were being turned into offices or pulled down to make way for hotels, while the well-to-do were turning their large town houses into flats or moving into smaller, more easily run establishments.

Women had begun to bob their hair during the last years of the war, but with the peace they tended to wear it longer again. Skirts were still rather long—an average of three to four inches above the ankles, though the bright young things of society were wearing them considerably shorter. Tunics were the fashion, long and straight by day, looped and draped for afternoon and evening dresses. Wartime economies were still in force and during the summer simple, shapeless cotton dresses, with short sleeves and round necks, so plain that any amateur dressmaker could make one in an evening, became the rage. At the same time the big stores began to sell far more ready-made clothes. Women who had spent hours at their dressmakers in the old days found that the new ready-made clothes were almost as good, were cheaper and saved them hours of time. The shops developed their ready-made departments and before long were inaugurating the first mannequin parades.

By 1920 skirts were lengthening and there was a craze for home-made knitted jumpers. Everyone knitted them and they were loose, shapeless and incredibly dreary. Evening frocks, however, became increasingly diaphanous. The skirts were long but wispy and the tops extraordinarily scanty, backless and often suspended by only one thin shoulder strap.

By 1923 skirts were down to the ankles again and everyone looked svelte and slinky. There was a craze for large, brightly coloured prints. Sometimes they were floral patterns but more often hard, geometric ones, derived and ill-adapted from those of the Cubists, Georges

In 1922 women still wore their skirts long and the whole effect was tubular and shapeless.

Braque and Picasso, with no regard for the purpose of these artists' work, which primarily was to reduce objects to their most primitive form, in order to convey the idea underlying their existence. The 'cubist' patterns of the fabrics which were now being printed bore no relation to these sophisticated mental and emotional processes and were, for the most part, devoid of meaning, composed of bizarre triangles, spots and squares in ugly, unsubtle colours.

In 1924 skirts for daytime suddenly became very short. To make matters worse, the waist line was so low that the length of skirt was considerably shorter than that of the bodice and the whole dress was out of balance and extremely unattractive and inelegant. Skirts became shorter and shorter until 1927, when they barely covered the knees, and by now backless evening dresses were short too. To balance the short skirt, hair was bobbed again. Then it was bingled; then shingled; and in the end the Eton crop arrived. The cloche hat grew ever more enveloping until in the end it was perched low over the eyebrows, and

WHAT OUR LEGS HAVE TO PUT UP WITH.
Variety in Bond Street.

© *Punch*

The Smart Set, 1925.

there was a vogue for very mannish tailor-mades, women even taking to men's dinner jackets for a time in the evening, worn with straight, tight skirts. Bathing costumes became brief, one-piece affairs, in which women could enjoy to the full—or very nearly so—the new cult of sun-bathing, and they took to slacks for games and country week-ends.

When skirts could grow no shorter they inevitably began to lengthen, and there was a trend towards frills and flounces again. The first move was with evening dresses, which became long at the back while remaining short in the front, thereby making the most perfect pair of legs look bowed. Soon they were long all round and down to the ankles. Daytime dresses gradually followed the same trend. Hair was grown long to match and by 1929 Eton crops and shingles were replaced by rolls and curls. From America had come the fashion for Marcel waving and soon nearly every female head of hair in the country was tortured into hard, unrelenting ridges and furrows.

Silk stockings had become popular during the last years of the war, when women and girls were earning their own money and could afford them. After the war they became scarce and very expensive, and by 1922 the first artificial silk stockings came on the market. At first they were black, as the silk stockings had been. They were hard, shiny and ill-fitting, and when the first light ones appeared, in beige, blonde and startling flesh pink, they looked even worse. Once again, however, custom softened the first sharp reactions, and by the time the quality of artificial silk stockings had improved skirts were longer again and they were less obtrusive.

The changes in men's fashions were as well defined as women's. During the early post-war years plus-fours became popular for week-end sports and informal wear in country towns. They had evolved from knickerbockers and were loose and baggy, fastened below the knees, and usually of rough, large-checked tweed. As their popularity increased, however, and the manufacturers turned them out in ever-increasing quantities for the ready-to-wear repartments of men's outfitters, they became no longer high fashion and men took to plain flannel trousers again.

The formal top hat and frock coat disappeared from the streets of the City of London and the correct wear in conservative establishments such as the banks and the Stock Exchange, as well as for the West End, was the dark lounge suit and bowler hat. For social occasions, such as the summer race meetings, garden parties and weddings, the grey topper appeared with morning dress and became increasingly popular, till in time it completely replaced the old black top hat, except for diplomatic functions and funerals.

In 1925 Oxford introduced the fashion for Oxford bags. Trousers grew so wide that they fell over the back of the shoes. The fashion lasted

Men's fashions were also changing. In 1925 Oxford introduced the craze for Oxford Bags.

for only two years but not till the 1950's did trousers become really narrow again.

With the 1920's came the silent film craze. The British film industry had come into existence during the closing years of the nineteenth century, after the inventions of Eastman in America and Friese-Greene in London, and despite many setbacks and crises grew steadily during the opening years of the twentieth century.

The first moving pictures, as we have seen, were newsreels which were shown mainly as closing items in music halls. Robert Paul, an instrument maker, began to make improvements to film projectors and then experimented with the production of short comedy films. He formed a company, equipped a small studio at Southgate, and began to turn out numbers of these films, which were little different from dozens more which were soon being made in America and also in Europe, particularly France. Then Great Britain startled the world with a documentary film recording Queen Victoria's Diamond Jubilee procession. Nothing like it had ever been seen before or even conceived. It was an unqualified success and was shown not only in the music halls but in small parish and municipal halls which enterprising impresarios had hired for the occasion.

For some time after this there were no further developments. Paul and others like him continued to make short comedies, based mainly on music-hall acts, with perhaps two or three simple sets. Even the music halls began to lose interest in them but they were bought by showmen for the fairgrounds and also by small-time touring companies, making one-night stands in villages and provincial towns. Soon some of the fairground people went over entirely to the showing of films, touring the countryside with their expensive equipment and heavy trailers, from which they generated their own electricity. Their booths seated up to eight hundred people and the barkers stood at the entrances calling to the people to come and see the latest miracle of the age—moving pictures.

The next step was for young businessmen to hire local municipal halls for Saturday afternoon and evening film shows. They proved so popular and profitable that the exhibitors were soon renting halls for showing films every night of the week, and making good livings for themselves into the bargain. Paul supplied the projectors for these early ventures and also many of the films. In his studios at Southgate he continued to experiment. He mounted his camera on a trolley for tracking shots, introduced lighting and developed all manner of intriguing camera tricks. As a director he was soon outclassed by other film makers but in fact none of these early British shorts had any distinction, for they were made in the fairground tradition for unsophisticated, uneducated audiences who delighted in the antics of knockabout music-hall comedians and still thought that jokes about mothers-in-law and kippers were funny.

In France, Léon Gaumont and Charles Pathé were developing the art of the cinema more seriously. Léon Gaumont opened a London office in the late 1890's for the sale of French cinematograph equipment, appointing as his London agent Colonel Bromhead, and soon Gaumont was producing short films both in Britain and in France. Charles Pathé and his brother Emil were Paris agents for Edison's phonograph and while visiting London bought some of Paul's equipment. They secured financial support to an extent which astonished the less vigorous British film producers and had soon set up film production units in Great Britain and the United States, as well as in Italy, Germany, Russia and Japan.

London, still the financial heart of the world and the principal exchange mart, became also the world distributing centre for films, which by this time were being made mainly in Britain, France, Denmark, Germany and Italy, the Americans being still preoccupied with news and factual films. The audiences for the European films increased steadily. Programmes consisted of seven or eight ten-minute films and included a few documentaries and newsreels; and in 1910 the Pathé Gazette was shown for the first time.

America now set herself to catch up and followed *The Great Train Robbery* with more story films. The interest in film-going spread quickly. The audiences, still for the most part the simple and the young, liked the new method of pictorial story-telling. It made no demands on their intellect or their imagination. They did not have to read, except for the few explanatory sub-titles; and apart from the playing of the patient pianist, who for hours on end thumped out the appropriate background music, they did not have to listen either. They just sat passively and watched, identifying themselves with the characters on the screen, drifting into a fantasy world of high living and adventure, and before long of crime and violence.

In Britain, businessmen were buying up shops, roller-skating rinks and empty garages in their local towns and turning them into small cinemas. The average capacity was three hundred seats, admission was 3d. and 6d., and programmes, which lasted about an hour and a quarter, were changed twice a week. Then films became longer and more ambitious, appealing to a wider range of the public. Programmes became double the length, and in order to see a return on their money cinema owners had to build larger cinemas. In 1909 and 1910 the first cinemas were built. They were ornate but very comfortable, with elegant names such as the Elite, the Bijou and the de Luxe. They had marbled vestibules, palm courts and tea lounges, and the music was provided by small orchestras.

Businessmen began to buy chains of cinemas throughout the country and by 1914 there were over a hundred small cinema circuits in Britain, owning between them 15 to 20 per cent of the three to four thousand cinemas which had come into existence. As many as 75,000 people were employed in the distributing side of the business alone, exchanging and selling films and reselling them to the small proprietors, after they had been the rounds of the bigger circuits.

The early British story films remained of small significance and by 1909 America had begun to flood the market with domestic dramas, comedies and Westerns. But though Great Britain was slow in mastering the story film she made her mark with scientific, nature and travel films, for it was during these pre-war years that the gentle, unassuming Percy Smith, using apparatus which was astonishingly simple but highly ingenious, began making his wonderful nature films, showing in slow motion, by means of microscopes and speeded-up photography, the life cycle of plants and flowers. Percy Smith was dedicated to his work and by means of an alarm clock wired from his garden shed to his bedside was able to photograph his plants night and day throughout their growth. By 1914 he had already made fifty-four nature films and Oliver Pike was photographing nature and bird life for Pathé.

The longest British documentary of this time was the Scott Antarctic Expedition, made for Gaumont, which ran for an hour and a half; and Cherry Kearton, with his brother Richard, was making the first travelogues in Africa, Asia and North and South America, bringing the film home to their studio at Clapham to edit. During the two or three years immediately before 1914 several British film producers tried to beat the competition of American feature films by making improved British films, and there were thirty British film studios at work, the most important being centred in the London area, at Ealing, Shepherd's Bush, Elstree, Twickenham and Merton Park.

Dr. Jupp founded London Films at Twickenham Studios, in a gallant attempt to make films of an improved quality and content compared with those proving so popular from America, and he imported American directors and technicians to help the experiment. There was no lack of British acting talent and from the London theatres came

Henry Ainley, Sir Johnston Forbes-Robertson and Sir Frank Benson, playing mostly in silent versions of adaptations of Shakespeare. Unlike the Americans, however, the new British film actors did not at once adapt their stage technique to the equally demanding but quite different acting technique required by the film camera, in front of which every shade of emotion, the twist of a smile, the flicker of an eyelid, was minutely recorded and exaggerated. Their performances, therefore, attuned to a theatre stage, from which they had been used to projecting their emotions, thoughts and intentions across the foot-lights to the far reaches of the pit and gallery, appeared overplayed and, to the unsophisticated, almost ludicrous.

Before there was time for matters to right themselves came the war. Nearly all the film technicians and personnel were called into the army and although a handful of studios managed to keep open the British film industry as a whole almost disappeared. America, however, not involved in the fighting until 1917, forged ahead, so that during the war and throughout the 1920's it was mostly American films which were being shown in the cinemas of Britain.

Women and girls sighed romantically as they came to know and love the first American film stars, John Gilbert, Lionel Barrymore, Earl Williams, Adolphe Menjou, Ramon Navarro, Douglas Fairbanks and Rudolph Valentino. They were soon aping the fashions of Mary Pickford, Pola Negri, Lillian and Dorothy Gish, Ruth Roland, Nazimova, Theda Bara, Pearl White and Marion Davies. Not only did they copy their clothes and their hairdressing; they also copied their make-up, with all the exaggeration demanded by the film camera, so that the effect in the cold light of an English street was often startling to the point of being grotesque.

The Americans were still making a great many adaptations of the classics—Shakespeare, Dickens, Thackeray, Robert Louis Stevenson, Thomas Hardy, Dumas, Victor Hugo, Tolstoy and Ibsen—as the British producers had tried to do, though often the American versions were grossly bowdlerized. But now the Americans began to buy original stories and employ script writers with sufficient literary ability to make real contributions to this new technique of visual story-telling. For light relief they offered domestic comedies, some good Westerns, the improbable adventures of Pearl White, the exploits of Elaine, the slapstick, custard pie comedies of Mack Sennett and the Keystone Cops, and later the brilliant social comedies of Charlie Chaplin.

During the 1920's British film producers were at work again, but their productions were not in sufficient numbers to fill the cinema programmes, nor could they sell their films to America and thereby recover some of their costs. Moreover, America was by now making giant spectaculars, such as *The Birth of a Nation* and *The Four Horsemen of the Apocalypse*. In Britain the slump was beginning and there was no money forthcoming from the City of London to lend for competing productions on this lavish scale. Many attempts were made, but British films were still too understated and restrained to compete with the American brashness for which the cinema-going public had now acquired the taste. Nevertheless the young British directors who later were to make their mark in the business were learning their job during these years, albeit with pain and many disappointments. To assess public taste is the problem of every showman and it can be judged only by trial and error; and the errors of the twenties usually brought such financial disaster that there was seldom an opportunity for a second chance.

By November 1924 it was reported that not a single foot of film was being shot in any British studio, and increasing numbers of British actors and actresses went to Hollywood to find work. Then gradually the prestige of British films began to rise again, with the early work of Michael Balcon, Victor Saville and Alfred Hitchcock. A few years later Herbert Wilcox and Anthony Asquith were showing the promise of their future attainments.

It was a slow business and still British films did not sell in America. Nevertheless the prestige of the British documentary was maintained during these years by the work of Bruce Woolfe, who has been called the father of British documentaries. Working first at Elstree and then at Welwyn Garden City, he founded British Instructional Films, and with Percy Smith, Oliver Pike and Charles Head launched the delightful "Secrets of Nature" films. A few years later Mary Field joined him, re-editing the films and adapting their pace to the post-war taste. Bruce Woolfe also made several important war films, including *The Battle of Jutland* and *Zeebrugge*, using contemporary war film records and marrying them with scenes shot in his studio.

Yet by 1926 British films were occupying only 5 per cent of the time that the British public were spending in the cinemas—for the lack of British films did not deter them from flocking to see more and more American productions, which the American industry could afford to release cheaply. The exhibiting and renting side of the British business flourished and now began the age of the super-cinema. The Tivoli was built in the Strand, replacing the old Tivoli music hall. The New Gallery in Regent Street was rebuilt. The Capitol appeared in the Haymarket and the Plaza in Lower Regent Street. In 1927 the Astoria was built in the Charing Cross Road and the following year the Regal at Marble Arch and the Empire in Leicester Square, on the site of the most famous of all the Victorian music halls of London. They were provided with orchestras twenty strong, and then giant cinema organs were installed, which before long ousted the other musicians completely.

Germany, Denmark, France and Italy all suffered from the American supremacy and found their films unsaleable outside their own countries. In Germany in particular, however, film makers began to experiment with new camera techniques and lighting, with unusual angles to heighten dramatic and emotional tensions and thereby give more vigour and reality to their stories. These new German techniques impressed both the American and English directors and cameramen and began to influence their work, but the general public were not ready for change and preferred the mixture as before, so that throughout the twenties it was American and American-type British films which they were seeing with unfailing regularity. The cinema, with its spurious luxury, was for many of the working classes a refuge from homes overcrowded and uncomfortable, and amongst the poorer sections of the community it was not uncommon for young people to spend three or four nights a week at the pictures.

The intellectuals were by this time showing an interest in the possibilities of the film as an art form, and in 1925 the London Film Society was formed to study the work of the forward thinking film makers of Russia, France, Germany and central Europe, meeting each Sunday afternoon at the New Gallery in Regent Street; but within a few years small specialist cinemas as, for example, the Academy in Oxford Street, had come into existence for showing these films commercially to the general public.

In 1927, to help the British industry, the Government passed an Act to restrict the number of American films that could be shown in British cinemas. It was of little interest to the distributors but helped the film makers a great deal, for it required cinemas in Britain to show a proportion of one British picture in ten, the quota to rise annually, so that in time one in every four pictures would be British. The industry was stirred to fresh endeavours and the quota Act enabled young British technicians to receive a training during the twenties and thirties which helped them to produce the distinguished British films of the forties.

In the mid-twenties more changes were on the way. In 1926, the year that Greta Garbo arrived in Hollywood, Warner Brothers acquired a device for reproducing sound on a wax recording, which was synchronized with the film projector. It was the beginning of "Talkies". The first experiment was in the silent film *Don Juan*, starring John Barrymore, which was synchronized with a musical score. Then came Warner's *The Singing Fool*, with Al Jolson. The first all-talking film was released by Warner's in 1928 and was shown at the Regal, Marble Arch. In 1929 it was shown throughout the rest of the country and proved so popular that there was an urgent demand for more. The days of the silent film were numbered, and with the passing of the twenties the silent film passed too, into the archives of the film libraries.

As important in the social life of the twenties as the silent film was the radio. As early as 1904, when Professor Ambrose Fleming invented the thermionic valve, it had been possible to relay speech and music by wireless telegraphy, as well as Marconi's original Morse signals; and during the war speech had actually been relayed to an aeroplane in flight.

In 1920 the Marconi Company opened an experimental station at Chelmsford, from which they relayed readings and music, which were picked up by enthusiastic wireless amateurs. Interest in the possibilities of wireless as an entertainment medium quickly grew, especially after Dame Nellie Melba had broadcast from Chelmsford and her voice had been heard as far away as Paris and Berlin.

There was soon a demand for a regular service of entertainment programmes. Wireless telegraphy was under the control of the Post Office and in 1922 the Postmaster-General decided to hand the responsibility to the British Broadcasting Company, which had been formed by Captain Eckersley, with capital raised mainly from six manufacturers of wireless equipment. He operated from Savoy Hill and the Post Office charged listeners ten shillings a year for a licence, half of which went to the new company and half to the Post Office. Within twelve months the number of licence holders rose from 10,000 to half a million and by 1924 it had risen to well over a million. Equipment was crude at first, with headphones and batteries which had to

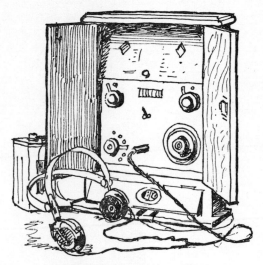

An early battery-set radio.

be frequently recharged, but soon they had given way to loudspeakers and transformers run from the mains, while indoor aerials replaced the long bean poles which, in the early days, were perched on rooftops or sprouted from so many back gardens.

The first programmes from Savoy Hill consisted of news, children's programmes of songs and stories, talks, religious services and orchestral concerts. Many people resented the monopoly granted to the British Broadcasting Company and pleaded for commercial radio stations similar to those which had already come into existence in America, but the Government refused to consider them and in 1922 John Reith was appointed general manager. Eight stations were built for the company throughout the country, at London, Birmingham, Manchester, Newcastle, Cardiff, Glasgow, Aberdeen and Bournemouth, for purposes of relay, and in 1925 a booster station at Daventry to cover the scattered rural areas. As more and more parts of the country were able to receive the programmes, the number of listeners grew, till in 1927 it was estimated that two and a half million homes had radio sets.

John Reith took his task seriously—some said too seriously. He saw the radio as an important medium of communication, not only for entertainment but for education and enlightenment, an invention as important to twentieth-century humanity as Caxton's printing press had been in the fifteenth century. His programmes were of a high standard, and though many who saw the radio as a fresh means of dispensing light entertainment declared that he had no right to decide what people should hear, he was never persuaded against his will and was quite impervious to the blandishments of vested interests. In 1927 the British Broadcasting Company became the British Broadcasting Corporation and John Reith, afterwards knighted, was appointed Director-General.

In those early days at Savoy Hill the announcers, whose voices and accents were impeccable to the point of irritating some of their inevitable critics, always wore full evening dress in the evenings, the studios from which they made their broadcasts were shrouded in long, heavy curtains, to absorb any extraneous sound, and the atmosphere was one of cheerful elegance. Of the educational programmes, perhaps the most loved were Monsieur Stephan's French lessons and Sir Walford Davies's talks on musical appreciation. Both were natural broadcasters and are so well remembered because the warmth of their personalities and the clarity of their expositions, which only such supreme masters of their crafts could ever have achieved, were carried to the heart of every listener.

An outstanding date in the history of broadcasting was 1924 when, on the occasion of the opening of the Wembley Exhibition, King George V's speech was broadcast to some six or seven million people, who were able to hear his voice for the first time.

Sir John Reith confessed to a fondness for dance music and the late night broadcasts of the Savoy Orpheans, Paul Whiteman, Jack Hylton, Jack Payne and later Henry Hall gave untold pleasure to thousands. More important still, the British public were able to hear, through radio—many of them for the first time—the music of the masters and the great orchestras of the world, including the B.B.C. Symphony

Orchestra itself, under the direction of Sir Adrian Boult, and with guest conductors such as Sir Landon Ronald, Sir Edward Elgar and Sir Thomas Beecham. Sir Henry Wood's promenade concerts were broadcast from the Queen's Hall, and Galli-Curci was heard from Covent Garden.

People to whom serious music had been incomprehensible began to hear it afresh and with understanding, and then with appreciation and delight. And it was to Sir John Reith that they owed their musical education and the hours of infinite pleasure it gave them.

Variety programmes, plays, sports commentaries and outside broadcasts of important national events were soon included in the regular B.B.C. programmes, as well as talks and discussions, appeals for charities and SOS appeals. In 1926 a device was invented for bottling programmes, so that they could be recorded and repeated at a future date. This was the year that John Logie Baird, working in a small room in Frith Street in Soho, succeeded, after years of experiment and frustration, in transmitting a picture by wireless. It was the beginning of television. Many years and another world war were to pass into history before television became familiar to everyone, and who would have dared say, in 1926, that the popularity of radio could ever be superseded by any other form of transmission?

London's theatres were gay and glittering during the twenties, though theatre-going was less formal and fewer people wore evening dress. The restaurants, for theatre dinners and suppers, soon re-established their pre-war standards and more of the inexpensive foreign restaurants appeared in Soho—French, German, Austrian and Italian; while for the timid souls, with more conservative tastes and little money to spend, there were the marble halls of the Lyons Corner Houses, which gave excellent value and service, with music thrown in.

For the feather-brained and those who wanted a good laugh there were the Ben Travers farces at the Aldwych, with Ralph Lynn, Robertson Hare and Tom Walls. André Charlot and C. B. Cochran were staging their sumptuous, brilliant revues, in which the young Noël Coward had his first chance as both an actor and writer, and stars such as Beatrice Lillie, Jack Hulbert, Jack Buchanan, Gertrude Lawrence, Jessie Matthews, June Inverclyde, Alice Delysia, Peggy Wood, Evelyn Laye, Nelson Keys and Sacha Guitry all made their mark and delighted their audiences. *The Co-Optimists* were at the

Palace and *Rose Marie* at Drury Lane. Later came *No, No, Nanette,* and Nigel Playfair presented *The Beggar's Opera* at the Lyric Theatre, Hammersmith.

In the straight plays of the twenties there was a vogue for drawing-room comedies of high society, the most famous being Frederick Lonsdale's *The Last of Mrs. Cheyney.* They were all in the tradition of the pre-war era and looked backwards rather than forwards, but two famous plays, *White Cargo* and *Young Woodley,* attracted attention for their handling of social problems; and *Journey's End,* the first of the war plays, underlining the miseries of war, strengthened the current thinking that such a disaster must never again befall mankind. Some of Somerset Maugham's plays, such as *The Circle,* first appeared at this time, but Noël Coward's brittle comedies and dramas, running all through the twenties—*I'll Leave It To You, The Young Idea, The Vortex, Fallen Angels, Easy Virtue* and *The Queen Was In The Parlour*—were perhaps most characteristic of the mood of the younger generation of the decade, with an understatement of emotion, a very tentative approach to the serious business of living and a restless cynicism. In 1928 appeared the Cochran revue *This Year of Grace,* most of which was written by Noël Coward, and the following year perhaps the most successful of all his musicals, *Bitter Sweet.*

Bernard Shaw was at the height of his powers and his play *St. Joan* was produced at the New Theatre, with Sybil Thorndike playing the part of St. Joan, a Shaw season was held at the Regent Theatre, King's Cross, and Barry Jackson presented *Back to Methuselah* at the Court, Sloane Square, with the Birmingham Repertory Company. At the Old Vic, Lilian Baylis had been presenting Shakespeare and opera since before the war, but in the twenties she strengthened her position and the Old Vic Foundation bought the theatre and site of Sadler's Wells in Islington.

It was in 1912, when Miss Emma Cons died, that her niece Lilian Baylis, who for the previous fourteen years had been acting manager, became the new licensee and manager of the Old Vic. Lilian Baylis was a passionate believer in the need for art in the lives of all human beings, and the theatre, she said, "is perhaps the most important and accessible and the most easily understood branch of art for the men and women in the street," for "all art is a bond between rich and poor; it allows of no class distinctions; more than that, it is a bond between nations and nations, and may do much to help widely differing peoples to understand the peculiar problems of life in each country." She believed with Dr. Dearmer that "Art is a spiritual necessity. Civilization cannot exist in its absence, for without it civilization is but organized savagery."

Miss Baylis therefore set to work to make the best of dramatic art "within reach of the poorest". The Old Vic had been a music hall at the end of the nineteenth century and in the early days of the cinema it had included short films in its programmes. But as films became more ambitious and at the same time more violently realistic and charged with false sentiments and emotions, they fell below the standard of artistic integrity which Lilian Baylis set for all her presentations. Though always hard pressed for money, despite bequests from various benefactors who deeply admired the seriousness and importance of her work, she began to produce opera, and by the autumn of 1914 had also collected a stock company of first-class actors for the production of the plays of Shakespeare.

Matheson Lang and his wife helped in the early days and Andrew Leigh and J. Fisher White both acted and produced. During the war years Miss Baylis carried on, producing both opera and Shakespeare, as well as other plays of the classical dramatists and a few of the moderns, including Laurence Binyon. Despite the shortage of male actors she provided first-class entertainment for the thousands of soldiers and sailors passing through London and staying at the nearby Union Jack Club in the Waterloo Road, and its wartime annexe, Morley College, the working men's college, which had been founded by Emma Cons and was at that time housed in the Old Vic premises. Miss Baylis also gave special matinées of Shakespeare for children of the L.C.C. schools, and during the twenties thousands of boys and girls went there to enjoy their first experience of the theatre.

Though there was seldom a time when a play of Shakespeare's was not being produced in the West End—in 1925, for example, John Barrymore produced *Hamlet* at the Haymarket—the Old Vic and the newly acquired Sadler's Wells provided two permanent homes for Shakespeare, as well as offering opera, on a self-supporting basis, six times a week for nine months of the year.

The quality of Lilian Baylis's productions was always high. From 1920 to 1925 Robert Atkins produced all the Shakespeare plays at the

Old Vic. Andrew Leigh followed and in 1929 Harcourt Williams became a resident producer. It was an invaluable training ground for many young actors who were later to win fame, amongst them such stars as Edith Evans, John Gielgud and Donald Wolfit.

In 1924 Ninette de Valois, a young Irish ballet dancer, joined the Diaghilev ballet company. Like Lilian Baylis she had an impeccable standard of artistic integrity. Interested more perhaps in the ballet as a form of artistic expression and in its relation to drama than in the dancing itself, and dissatisfied with the limitations of her work with Diaghilev, she left after two years to found her own school of ballet, the Academy of Choreographic Art. Though it was not till the 1930's that Ninette de Valois was to join Lilian Baylis and create the distinguished Sadler's Wells Ballet Company, the foundations of her work were already being laid during the twenties.

The world of literature was no less alive than that of the theatre and this was a period of intelligent, though unfortunately short-lived, literary journals, which included the *Adelphi*, the *London Mercury*, *Life and Letters*, the *Bookman* and the *Athenaeum*. Bernard Shaw was probably the most distinguished man of letters in Britain at this time, but Aldous Huxley quickly came to fame with his novels *Crome Yellow*, *Antic Hay*, *Those Barren Leaves* and *Point Counter Point*, all of which were published during the twenties, and D. H. Lawrence, who died in 1930, was also writing many of his important novels during these years. Hugh Walpole and Somerset Maugham were both writing and in 1928 Evelyn Waugh achieved fame with his first novel, *Decline and Fall*, which he followed with *Vile Bodies* in 1929, the year that J. B. Priestley published his first best-seller, *The Good Companions*. Amongst the women writers the most distinguished were Virginia Woolf and Rose Macaulay; and in the realm of crime and detective fiction, perhaps the most famous of all thriller writers, Edgar Wallace, was in his heyday, publishing story after story at a bewildering speed, many of which were filmed or dramatized.

Amongst the most widely read poets of the decade were Hilaire Belloc, G. K. Chesterton, Edmund Blunden, Maurice Baring, Gordon Bottomley, John Freeman, John Masefield, John Drinkwater, James Stephens, Victoria Sackville-West, Edith Sitwell and Harold Monro, who gave readings in his Poetry Book Shop in Bloomsbury. Most of these poets—the Georgian group—wrote with a "timeless lyricism" and a yearning for the pre-war life, which in contrast to the bustling twenties seemed by now to have been so uncomplicated and sweet.

The 1920's were the years of the first long-distance air flights. On 1st May 1919 civil flying was authorized in Britain and the following month John Alcock and Arthur Brown flew non-stop across the Atlantic to make aviation history, completing the flight in just over sixteen hours. In November 1919 the Smith Brothers flew a Vickers Vimy from London to Australia in just over four weeks and in 1922 James Doolittle flew across the United States in a day. There followed a long sequence of first flights to distant parts of the world, till a wondering public could wonder no more and began to realize that the whole world, so vast and complicated, was, in terms of physical accessibility, becoming very small indeed. Alan Cobham was the first man to fly to Australia and back. In 1927 Charles Lindbergh flew solo, in a monoplane, from Long Island to Paris in $33\frac{1}{2}$ hours. Bert Hinkler flew to South Africa and then to Australia. Women took to the air. Lady Heath and Lady Bailey both flew from South Africa to London and Amelia Earhart across the Atlantic. The woman who created most attention was Amy Johnson, who, with little flying experience, flew alone in her second-hand Gypsy Moth, *Jason*, from London to Australia.

The first flying club was at Hendon but very soon flying clubs and aerodromes were to be seen all over the country. The Royal Air Force was created, from the nucleus of the old war-time Royal Flying Corps, and the first commercial air companies were formed, for regular passenger services from London to the Continent.

Air travel was still far too expensive for ordinary tourists, however, and in any case they were still too interested in their new motor cars. British-made cars were expensive to buy and to run at first, for manufacturers were still concentrating on luxury cars for the rich, but Ford's were exporting cheaper cars from America and within a few years had established an assembly plant at Manchester. William Morris, afterwards Lord Nuffield, was the principal maker of cheap British cars after the war and his Morris Cowleys and Morris Oxfords were soon competing favourably with Fords. With the onset of the slump he reduced his prices in a successful attempt to promote sales. By 1925 he was selling nearly 50,000 cars a year. Other British com-

10

panies joined the Morris group and by 1939 they were producing a Morris Minor for £100.

For the rich there were the Rolls-Royce and the Daimler, but Morris's cheap cars made motoring possible for thousands of the middle classes. They began the motoring craze, and at week-ends the countryside and the roads to the coast became busy with people en-

The Morris Oxford, one of the cheaper family cars which began the motoring craze for the middle classes.

joying themselves as never before, on pleasure jaunts and exploration of the isolated hamlets and villages of England, which hitherto had almost escaped the onslaught of twentieth-century civilization and were still dreaming away their placid existences in an atmosphere of eighteenth-century feudalism.

Housing was one of the most pressing of the post-war social needs. There had been little building during the war and men returning from the forces, many to marry and have families of their own, found it almost impossible to obtain homes. With the increase in wages demanded by the trade unions, and a general rise in the standard of living, apart from those who were unemployed, their requirements were higher. No longer would they be satisfied with two or three rooms in someone else's house. They wanted a home of their own, with a garden and possibly a garage as well. To add to the problem the population was increasing and more people were flocking to London and the South from the half-derelict manufacturing and industrial regions of the North and the Midlands. Building costs were high and the houses and housing estates that were devised were hastily planned and ill-conceived. It was a case of more and more houses as quickly as possible, regardless of the overall appearance. The result was endless, dreary rows of small, ill-equipped houses and long, cheerless roads, devoid of trees and flowers. In design they were mostly the local builder's fancy but the most popular style was imitation Tudor, which came to be known as "Tudor Georgette".

Rooms were small and, partly through necessity, there was a fashion for austerity. Wallpapers disappeared and walls were distempered, more often than not in a dull, thick cream colour. Pictures were unfashionable and were rarely seen, while furniture was both expensive and shoddy, often of varnished oak. The three-piece suite was the mark of respectability and it was invariably upholstered in a fabric of pseudo-Cubist pattern, like the women's frocks, the favourite colours being brown, beige and a dull orange; carpets and curtains were of a similar order, bespattered with jazzy, meaningless and harsh geometric shapes.

These were the homes of the new lower middle classes. Most of the houses were bought through building societies and much of the furniture was being acquired through the steadily increasing menace of hire purchase.

During the first half of the twenties less than half a million houses were built, but by 1924 the housing shortage had become so desperate that within the next six years well over a million more had been put up. In building these sad housing developments no thought or direction was given to planning garden suburbs such as Canon and Dame Henrietta Barnett had created at Hampstead early in the century, or to the garden cities that Ebenezer Howard had advocated and brought into being at Letchworth and Welwyn. His purpose had been to decentralize industries and create self-supporting industrial towns in virgin countryside, where land was relatively cheap, with factories in pleasant surroundings, parks, civic buildings, shops, facilities for entertainment and sport and houses and gardens for the community, all within easy distance of one another. A great deal of Welwyn Garden City was developed during the 1920's, the architect responsible being Louis de Soissons, and the attractive, matured result is a salutary reminder of what might have been accomplished elsewhere. But the greater part of the building went on in endless ribbon development, eating up the countryside and transforming it to total urbanization. Within a very short time the tenants of these new houses realized that no thought had been given to the provision of playing fields and most of the children were playing in the streets. There were no football fields, cricket pitches or tennis courts. The National Playing Fields Association was formed to try to solve the problem by acquiring sites which could be used for sport, and branches were soon being established all over the country, their ultimate purpose being to promote facilities for open-air recreation in every city, town and village.

The 1920's showed an increasing interest in sport amongst the British, particularly in watching it. With shorter working hours and more leisure, their enthusiasm for cricket, football, boxing, lawn tennis, golf, athletics, horse and motor racing became almost an obsession. Racing and football drew the most spectators. Thousands went to the Grand National and the Derby and 100,000 was a usual attendance for the Cup Final at Wembley. The crowds watching the Oxford and Cambridge boat race and flocking to Lord's or the Oval for the test matches seemed to grow bigger every year, and after the new ground and the Centre Court Stadium of the All England Lawn Tennis Club were opened at Wimbledon in 1922, Wimbledon fortnight became for many a part of the summer social round.

There was an infinite variety of things to do and see during the 1920's—motoring and sport, the radio and the films, new books by the score and new ways of living. Women entered the professions and began to approach terms of equality with men. Life was freer and horizons were widening. But what were people thinking? Were they really enjoying themselves?

The problem of the unemployed was an ever-present shadow. To those who came in contact with them it was a grief, but many living in the prosperous South were able to spin through the new gay life without ever meeting or considering them.

During these restless years the power of the Christian Church declined. Fewer and fewer people concerned themselves with orthodox religion. Instead they had acquired a facile rationalism, fortified by the popularity of psycho-analysis and psychotherapy, though even the broad principles of these sciences were often ill-assimilated.

Psychotherapy was being used with good effect in the treatment of shell-shocked soldiers suffering from mental disorders such as obsession, worry, fear, morbidity, a sense of inferiority and lack of confidence, with all their resultant physical disorders, as, for example, hysterical paralysis, functional blindness and nervous dyspepsia; and it was also being used in the treatment and cure of certain moral conditions, such as delinquency, stealing and lying.

Too many people now tried to justify their own peccadilloes and more serious misdemeanours with psycho-analytical interpretations, without any regard to the blatantly obvious, commonsense explanations. To be psycho-analysed became a favourite pastime for those who could afford the expensive series of treatments, an indulgence for bored, rich men and women, sated with current diversions and eager for new ones. In the result they tended to lose faith in the ability to control their own destinies and adopted a bleak fatalism, believing themselves to be ordered by physical and deep-rooted emotional impulses more powerful than their own wills.

In contrast to this tendency, Émile Coué arrived in London early in the twenties to preach his gospel of auto-suggestion and the power of the imagination, the mind and the will to control the human flesh; and Dr. Frank Buchman founded the Oxford Group, in an attempt to win people back to Christianity, its four declared aims being absolute honesty, purity, unselfishness and love. He won a certain measure of success among the prosperous upper classes, but the bulk of the population was untouched by it. A few thousands joined the League of Nations Union, in an effortless acknowledgment that war was a bad thing which should be avoided at all costs, but that was about the limit of their public service or private contribution to a more spiritual way of life.

CHAPTER NINE

The 1930's

After the financial crisis of 1931 and the fall of the Labour government, Ramsay Macdonald was returned as Prime Minister of a National government, with Stanley Baldwin as second in command. Macdonald, who had founded the Labour-Socialist party, now found himself head of a predominantly Conservative government, in which the Labour Party held only fifty seats and the Liberals seven. It was a situation which created intense bitterness amongst the members of the Labour Party, who felt with justification that their leader had deserted them for the opposition.

When the National government set to work, Britain's financial position was considered by the rest of the world to be in dire jeopardy and international confidence in the value of British sterling was seriously shaken. Her international trade was dwindling. She was unable to cash her overseas investments, as they were made on long terms, and in any case had seriously depreciated as a result of the world slump, and she could not borrow for short terms in order to meet her immediate needs, for foreign countries were not prepared to make the loans.

To add to Britain's difficulties, Government expenditure had been rising rapidly. In 1929 the Government had been paying out £51 million a year in unemployment benefit, but by 1931, as a result of the Labour government's more generous treatment of the workless, the figure had risen to £125 million, of which only £30 million came from the weekly contributions of employers and employees.

The only hope of redemption lay in drastic economies. Everyone was urged to economize and save. Wages, salaries and incomes were all reduced and Britain was forced to suspend the repayments of her American war debt. To the indignation of the Labour Party and the bitterness of the unemployed, insurance contributions were increased and benefits reduced. For those who had been unemployed for so long that they had no insurance left, the hated means test was imposed, which meant that these people, who were paid what were hopefully known as temporary, transitional payments—their only means of keeping alive at all—had to declare every penny they and their families possessed, even to the few pounds a wife, son or daughter might have saved from happier days for a family nest-egg. The means tests were applied through Public Assistance Committees, which were associated with the Poor Law, and the unfortunate unemployed regarded this as the final indignity.

Though the unemployment figures rose during the early 1930's to the terrifying figure of nearly three million, the cost of the various types of unemployment payment fell from £110 million in 1931–1932 to £104 million in 1932–1933, the cost of payment to those who had been insured falling from £80 million to £54 million.

Life in England during the next year or two flowed, as Sir Winston Churchill put it, "placidly downstream". With work so difficult to come by, the wages of those unprotected by membership of a trade union were low and hours of work long. One of the Government's economies had been a reduction in the number of factory inspectors who had been appointed to see that the rules of minimum wages and hours of work laid down by the Trade Board Acts were being obeyed. The Acts covered some two million workers, but by 1934 there were only fifty-five inspectors, thirteen less than in 1930.

Some of the worst examples of sweated labour were to be found in the small tailoring and dressmaking businesses in the East End of London, where a high proportion of the country's ready-made clothing was manufactured. An embroideress in Hoxton, for example, worked from eight in the morning till half past six in the evening on weekdays and from eight till one on Saturdays for 25s. a week, out of which she had to pay for fares, meals, clothes and the rent of a room. Every second of waste time was eliminated in the factory and the girls had to work in complete silence. Girls working in Houndsditch and East End warehouses and textile firms, from nine in the morning till seven-thirty or eight in the evening, earned about 15s. a week; and these rates of pay and hours of work were legal according to the Trade Board Acts. A dressmaker, writing in 1934, said: "The firm I work for is one of the best in the trade, and compared with others we have not much to grumble at. We work from eight a.m. till six p.m. with an hour off at midday for lunch.... We get from 10d. to about 1s. 6d. for making a jumper or blouse, which is sold for anything from 12s. 11d. to 50s. and which takes from one hour and twenty minutes

to three hours to make, working at high pressure. Dresses we get from
1s. 10d. to 3s. 6d. each for making. These are day and evening dresses
sold in the West End for thirty shillings to four or five guineas. I saw
a jumper in Oxford Street priced at 29s. 11d. which we had made for
1s. 1d., and a dress marked 49s. 11d. which we had made for 2s. 3d.,
and which took nearly four hours to make.

"I remember working out my average wage for 1931, and it came
to 34s. 7d. a week for 51 weeks. . . . Of course we earn more when we
are busy and less when we are slack."

The outworkers fared worse, for there was little or no means of
investigating their pay and they were the victims of the seasonal
fluctuations of the clothing trade. Nine shillings a dozen was a usual
payment for making dresses, each of which took nearly a day to complete. Children's embroidered and smocked silk dresses, which sold in
Mayfair for four and a half guineas, were made for 3s. 6d. each.

Another aspect of the employment problem of the thirties was that
many more women were being forced to earn their livings. In the
1931 census figures it was estimated that of the nine million women
over 35, one and a half million were unmarried, and that one girl in
six must expect to remain unmarried all her life. In this year there
were 943,000 married men out of work and it was estimated that
nearly 80 per cent of women had to enter the labour market at some
time during their lives, while one in five women must expect to continue working all through her adult life, whether she married or not.

Great Britain did not go bankrupt during the 1930's as some had
feared. Instead she made a slow recovery and her international credit
was gradually restored, but the cuts in the pay to the unemployed
were not restored and they suffered terribly. Writing in the *Bookman*
in 1934, Walter Fancourt Bell described a case he had attended at the
Assizes in one of the large industrial Midland towns. An elderly man,
about sixty years of age, had tried to cut his wife's throat with a bread-
knife and was indicted for attempted murder. "The police read out
his record. He had worked all his life in the jewellery trade until
three years ago, when he had been sacked owing to the trade depression. His wife was called into the witness box. She appeared to be
of the same age as her husband, happily married to him for thirty-four
years. She gave her evidence quietly and with great dignity, striving
hard to suppress her emotion. The prisoner had long exhausted his

right to unemployment benefit. They had sunk into deeper and deeper poverty. The continual anxiety and lack of food had driven him to a state of chronic depression. Finally, throughout July of last year, they had subsisted on bread and blackcurrants which grew in the garden. One evening a friend offered him a drink—half a pint of beer—which went to his head, his stomach being weak through lack of food. He went home and tried to cut his wife's throat. ... The Public Assistance Committee had heard nothing of the case—I suspect the reason being that this couple, like many others of the working class, would sooner starve than submit to the inquisition of the Poor Law."

People in the depressed areas of Britain were literally dying of starvation. The *Lancet* of 12th January 1934 said that "the mass of middle-class people are only now beginning to learn of the type of physical privation possible in depressed areas, where hardly anyone has resources beyond insurance benefit or relief." The British Medical Association reported that in Newcastle-on-Tyne there was a deficiency of proteins in the diet of the unemployed of 50 per cent in the slums and 65 per cent in council houses, where since rents were higher there was less money over for food. At Stockton-on-Tees, where the rents of council houses were almost double those of slum properties—8s. 10½d. a week as against 4s. 7½d.—the death rate between 1931 and 1932 rose by 40 per cent.

From time to time the workless would rouse themselves from their bewildered despair and organize protest marches to London, which was gradually regaining its prosperity, but the Government could conceive no plan which would help them. The most famous march of all was the Jarrow Crusade, which was led by Jarrow's Member of Parliament, Ellen Wilkinson.

In 1851 Jarrow had been a small mining village, with a population of 3,500. Then Charles Palmer arrived and built a shipyard. As steel-plated armoured ships developed, Jarrow, with its resources of coal and iron, became one of the most important shipyards in the country. It made floating batteries for the Crimea and, with the passing years, iron ships, screw colliers and liners for the big shipping lines, until by 1921 its population had risen to 35,000. True it was a murky, hideous, insanitary place, one of the worst examples of nineteenth-century unplanned industrial development to be found in the whole country. Nevertheless, Palmer's had provided work for nearly all its inhabitants. With the slump Palmer's collapsed and Jarrow's source of livelihood went with it. Moreover, many of the older workers had invested their savings in the shipyard, some as much as £300, which in those days was a small fortune for a working man. Every penny was lost and none was ever recovered. The derelict yard was bought by National Shipbuilding Security, Limited. The cranes and machinery were dismantled. Jarrow waited hopefully but nothing happened. There was a suggestion for promoting a new steelworks, but the idea was turned down by the Iron and Steel Federation. Jarrow was abandoned.

"Jarrow in that year, 1932–1933, was utterly stagnant," wrote Ellen Wilkinson. "There was no work. No one had a job, except a few railwaymen, officials, the workers in the co-operative stores, and the few clerks and craftsmen who went out of the town to their jobs each day. The unemployment rate was over 80 per cent."

In her book *The Town that was Murdered* she wrote: "Charles Palmer started Jarrow as a shipbuilding centre without considering the needs of the workers. They crowded into a small colliery village which was hurriedly extended to receive them. They packed into insanitary houses. They lived without social amenities. They paid with their lives for the absence of any preparation for the growth of such a town. And in 1933 another group of capitalists decided the fate of Jarrow without reference to the workers."

Ellen Wilkinson fought hard for her constituents. In 1934 she led a deputation of three hundred to see Ramsay Macdonald, who was on a visit to his own constituency nine miles away, walking every step of the way through a fierce gale. Macdonald agreed to see her and eight of the marchers. He said he would bear them in mind and his advice to Ellen Wilkinson herself is a terrible indictment of his own futility. "Ellen," he said, "why don't you go out and preach Socialism, which is the only remedy for all this?"

She led another deputation to see Walter Runciman, the President of the Board of Trade, but no help whatsoever was forthcoming. "Jarrow", said Runciman, "must work out its own salvation."

In 1936 she organized the Jarrow Crusade, in which she led two hundred men from Jarrow the long 280 miles to London, bearing a petition to the Government from twelve thousand of their fellow citizens. They were a month on the road but nearly everywhere they were welcomed with sympathy and given food and shelter for the night. By this time Mr. Baldwin had changed places with Ramsay Macdonald, whose ineptitude and failing powers prevented him from holding such high office any longer, so it was to Baldwin, as Prime Minister, that Ellen Wilkinson presented the Jarrow petition when they at last reached Westminster. She was received politely but no promises were made. The marchers were given tea at the House of Commons and the following day they left by special train for Jarrow again. Nothing was done for them and when they reached home they found that the Unemployment Assistance Board had deducted from 4s. to 11s. from their pay for the period when they were away, because "they would not have been available for work if it had turned up".

While Britain was preoccupied with her own domestic troubles during the twenties and early thirties, events were happening in Europe the dangers of which she did not heed until it was too late. The civil war in Russia had ended with the total success of the Communists. Little news was coming from Russia during these years, apart from rumours that Stalin's Five Year Plan to build up a workable economy for the people had failed and that they were starving. There were also grisly tales of the murderous activities of the OGPU, the secret police, and the sufferings of the enemies of the régime, who were sent to the concentration camps and labour gangs in Siberia. The Communist revolution had not extended beyond the boundaries of Russia, despite many periods of near victory when Communist forces or powerful propaganda had almost won over Poland, Italy, Germany and Hungary, and by the thirties Russia's western frontier was flanked by states which were, generally speaking, anti-Communist— Poland, Czechoslovakia, Hungary, Rumania and Bulgaria.

In Italy, Mussolini rose to power during the twenties with his new doctrine of Fascism, devised to combat Communism and restore Italy's economy after the devastation of the 1914 war. In the early years of his régime Italy's prestige rose steadily. The standard of living of the peasant population remained low but her former commerce in silk, fruit and wine was resumed and the motor car and other industries of the north were firmly established. Mussolini was responsible for the building of Italy's fine motor roads and he also did valuable work in preserving and restoring the country's priceless antiquities and ancient monuments.

In 1925 Friedrich Ebert, the first President of the German Republic, died, and Field-Marshal von Hindenburg, then seventy-seven years of age and living in retirement, was induced to stand for the presidential election. France was apprehensive of the reappearance of any signs of the old militaristic spirit in Germany, but Hindenburg was duly elected, although by only a small majority, and the fears of the French were allayed by the knowledge that Germany, by the terms of the peace treaty, must remain unarmed.

After the Treaty of Locarno, when Germany joined the League of Nations, it seemed that Europe's problems were solved. Germany had no arms to attack France, and though France was armed it had been laid down that if she should attack Germany, Britain would go to Germany's help. Thus equilibrium between the old enemies seemed to have been attained. However, despite the vigilance of the Allied Military Commission of Control in Germany, early in the 1920's the Germans began, in the greatest secrecy and with many subterfuges, to re-arm. Under cover of various youth movements, such as the Boy Scouts and Cadet Corps, she laid the foundation of a vast new organization which could quickly be transformed into an army. Civil aviation was developed, the personnel of which could soon be trained for a purely military air force, and with American and British loans, which had been advanced for the re-establishment of her industry, she was soon manufacturing, along with peacetime commodities, hidden stocks of armaments.

During the 1914 war Adolf Hitler had been an obscure Austrian corporal in the German army. Hitherto his life had been a failure, for he had aspired in vain to earn his living as an artist. Filled with rage at his country's defeat, an emotion not unmixed with resentment at his own personal failure, he felt that Germany's troubles had come about through the activities and betrayals of the Communists, with whom he also identified the Jews. He remained in the army for a while after the armistice as a political education officer, investigating the activities of the revolutionary Communist groups in Germany during the first confused months of the peace. In the course of his work, Hitler attended political meetings of all shades of opinion throughout Bavaria, where his regiment was stationed, and one night chanced on a meeting of the German Workers' Party in Munich, a group which he found shared his own views in regard to Communism and the Jews. He joined the party and when he was demobilized a few months later gave the whole of his time to its work. Soon he became its leader and saw himself as the saviour of Germany. The Communists in Bavaria took warning and attempted to break up his meetings. Hitler countered with the formation of the first bands of his Storm-troopers.

Before long the whole of Germany, smarting with anger at the French occupation of the Ruhr and already suffering gravely from the decreasing value of the mark, was taking notice of Hitler's party and its avowed aim of restoring Germany to its former power. By the end of 1923 Goering, Hess, Rosenberg and Roehm were all closely associated with Hitler. They planned to seize power in Bavaria by force. The venture failed and Hitler was arrested and sentenced to four years' imprisonment, but popular feeling against the punishment was so strong that the sentence was reduced to thirteen months.

It was during this time in prison that Hitler wrote *Mein Kampf*, which was a statement of his creed and his particular brand of Fascism. In it he declared that it was a fallacy to assume that all men are equal and pointed out that all the inventions of material civilization have been made by individuals especially endowed with superior mental qualities. "Accordingly a human community is well organized only when it facilitates to the highest possible degree individual creative forces and utilizes their work for the benefit of the community. . . . This common interest is surely not served by allowing the multitude to rule, for they are not capable of thinking nor are they efficient and in no case whatsoever can they be said to be gifted. Only those should rule who have the natural temperament and gift of leadership," he wrote, which was a statement extreme enough to rouse the resentment of the mildest of democrats.

Of Communism he said: "The Jewish doctrine of Marxism repudiates the aristocratic principles of Nature and substitutes for them the eternal privilege of force and energy, numerical mass and its dead weight. Thus it denies the individual worth of the human personality, impugns the teaching that nationhood and race have a primary significance, and by doing this it takes away the very foundations of human existence and human civilization. If the Marxist teaching were to be accepted as the foundation of the life of the universe, it would lead to the disappearance of all order that is conceivable to the human mind. And thus the adoption of such a law would provoke chaos in the structure of the greatest organism we know, with the result that the inhabitants of this earthly planet would finally disappear."

Though Communism and Fascism both bear the label of democracy, neither is true democracy, in which the holders of political office not only expound the law and enforce it, but are themselves subject to it. In fact in both doctrines the State is reckoned greater than the individual and the rulers are regarded as above the law, so that in practice, though their approaches appear to be completely divergent, there is little to choose between them, so far as the lack of freedom of the individual is concerned.

It is a fundamental law of nature that living creatures can survive only through ceaseless struggle and adaptation to changing physical and economic environments, but Hitler interpreted this by asserting that a race, in order to survive, must fight its neighbours and win supremacy by brute force. It was a philosophy so utterly opposed to the pacifist Socialists of Britain that the strength of Hitler's following in Germany at this time, had they realized it, must have filled them with the gravest foreboding.

The struggle for power in Germany continued throughout the twenties and early thirties and by 1932 Hitler's party, now called the National Socialist Party, whose members were known as the Nazis, won a decisive majority of 230 seats in the biennial elections to the Reichstag, and from the small force of original Storm-troopers, the Brownshirts, had developed the formidable S.S., or Blackshirts, who were, in effect, Hitler's private army.

The Nazis had formed a revolutionary movement arising from the chaos and misery of the economic depression, which had gripped Germany as well as the rest of the world, and the army chiefs of Germany, who had hitherto wielded the real power behind Hindenburg, felt compelled, for the sake of maintaining the unity of the country, to join with it. There followed intrigues and bitter, violent riots between the various minority political groups in Germany, but in January 1933 Hindenburg was persuaded, against his better judgment, to invite Hitler to become Chancellor of Germany.

Once he had come to office Hitler set about destroying the opposition, and Communists and Jews were ruthlessly persecuted and deprived of their civil rights. Hitler in fact began putting into practice the theories he had expounded in *Mein Kampf* and pursuing them to their logical conclusions. In the face of all treaties and promises, he armed Germany and prepared to wage war against her erstwhile victors, for the greater glory of the Fatherland.

In Britain the Macdonald-Baldwin government, blind to the developments in Germany, was bent on increasing economies, which now included a reduction in armaments. As Hitler armed Germany, Britain not only disarmed herself but, through the League of Nations, pressed France to do the same. Disarmament conferences were held, at which German representatives were present, where Mr. Macdonald put forward idealistic plans for France and Britain to reduce their arms to the theoretical state of disarmament which had been imposed on Germany at the Versailles Treaty fifteen years earlier; but by the end of 1933 Hitler, no longer troubling to conceal the contempt he had for all treaties and honourable agreements, ordered his government to withdraw from the conference on European disarmament and also to resign from the League of Nations. It should have been the final warning to Great Britain, but by this time most of her people were imbued with a woolly pacifism which demanded peace at any price.

In 1934 the British Fascist Party, led by Sir Oswald Mosley, first came to the public notice when they took over the stadium at Olympia for their first large-scale rally. The meeting was characterized by the unjustifiably brutal manhandling of the few who had the temerity to interrupt and disagree with the speeches advocating the virtues of National Socialism and preaching the Fascist gospel of racial purity. In a country such as Britain, which has been subject to the most extraordinary infiltration and mingling of the races of Europe and western Asia, this could in any case make little sense. Yet onlookers at the scenes which took place that night at Olympia, and subsequently in the Fascist demonstrations in the East End of London against Jews and Communists, remained curiously unperceptive and unmoved by the potentialities and implications of the movement.

In 1926 the Communist Party of Great Britain had 10,730 members. During 1930 the numbers fell to 1,376, but throughout the following years, as the menace of Fascism became apparent to those who took the trouble to study what was happening in Germany and on a minuscule scale in London, the number of Communists, particularly amongst the young intelligentsia, steadily grew, until in 1939 it had risen to well over fifteen thousand.

There were many shades of opinion in Britain, between the extreme Fascists and the extreme Communists, for compromise is a particularly British characteristic. Ramsay Macdonald even maintained that his own brand of Socialism had nothing to do with the Communism of the Soviet Union. The majority of the Socialists in Britain might be described as democratic Communists. In other words they desired a State where the workers had full democratic rights, a stake in the main industries and a fair share of the government, but they wished the leaders to remain of the people and to refrain from acquiring the powers of absolute autocracy. The Conservatives, who were in the majority, pursued their policy of maintaining the traditional way of British life, upholding the dignity and liberty of the individual, and encouraging private enterprise and the extension of the ownership of property, rather than restricting it—though this, of course, meant little to those members of the community who had long ago given up all hope of ever owning anything, apart from their few sticks of furniture.

In 1935 King George V celebrated his Silver Jubilee. A few years earlier he had been seriously ill and the British people during those anxious weeks had shown a sympathy and affection for him which had hardly before been apparent and which touched him deeply. Once more, during the Jubilee celebrations, they displayed their loyalty and love to the ageing king, but he was a sick man and by the end of the year was struck once more by the illness from which he died. The Prince of Wales, the prince who had worked so tirelessly for most of his adult life as Britain's ambassador to the countries of the Empire, was proclaimed Edward VIII. However, he declared his intention of marrying Mrs. Simpson, an American who had twice been divorced, and Mr. Baldwin and the archbishops would not countenance the alliance. The King's wife, by British law, would automatically become queen, for the constitution did not provide for morganatic marriage; and Mrs. Simpson was not acceptable.

After days of anxiety, during which the whole of Britain argued the rights and wrongs of the case, the King, refusing to give up Mrs. Simpson, took the only alternative, which was abdication. His brother and sister-in-law, the Duke and Duchess of York, became King George VI and Queen Elizabeth, embarking with great courage on their unexpected duties, which were to be undertaken throughout one of the most perilous periods of Britain's history.

In Europe events were moving fast. In France the Daladier government fell in February 1934 and Monsieur Doumergue became Premier with Monsieur Barthou as Foreign Minister. Monsieur Barthou succeeded in persuading Russia to join the League of Nations, a vitally important step towards the maintenance of European peace, but only a few weeks later, during the fateful visit of King Alexander of Yugoslavia to France, the assassin who killed the King also killed Monsieur Barthou. He was succeeded as Foreign Minister by Pierre Laval, who once had been a Communist but now was not unsympathetic to the principles of Fascism. Later that year the Nazis in Austria, organized by Hitler's party, murdered their Chancellor, Dollfuss, in an abortive attempt to overthrow the government and bring Austria under German control. Austrian independence was preserved for another year or two, but in the midst of these tragic deeds Hindenburg died. This time there were no presidential elections. Hitler, while still remaining Chancellor, became also the head of the German State.

In 1935, Italy, in a desire for colonial empire and also to avenge her humiliation at the hands of the Abyssinians at Adowa forty years earlier, suddenly made an unprovoked attack on the country, despite a treaty of friendship which had been signed in 1928. Helpless, primitive tribesmen, quite powerless to defend themselves against any modern weapons, were mercilessly dive-bombed and machine-gunned. Their emperor, Haile Selassie, appealed to the League of Nations for help. Anthony Eden, who had been appointed British Minister for League of Nations Affairs, at once demanded that economic sanctions be applied against Italy. This meant that Italy would be cut off from any financial help and denied the supply of imported commodities for her ordinary economy. Mussolini defied the threat and prosecuted the war. Afraid that the sanctions against Italy would mean European war, the League applied them in such a way that Italy was little affected. Sir Winston Churchill said that "the League of Nations therefore proceeded to the rescue of Abyssinia on the basis that nothing must be done to hamper the invading Italian armies".[1]

Italy conquered Abyssinia, her friendship to Britain turned to enmity, and Hitler, watching events with gleeful cynicism, was encouraged to develop his own plans for future aggression, increasingly confident that the peace parties in France and Britain would prevent any armed resistance, even to his most audacious moves. Though Mussolini disliked both Hitler and his particular brand of violent Fascism, the two States now established friendly relations.

By 1935 the time had come for a general election in Britain and Mr. Baldwin was returned with a triumphant majority of 247. Two years later, in failing health, he retired, and the premiership was assumed by Mr. Neville Chamberlain, who for the previous five years had been Chancellor of the Exchequer.

The Rhineland had been an important point of discussion at the Versailles Conference and in order to protect the French frontier Germany had been forbidden to build any military defences or permit any armed forces within the zone. For several years the Rhineland had been occupied by Allied troops. They had withdrawn before the time laid down in the peace treaty, as a concession to Germany, at the time of the Locarno Pact in 1925, when she joined the League of Nations, but it was on the understanding that the Rhineland be still regarded as a demilitarized zone.

Suddenly, in March 1936, Hitler poured 35,000 of his troops into the Rhineland for a military occupation. It was a deliberate flouting of the Versailles Treaty and Locarno Pact and placed France in her old position of jeopardy. She protested angrily that it was an act of aggression which should be met with counter-aggression and turned to Britain for advice and support. Both countries were torn between a desire to see justice done and the Locarno Pact upheld, on the one hand, and a desire for peace on the other. In the end the pacifists won again. Hitler offered a non-aggression pact for the future, convincing all too many people of his sincerity, and justifying his occupation of the Rhineland by declaring that he was merely endeavouring to reunite the German people.

Nothing further was done and Hitler's army remained in the

[1] Winston Churchill, *The Second World War.* Vol. 1, *The Gathering Storm* (Cassell, 1948).

Rhineland, but tension between Fascists and Communists throughout Europe was rising. Their first armed clash came during the Spanish civil war, which broke out the same year. Spain had played little part in European affairs since her brief flash of power and glory during the sixteenth and seventeenth centuries, the years of exploration and overseas colonization. With her years of decline, after the rise of British and Dutch commercial and sea power, she had turned in upon herself and remained aloof and introverted in her harsh, arid, mountainous peninsula. The peasants, who represented 85 per cent of the population, were dominated by an autocratic monarchy, a small but immensely rich ruling class, and the priests of the Roman Catholic Church.

King Alfonso, who had come to the throne in 1902 at the age of sixteen, ruled with the traditional despotism of his ancestors, having little contact with his people. His right-hand man was General Primo de Rivera who, with leaders of the army and the Church, shielded him from contact with the rest of Spain. The first signs of the stirrings of democratic philosophies amongst the Spanish people were quickly repressed. The Press was stifled and orders went forth from Madrid that the Church was to demand absolute obedience from her people and control their education.

In 1930, as had happened in France in 1789, a revolution of the people broke out in Spain. General Primo de Rivera fled to Paris, where shortly afterwards he died, some said of a broken heart. In April 1931 municipal elections were held throughout Spain and the results were an overwhelming victory for the Republican Party. The Republic of Spain was declared and King Alfonso abdicated.

For the next few years Republican Spain endured, but the country was torn by internal dissension. The central government tried to rule democratically but was constantly beset on the one hand by riots, murders and strikes amongst the peasants, fighting their own battles against their landlords in the distant provinces of Aragon, Catalonia, Navarre, Asturias, Valencia and Andalusia, and on the other by the retrogressive Right Wing, who wanted to restore the monarchy and the old order. One of the Right Wing leaders, who was subsequently shot by the Republicans, was José Primo de Rivera, founder of the Falange, the Spanish Fascist Party, and son of the general. The Carlists were also of the extreme right, their motto being "The King, Christ and the Holy Virgin", at a time when the peasants were desecrating the churches and murdering the priests.

In 1936 civil war broke out in Republican Spain, touched off by the landing of General Franco, the Governor of the Canary Islands, who declared himself leader of the Spanish Nationalist Party and, with the support of the Spanish army and the Carlists, set to work to overthrow the legally appointed Republican government. There followed three years of fierce and bitter conflict. The Communists and Fascists in other parts of Europe saw the Spanish war as a struggle between their own two factions and a preliminary of the greater issue to come, though in fact this was an over-simplification of the Spanish civil war, which was in the main a domestic quarrel, prosecuted with all the national characteristics of violence, cruelty and stubborn passion.

The official attitude of Great Britain towards the Spanish conflict was one of strict neutrality, and Britain, Italy, Germany and Russia all signed an agreement of non-intervention. Nevertheless, every Communist Party in Europe sent representatives to Spain to observe the fighting and learn what they could from it, and Russia soon went back on her agreement of non-intervention, arguing that the pact had already been broken by the other signatories, and sending men and arms, guns, tanks and aeroplanes for the Republicans, while Italy and Germany sent help to Franco.

The International Brigade formed to help the Republicans included many young men from Britain who had sickened of the years of appeasement towards Hitler and believed that the time had come when the cause of democracy could be defended only by fighting, thereby shattering the policy of pacifism which had so long prevailed among the Socialists of Britain. After the first few months, enlistment for the fighting in Spain was forbidden by the British Government, but the volunteers—amongst them many young British poets and writers such as W. H. Auden, Louis MacNeice, Roy Campbell, John Cornford and George Orwell—reached Spain by devious ways. They embarked like young crusaders, with a burning conviction of the justice of their cause, but many found only disillusionment and were sickened by what they saw. Neither Spanish Republicans nor Spanish Revolutionaries gave any quarter and both sides were equally matched in cruelty. By the end of the war, in March 1939, they had between them executed 800,000 of their fellow countrymen—twice the number killed in the actual fighting.

Of nearly 3,000 British volunteers, 543 were killed and 1,763 wounded in the cause of the Republic, and 30,000 Germans and 80,000 Italians fought with Franco. The trained armies won the day and General Franco became and still remains dictator of Spain.

Hitler, watching events carefully, saw that the desire for international peace amongst the democracies still outweighed their inclination to reassert their authority in the conduct of European affairs. In sending help to Spain he had demanded in return supplies of Spanish iron ore to keep his armament factories working at full pressure, and by 1938 he was ready for his next move. After "diplomatic" talks with the Austrian Chancellor, which were nothing more than threats of armed aggression if his wishes were not granted, he ordered his troops, on 12th March 1938, to occupy Austria, and it became part of the German State. Hasty and alarmed discussions between Russia, France and Great Britain led in the end to nothing, and the way was left clear for Hitler's subsequent occupation of Czechoslovakia. In the first instance diplomatic exchanges took place between Hitler and the President of Czechoslovakia in regard to the Sudetenland, the region of the north-east of Bohemia, just south of Germany's south-eastern frontier. Hitler's sequence of moves was similar to his previous exchanges with the Chancellor of Austria. His ultimate aim could hardly have been misinterpreted and tension in Europe mounted. If Hitler struck yet again, war would surely be inevitable. Appeasement, it seemed, could go no further. Three times during September 1938 Neville Chamberlain flew to meet Hitler and discuss his aims for the Sudetenland. At the last there was more appeasement and a new victory for Hitler, for Britain abandoned Czechoslovakia's cause and allowed Hitler to annex the Sudeten area, in order, so it was said, to prevent his invading the whole of Czechoslovakia. In a joint declaration signed by Chamberlain and Hitler they said: "We regard the agreement signed last night ... as symbolic of the desire of our two peoples never to go to war again", and Hitler afterwards announced that "with this problem solved, Germany has no more territorial problems in Europe".

When Chamberlain arrived back in London from Munich he was hailed as the saviour of peace by most of the British public, who, with still only a vague grasp of what was going on—for history is not easy to comprehend while one is living it—were devoutly thankful. "What Munich showed to many people was the need to prepare for war; but many others, like James Maxton and George Lansbury, thanked Chamberlain for preserving peace, and hoped that the peace might be permanent because the alternative was so terrible to contemplate; and to supporters of the Popular Front, Munich was merely one more proof of the need for collective security, something that they took metaphorically in their stride. Their reaction was neither to wish for British rearmament nor to thank Chamberlain; it was rather to feel that although war would have been terrible, peace on such terms was even worse", wrote Julian Symons,[1] describing the attitude of the British people in September 1938.

It was all of no avail. Six months later, on 15th March 1939, Hitler marched into Czechoslovakia and the whole country was incorporated in the Reich. It soon became apparent that Hitler's next prey was Poland. At last Chamberlain knew that peace could never again be bought with dishonour. Britain and France must make a pact to protect Poland and halt Fascist aggression farther into north-eastern Europe. By now, however, Britain had allowed herself to be confronted by a truly formidable army. Moreover, on 7th April Italian forces landed in Albania and occupied the country as a springboard for future action against Greece and Yugoslavia. The pattern of future Fascist aggression became all too apparent.

The key to the balance of power was now Russia, the avowed enemy of Fascism. If she allied herself with Britain and France the prospects would be brighter, but Russian policy remained enigmatic. Then on 23rd August 1939 came the bombshell. Stalin and Hitler, after secret talks throughout the summer, had signed a ten-year pact of non-aggression. It was the most shameful and cynical of treaties, betraying on both sides all honour and avowed principles. Britain now knew that all hope of averting war was gone. Mobilization was ordered and Chamberlain wrote to Hitler reaffirming Britain's intention of honouring her obligation to Poland if Germany invaded.

At dawn on 1st September 1939 Hitler's armies marched into Poland. A British note was sent to Germany the same day, followed by

[1] Julian Symons, *The Thirties* (Cresset Press, 1960).

a final ultimatum on the morning of 3rd September. There was no reply from Germany and at a quarter past eleven on that lovely, sunny, tragic Sunday morning of high summer Mr. Neville Chamberlain had the melancholy task of broadcasting to the people of Britain that the nation was once more at war with Germany.

CHAPTER TEN

Britain during the 1930's

While Britain became ever more deeply implicated in the politics of Europe during the 1930's, a new generation was growing up which had no memory of the 1914 war; even to those who had lived through it, it had become for most nothing but a bitter memory—a nightmare so terrible that they hardly dare contemplate it ever happening again. So life went on for a while, with all its changing fashions in dress and habits, manners and modes, entertainment, art and literature.

With the years of depression, the tendency towards a social levelling between the classes became more marked. During the financial crisis of 1931 many of the rich lost fortunes overnight and were forced to change their standard of living drastically. Those who were still living on private incomes, with much yet to lose, had become apprehensive after the General Strike of 1926 and the election of the Socialist government in 1929, wondering how much longer they would be able to survive in their present way of living. If for no more moral reason, they deemed it expedient to adopt simpler ways. Any form of ostentation was considered bad taste, and although a generation or two earlier it would have been thought the height of bad form to talk about money, it was now fashionable to discuss it freely and announce to the world that one was hard up.

As the more prosperous South gradually became aware of the plight of the unemployed, many developed a sincere social conscience and saw clearly, for the first time, the essential morality of Socialism. Some adopted an unemployed family as a salve to their own consciences, taking a personal interest in them, visiting them—rather in the manner of the Lady of the Manor calling on the poor villagers at first, it must be admitted—and offering what material help they could, in money, food and clothing, to supplement the inadequate unemployment pay and national assistance.

Many were now advocating a classless society and it was fashionable to be, if not avowedly Socialist or Communist, at least slightly "pink" in political belief. Yet Britain did not lose her deep-rooted class consciousness and the old pattern of social life persisted, for there was as yet nothing to take its place. Entertaining was less lavish but the upper crust still followed the routine of the social season, beginning with the opening of the summer exhibition at the Royal Academy and plodding through the parties and dances to Ascot, Goodwood and Cowes. "Deb" dances were now often shared to save money, and with very few exceptions girls prepared as a matter of course to earn their own livings after they had been socially launched. They trained to be secretaries or mannequins or became salesgirls in the more exclusive Mayfair shops. They appeared as models in newspaper and magazine advertisements, proclaiming the virtues of anything from patent medicines to underclothing. Decorum was outdated, for to be modest was now, in the jargon of the psycho-analysts, to be inhibited, and although no one ever quite knew the precise disadvantage of this state, it was considered to be a "bad thing". Some girls ran their own businesses, many of them the new sandwich bars, which became very popular during the thirties. They were cheap, they suited the new craze for slimming and eating lightly at midday, and they were very convenient.

These were the years when it was smart to turn the mews of large establishments, which only a few years earlier had housed horses, carriages, and the coachmen and their families, into mews flats and maisonettes. They were seldom convenient to run and usually uncommonly cold and draughty, but they were amusing and comparatively inexpensive. Bottle parties became the rage, for with every guest arriving with his own bottle of drink, and often with food as well, it was the cheapest form of entertaining, particularly favoured by the gay young things setting up house for the first time, in either married or bachelor establishments.

Early in the thirties, when the depression was at its worst, there were no outstanding styles in women's dress. Everyone looked alike and it was difficult at first glance to distinguish between a duchess and a shopgirl. Skirts were longer but dresses were very simple and rather shapeless, so that the most expensive models could easily be copied and made at home. A picturesque informality and anonymity was the effect most women fancied for themselves, many achieving it by wearing during the daytime a copy of Greta Garbo's old trench coat, pulled in at the waist, with something like her rakish felt hat or a beret clapped on the side of the head. The beret craze was varied by the brief vogue for the small, tip-tilted bowler and then the tricorne, while for a few

163

months after Princess Marina arrived in England for her marriage to the Duke of Kent, every other woman seemed to be wearing a copy of the jaunty little round pork-pie hat in which she first showed herself, which became known as the "Marina" hat.

In 1935 Schiaparelli introduced the fashion for squared shoulders, which soon reached London from Paris. To students of the history of

The squared shoulders of the fashions of 1935 gave an ominously military air to the people, as though they were aware of things to come.

fashion it was the ominous military look, associated with war, and it persisted for the next ten years or more. About the same time Chanel brought in her famous cardigan suit, simple and elegant, which women adopted enthusiastically and have been wearing, in one form or another, ever since.

For Ascot and for fashionable weddings and garden parties, however, dress remained as formal as ever, women wearing large, flowery hats and light, fragile dresses down to the ankles, the men their light grey toppers and morning dress. The conventions, too, were still maintained in the evenings. For dances men wore white ties and tail coats, and the upper and upper middle classes, both in London and the country, changed into dinner jackets for dining at home. Women's evening dresses were long, backless and diaphanous, often tight to the knee and then breaking out into flounces and godets; and the process of pouring oneself into one of these frocks was made a good deal simpler by the timely invention of the zip fastener, which has been with us ever since.

Hair, in imitation of Greta Garbo and equally favoured film stars, was worn progressively longer throughout the thirties, until by 1939 it was down to the shoulders, after which everyone scraped it into a bun or pinned it precariously to the top of the head. Make-up became almost universal, and in addition women took to nail varnish. Formerly a little colourless powder polish on the nails was the limit that etiquette and good taste would allow. Now came a craze for brightly varnished nails, usually in blood red, and with it the nails were worn extremely long and pointed.

By 1939 skirts had become very short again for daytime, till they were only just below the knees. All suits and coats had square, padded shoulders and looked like military uniforms. Shoes were square-toed and tended to be rather low-heeled. Hats though small were high and conical, often with a single straight feather, like the headgear of one of the seven dwarfs.

As economic conditions gradually improved throughout the thirties, people of all classes began to go abroad for holidays, to France, Belgium, Holland, Austria, Italy and Switzerland. Travel was cheap and the shipping lines organized short cruises to the Mediterranean and to the "northern capitals" of Europe. The smart set cruised the Mediterranean in private yachts and made the Venice Lido an international playground; and before long, in retreat from the increasing crowds of tourists, they were reaching the eastern Mediterranean and the Dalmatian coast. The cult of sunbathing flourished, oiling and frying becoming a ritual and a deep tan a status symbol. To the best of their ability people sunbathed in Britain too, in parks and open spaces, at George Lansbury's new lido by the Serpentine in Hyde Park, or in their own back gardens; and the moment the sun broke through Britain's almost eternal pall of grey cloud it became the accepted thing to put on dark sunglasses. Hitler's cult of physical fitness—the Strength through Joy movement—reached England. People began to talk about proteins and vitamins. They considered their diet and watched their weight. The League of Health and Beauty was begun by Mrs. Bagot Stack and her daughter Prunella, and Health and Beauty classes were soon being held in every town and village throughout the country—fat women and thin ones, young and very far from young, rich and poor all getting themselves into white blouses and black shorts and exercising to music.

Sunbathing and sea bathing costumes became scantier than ever, for no one must be thought inhibited, but bathing costumes were now made of fine wool, and though they took a long time to dry they were a good deal more shapely and becoming than the drooping cotton ones of earlier years. Early in the thirties women took to beach pyjamas during their summer holidays. They consisted of short jackets and trousers with immensely wide legs, usually made of brightly patterned cotton or cretonne, but they soon tired of them and wore blouses and shorts instead for parading the promenades of the seaside resorts.

As the thirties continued though behaviour in general became progressively less formal, there was a brief return amongst the upper classes to Victorian decorum. The chaperone reappeared for young girls at dances. It was a last gesture of the old régime before the Second World War ended all such manners and modes, and quite pointless and artificial, for in other aspects of their lives the most carefully nurtured girls were as free as their elder sisters had been during the twenties.

It was the cinema, with its new talking films, which dominated the entertainment of the thirties. American films remained the more popular, for British films, after a promising start with Alfred Hitchcock's *Blackmail*, were slow in making their mark and achieving solid success. By 1933, despite many British efforts, it was all too apparent that the British public preferred the film products of America. In his book *Where We Came In*, C. A. Oakley, writing of American films at this time, says: "The shrill and raucous intonations which had made some voices unacceptable in 1930 disturbed few people a year or two later; and by contrast some English voices had become unpopular—a change in public attitude of considerably greater social significance than has so far been recognized."

By now people had been listening for more than a decade to the voices of the B.B.C. announcers, with their excellent production and quality and usually impeccable pronunciation, yet there is no evidence that the manner of speech of the British people was in any way influenced by them; yet with the arrival of American talkies, American ways of speech were so quickly accepted that they very soon became part of the language. The laconic O.K. and Oh yeah were heard everywhere. Women were dames, men were guys, corpses were stiffs, guns were rods and the humble choc-ice became an Eskimo pie.

A Scottish accent was said to be incomprehensible to Londoners, a West Country accent to people of the North of England, and Americans, particularly the audiences of the Middle West, declared they could understand none of them; but American talkies were understood by all English-speaking peoples and American became the universal language.

Too many British producers were still using adaptations of stage plays with stage players, and filmed stage plays proved unacceptable to audiences who went to the cinema to enjoy pictorial story-telling. American films used sound to support the picture rather than the picture to illustrate sound. The dialogue in the films was relatively sparse and plot points were always established visually, with underlining by the camera, the director never relying solely on the spoken word for their exposition. In this way American films achieved more action and pace, every sequence contributing to the movement of the basic plot and "propelling a gimmick".

British companies made a number of financially successful cheap farcical comedies during these years, using music-hall comedians such as Leslie Fuller, Ernie Lotinga, Sandy Powell and Jerry Verno, and aiming specifically for the industrial North of England audiences; of the big musicals of the early thirties *Congress Dances*, with Lilian Harvey and Conrad Veidt, was the most notable. The film craze grew so frenzied that the theatre began to suffer. Several West End theatres closed or changed to cinemas, and in the provinces theatres which had already deserted repertory for visiting companies touring with West End successes found it increasingly difficult to keep going.

The Government was well aware that excessive filmgoing was having a marked and by no means desirable effect on audiences. Films were growing tougher, sexier and more violent, and despite the oracles, many claiming to be psychologists, who maintained that children and young people were uninfluenced by Westerns and gangster films, their influence on speech, fashion, manners and general conduct was all too obvious. "Mindful of the contribution the cinema had made during the 1920's in spreading the presumption of America's omnipotence, it was worried—and with good reason—about what these new films might be doing," writes C. A. Oakley. "But the needs of business came first and the American film industry pushed ahead, with its eye focused particularly on the English-speaking market. It wanted, as was said at the time, 'every cent it could get from Britain'—because of the reduced value of sterling and because of its own economic pressure."

British producers tried to improve the standard of films but failed financially under the pressure of the flood of American films. They were crowded out of British cinemas by the American-controlled circuits and did not get a proper showing in America itself. In 1932, at Gaumont British studios at Shepherd's Bush, Michael Balcon produced one of the first important British talkies, *The Rome Express*, and followed it with several more successes, including the film version of Priestley's *The Good Companions*. In 1934 Alfred Hitchcock joined him and made a series of entertaining thrillers, including *The Man Who Knew Too Much*, *The Thirty-nine Steps* and *Secret Agent*. Jessie Matthews starred in several popular musicals made at Shepherd's Bush during these years, *Evergreen* in particular being acclaimed almost as warmly in America as in England, and the famous documentary *Man of Aran* was also a Gaumont British production; but by 1937 the company was losing money and Shepherd's Bush studio closed down.

Early in the 1930's the Hungarian film director Alexander Korda came to England to found London Films at the British and Dominion studios at Elstree. His first outstanding success, released early in 1934, was *The Private Life of Henry VIII*, with Charles Laughton playing the part of Henry. It was immensely popular, paid for itself ten times over and is still revived from time to time. It had its critics, however, including many British people who asked why a Hungarian director "should be allowed to come here and launch cheap insults at the British monarchical tradition". The sets were oddly artificial and clean-looking and the film was episodic, with little regard for the historical and social background of Henry's numerous and ill-starred marriages, but as a contemporary critic, Charles Davy, wrote: "A film directed by a Hungarian and photographed by a Frenchman (Georges Périnal) can hardly be acclaimed as evidence of pure British genius. But our native geniuses may well feel grateful for the handsome advertisement *Henry*

has given to the entire British film industry." The studio correspon-
dent of *Cinema* said that "Without the Charles Laughton picture,
Broadway could still raise a cynical eyebrow at the mention of
the British picture industry."

The Prudential Assurance Company gave Korda financial backing
and plans were drawn up for the building of Denham Studios, which
were to be the best-equipped film studios in the world. During the
next few years Korda made films which met with varying success, but
the outstanding ones were Baroness Orczy's story *The Scarlet Pimpernel*, with Leslie Howard, Edgar Wallace's *Sanders of the River*,
H. G. Wells's *The Shape of Things to Come* and *The Man Who Could
Work Miracles*, and J. B. Priestley's *Laburnum Grove*, which was
directed by Carol Reed. Throughout the thirties the studios at Elstree
and Welwyn were busy turning out a variety of relatively low-priced
films for the British market, but by 1936 it was found that Britain was
still importing £5 million worth of films, mainly from America, and
selling back to them only £100,000 worth, with £500,000 worth to
other foreign countries.

It was at this point that J. Arthur Rank stepped on to the scene. A
rich miller and devout Methodist, his first interest was in religious
films, but he was soon thinking about the industry as a whole, which
he decided "had got into the hands of the wrong people". Great Britain
was now turning out two hundred films a year, through Gaumont
British, Associated British Picture Corporation, London Films, the
English studios of Warner Brothers at Teddington and Twentieth
Century-Fox at Wembley, and from various independent producers,
who rented one or other of the studios for the duration of their particular productions. In 1934 Arthur Rank founded British National
Films at Elstree with Lady Yule and within a few years had gained
control of Oscar Deutsch's 142 sumptuous cinemas which formed the
Odeon circuit, the Gaumont theatres, not quite so gorgeous, as well as
the studios at Denham, the newly built Pinewood studios a few miles
away, and the Shepherd's Bush studios.

In 1933 the British Film Institute, financed by the industry, had
been established "to promote the development of the film as a means
of entertainment and instruction". It began publication of the film
quarterly *Sight and Sound* and also formed a valuable library of films,
both British and foreign, but its influence on film-making did not

match its high-sounding terms of reference and by the end of 1936 there was talk of another slump. The cause, apart from allegations of muddled and wasteful production methods, was attributed to the old trouble—the competition of American films and evasion of the quota Act. British films were not getting an adequate showing in America and Americans, with four times the market, which meant four times as great a return for their initial expenditure, could afford to sell their films cheaply to the British circuits.

In 1937 Britain produced 225 films, many of them excellent, particularly Herbert Wilcox's *Victoria the Great*, René Clair's *The Ghost Goes West* and Hitchcock's *Sabotage*. *Wings of the Morning* was the first British film to be made in colour. There were also the Jessie Matthews, Gracie Fields and George Formby films for the home market, but the financial position was unimproved and film people began to fight shy of production and concentrate on the exhibition side of the business, as being obviously more profitable. Associated British now increased the number of cinemas in their circuit to 500, Gaumont British to 350 and Odeon to 250, and to fill them came more American films, for during 1938 the British film industry made only 116 films, the most notable being Hitchcock's *The Lady Vanishes*, Korda's *The Four Feathers* and the first adaptation of a Shaw play, *Pygmalion*. When Herbert Wilcox returned from America at the end of 1938, he reported that "British pictures have never been so scornfully despised in the United States as at this moment."

While filmgoing was undoubtedly the principal diversion, outside the home, for the mass of the British people during the thirties the radio had become part of their daily lives. Nearly every household possessed a wireless set, which all too frequently was turned on first thing in the morning and left, often scarcely heeded, till it was time to go to bed. People were becoming attuned to a "background noise" and unselective in their choice of programme. They formed the habit of hearing without listening, and a good deal of what they were hearing was the new technique of the crooner.

The story of Baird, the inventor of television, was tragic. After his first demonstration, in 1926, he set to work to perfect his apparatus and by 1928 was successful in transmitting pictures to America and had also begun promising experiments with colour television. He demonstrated at the National Radio Exhibition at Olympia in 1929, and the B.B.C., after a first successful television broadcast the same year, undertook the responsibility for public television in 1932. In the meantime, many other inventors both in Britain and in America were working to develop television, and when Baird visited the United States to demonstrate his own invention and apparatus, no one was interested and he returned empty-handed, to find that other English inventors were devising alternative systems of broadcasting. He moved his laboratory to the Crystal Palace, where he set to work to perfect his colour system and to try to transmit a television picture on to a cinema screen. Then the Crystal Palace caught fire and was burnt out. A great deal of his apparatus was lost and when he had salvaged what he could he learnt that the B.B.C. had adopted an alternative to the Baird system, making their first public television broadcast from Alexandra Palace in 1936. Bitterly disappointed, Baird continued his researches and experiments in colour television, of which his company still held the monopoly, and made a successful demonstration of colour television at the Radio Exhibition of 1939. Then came the Second World War. All television transmissions ceased and in 1946, his knowledge and inventive genius ignored and unused during the war years, he died.

Television sets were expensive in the early years, and though the B.B.C. were making regular broadcasts for the three years before the outbreak of war, the television craze did not get under way until they had resumed their broadcasts in the late forties.

The theatre, struggling against the competition of the cinema, went through a bad period during the thirties and many stage people were unemployed. Unlike many of the poets and writers, the contemporary dramatists showed in their work little concern for the menacing problems of international and domestic politics, which each year grew more acute. One of the few plays of the period which exposed social conditions was the dramatization of Walter Greenwood's novel *Love on the Dole*, but those which made the money and pulled in the audiences were of an utterly different kind, unconcerned with any social conflict or political message, and concentrating, like the feature films, on purely escapist entertainment. They included James Bridie's *The Anatomist* and *Tobias and the Angel*, at the Westminster, Ivor Novello's musicals, *Glamourous Night* and *The Dancing Years*, Nigel Playfair's production of A. P. Herbert's *Derby Day*, at the Lyric, Hammersmith, and Noël Coward's *Cavalcade*, which was well timed but looked nostalgically backward, to the changes brought about by the First World War, rather than forward, to warn of what might be coming next.

Writing in March 1934, in a review of John Gielgud's first production of *Henry V* at the Alhambra, Aubrey Menon said: "As I write this, the proletariat of two European capitals have been bombed, machine-gunned and ridden down since 9 o'clock yesterday morning. It is now exactly 8.30 p.m., and of theatre audiences in London at the moment, the only one which will see a production with the faintest political flavour will sit through a play about a king who died five hundred and twelve years ago, written by a grossly misinformed playwright with the social conscience of an Australian aborigine. And in that play [the Alhambra *Henry V*] we are presented with the spectacle of fifteenth-century Englishmen making wanton war on their nearest neighbour for no sane reason at all."

There were, however, three experimental theatre groups in England at this time. The Cambridge Festival Theatre, under the direction of Terence Gray, was concerned with the interpretation of drama through mime and ballet, as well as or instead of the spoken word, Terence Gray maintaining that the human body is man's "instinctive and immediate means of expressing the emotions which arise within him". The Group Theatre, which had its first public season at the Westminster Theatre in 1935, was also concerned with ballet and movement in relation to dramatic representation and interpretation, and Rupert Doone, who was responsible for most of the productions, had trained with Diaghilev. He contended that theatrical art was "an art of the body, presented by living people in action". W. H. Auden, Christopher Isherwood, Benjamin Britten, Tyrone Guthrie, John Piper and Henry Moore all worked at one time or another with the Group Theatre, and unlike the movement at the Cambridge Festival Theatre, which was concerned purely with its own form of dramatic interpretation as such, the members of the Group were out to demonstrate immediate social and political problems; but their methods of presentation, with the use of masks and the introduction of fragments of ballet, their attempts at satire and lapses into levity, though brilliant in patches and imbued with sincere social observation, were too stylized and obscure to appeal to any but small specialized audiences.

The third group was the Unity Theatre, the theatre of the Left, which was an attempt on the part of the trade unions and the Labour movement to voice their own problems and struggles in the form of social dramas. The Unity Theatre was converted from a Methodist chapel in Camden Town and most of the actors were unpaid amateurs, though a few unemployed professionals gave their services free in return for expenses. In many of the plays, for example *Waiting for Lefty*, the actors spoke directly to the audience, who at the appropriate moments joined in, for the purpose of the Unity Theatre was to stir the workers to positive action against their social conditions. This method of presentation is the "audience participation" advocated by Joan Littlewood.

The story of British ballet during the thirties is a far happier one, for it was during these years that it began to wax strong and vigorous, to take its place in due course amongst the most distinguished in the world. It was early in the thirties that Lilian Baylis invited Ninette de Valois to join her at the Old Vic and Sadler's Wells, to work in the first place on the ballets associated with the operas. Ninette de Valois closed her school, which was beginning to prosper, and took her pupils, and the accomplished and delightful dancer Ursula Moreton as an assistant, to help build up a ballet company.

The Wells engaged Alicia Markova as their star ballerina and from time to time Anton Dolin was invited as guest artist. During the early years the young ballet company remained as a background for Markova, but when she decided to leave Sadler's Wells it was found that the company had been so intelligently and intensively trained that they were ready to stand on their own.

During the thirties lovers of ballet watched with delight the growing strength of the Sadler's Wells ballet and the performance not only of classical ballets but of many new ones. The choreography of some of these, for example *Job*, with music by Vaughan Williams, *Bar aux Folies Bergère*, *The Rake's Progress* and *Checkmate*, with music by Arthur Bliss, was by Ninette de Valois herself, and Frederick Ashton, who joined Sadler's Wells after working with the Camargo Society, contributed the choreography of *Façade*, with music by William Walton, *Les Patineurs*, *Les Rendezvous* and *Horoscope*, with music selected or composed by Constant Lambert, one of the resident directors of music at the Wells, and *The Wise Virgins*, with Bach's music orchestrated by William Walton. For the crowds of ballet-lovers who flocked each night to Rosebery Avenue these were exciting days, for they felt themselves watching from the beginning the birth and development of a great artistic achievement which was destined to win worldwide acclaim.

In the world of painting, the New English Art Club, the Slade School, under the direction of Henry Tonks, and the Royal College of Art at South Kensington were the most important influences on British art during the twenties and thirties, and Walter Sickert, William Orpen, Augustus John, Frank Brangwyn, Stanley Spencer and John Nash were among the distinguished artists working and exhibiting. Jacob Epstein was producing his magnificent bronzes and controversial stone sculptures, and Frank Dobson and Henry Moore were also achieving first scandalized notoriety and later appreciation and distinction.

Very early in the century the experimental artists, the English group led by P. Wyndham Lewis, had displayed in their abstract paintings a premonition of the days of merciless aggression which were shortly to descend on the world; but when the First World War finally broke there was a return to realism. After 1918, however, the experimentalists were soon at work again—the Vorticists, the Cubists and the Futurists. In the 1930's the Surrealists arrived, though very few people could understand what they were trying to say. At the International Surrealist Exhibition held at the New Burlington Galleries in the summer of 1936 Salvador Dali attended, wearing "a diving suit decorated like a Christmas tree, with a motor-car radiator cap on top of the helmet and plasticine hands stuck on the body of the suit, to deliver, in French with a strong Spanish accent, a lecture which was relayed through loudspeakers. When the lecturer grew hot and asked that the helmet should be taken off, this was found to be difficult; it was finally prised up with the billiard cue he carried. Two Irish wolfhounds stood by docilely while Dali described his encounters with that phantom, Reality."[1]

The Surrealists declared that they were interested in the association of ideas and the significance and omnipotence of dreams, in their struggle to solve the problems of life, and their cult was vaguely associated with revolutionary Communism, but they made little impact on English artists and writers and J. B. Priestley, for example, angrily

[1] Julian Symons, *The Thirties* (Cresset Press, 1960).

dismissed them as "the equivalent in art of the Fascist gangs in politics. They stand for violence and neurotic unreason. They are truly decadent."

Motoring became more popular than ever in the thirties and more people bought cars for week-end jaunts, while roadhouses were strewn along the main roads in increasing numbers, where the young could dance and swim, eat, drink and enjoy themselves. The architecture of these new playgrounds was often imitation Tudor, like so many of the contemporary houses, but a few buildings were now being put up in the new Swedish style, plain, functional and sometimes flat-roofed, as for example the interesting houses on the hillside at Amersham in Buckinghamshire and the first block of "modern" flats near Highgate village.

Gradually the cult of functionalism in architecture gained ground over the school which built in imitation of the styles of the Tudors, Jacobeans, Georgians or Victorians, but then came the slick imitators of the modern architects, copying the new forms without consideration or understanding of the basic principles in their design and construction, and producing buildings as unattractive as the worst of the imitative traditional styles. To brick, stone and wood were added new building materials, for engineers now joined architects in erecting steel frames reinforced with concrete for large public buildings and blocks of flats, and soon architects were also using plastics, aluminium, rubber and asbestos in their buildings.

Change assaulted and battered people from all directions during the thirties, for it was, amongst many other things, the era of the Press Lords. The first was Lord Northcliffe, who came to own *The Times*, the *Daily Mail*, the *Daily Mirror*, the *Evening News*, the *Weekly Dispatch* and the *Glasgow Daily Review*, as well as dozens of weekly and monthly magazines. On his death his brother, Lord Rothermere, sold *The Times* to Major Astor and most of the magazines to the Berry brothers, who in time became Lord Camrose and Lord Kemsley. Then the Canadian Lord Beaverbrook entered the arena by buying the *Daily Express*, to which he soon added the *Sunday Express*. He and Lord Rothermere bought the *Evening Standard* from Sir Edward Hulton and also a number of provincial papers, which were resold to the Berry brothers at a handsome profit. The Berry brothers continued to buy up provincial papers, and Lord Rothermere, to maintain the balance of power, plunged into the fray once more to secure the more profitable of those still remaining. Lord Southwood, chairman of Odhams Press, which owned the *People* and many weekly journals, bought up the *Daily Herald*. So it happened that by the end of the thirties half the daily newspapers of the entire country were under the control of the five Press Lords.

The change in the character of newspapers was profound. Many small family newspapers, which had held independent views and had spread the news to their local readers honestly and efficiently, were forced out of business altogether or sold to the combines. The five big groups quickly grasped the opportunity for acquiring large advertising revenues, and as more and more large stores and manufacturers were persuaded that it pays to advertise the mystique of the advertising agency was created.

Advertising revenue depended on sales and the newspapers began to woo new readers by every means they could devise. There were the door-to-door salesmen, persuading people to take their newspapers for specific periods of time and tempting them with all manner of gifts when they had signed the necessary order forms. There were newspaper competitions with large cash prizes. But worst of all, the reading matter of the papers was changed in both style and content, in order to attract more readers. Journalism was no longer a profession. It had become a part of very big business. The policies of the newspapers were dictated to the editors and their staffs and the password to success was sales promotion. All restraint in the description of murders, scandals and crimes gradually fell away, until in the end no privacy was respected. Ordinary people whose claim to publicity was based on the slenderest of achievements acquired a spurious fame in the newspaper world, as twenty years later was to happen in the sphere of television, and in the dedicated cause of pleasing and entertaining the public an utterly false sense of values was established. The dubious and often crashingly boring life stories of criminals and other notorieties were bought and embellished by staff writers to titillate the public. Sometimes "vice" was "exposed", with a wealth of highly coloured detail, for the same purpose. Anything served, provided it made a good story and attracted the readers' attention. Some solemnly believed every word they read. Others lost all respect for the Press and believed nothing at all.

During these years the congregations in most of the churches gradually declined. By 1935 it was estimated that since the beginning of the century the Nonconformists had lost 7 per cent of their membership. The Roman Catholics, on the other hand, claimed a 10 per cent increase during this period, largely due to the immigration of unemployed Irish, who once they had obtained their independence from Britain paradoxically began to arrive here in large numbers to find work.

The Church of England remained firmly entrenched in its traditions, sadly contemplating its emptying pews. The bishops and clergy occasionally declaimed aloud the social evils that beset the times but were powerless to alter the tide of events. All they could do, as servants of a secular State, was to preach the gospel of personal morality and integrity to those who had an ear to listen and a heart to obey.

As for the social services in Britain during the thirties, the Education Act of 1918, drawn up by Dr. H. A. L. Fisher, could not be fully implemented for some years because of the financial economies necessitated by the depression. However, provisions were made for more advanced instruction in the senior departments of the elementary schools and there were plans for the part-education, in day continuation schools, of boys and girls between the ages of fourteen and eighteen who had left their elementary schools. In 1926 the Hadow Report first suggested a complete break for children after eleven years of age, and their removal to special schools for older children, where they should stay until they were fifteen. It also recommended technical high schools for older children, in addition to the secondary schools.

The number of secondary schools giving grammar school education increased slowly but steadily during the thirties and the arrangement for all children to stay at school until they were fifteen would have come into force in September 1939 had it not been for the outbreak of war.

In regard to the health services, there was a development in maternity and child welfare and there were national schemes for the control of tuberculosis and immunization against diphtheria. Hospitals also claimed that the standard of service was improved, though all too many of them were by now a century or more old and there was little money available for rebuilding and modernization.

The plastic surgeons were having valuable practice for the war years

177

ahead in operating on the rich, who had a fancy to improve their appearances. Hooked noses were straightened, snub noses given a line of patrician disdain, sagging jawlines were retrieved and unwanted chins removed, all with tremendous skill and at a deservedly high cost. New operative techniques in brain and thoracic surgery were devised and improved and in the sphere of medicine Dr. Wenyon, working at the Wellcome Research Institute, earned the undying gratitude of thousands of patients from the tropics with his discovery of the serum used in the treatment of yellow fever. For those suffering from only minor ills the ubiquitous aspirin was regarded as the panacea and sold by the thousand; and amongst the many names which have been given to this strange period of British history is that of the Aspirin Age.

Probably the most important advance in the treatment of wrong-doers was the Children and Young Persons Act of 1933, which was responsible for many improvements in the running of the juvenile courts. No child under the age of eight was now considered guilty of a legal offence in the United Kingdom, and between the ages of eight and fourteen the court had to be satisfied that the child knew he was doing wrong. Delinquents up to the age of seventeen were now to be tried in the juvenile courts and the magistrates had to be people with special experience of children and young people. The Act also required the court to concern itself with the well-being of the culprits and where necessary remove them from an undesirable background into the care of foster parents or hostels.

For older boys and girls who were persistent offenders the first Borstal institution had been established in 1902, to protect them from the prisons and contact with hardened criminals. A few more of these institutions were established but the prisons themselves remained grim, hopeless, soul-destroying places, unchanged since their establishment in early Victorian times, when the foundation stone of Holloway, for example, was inscribed with the chilling words: "May God preserve the City of London and make this place a terror to evil-doers." Moreover, with an increasing population and a proportionately increasing number of offenders, the prisons were already becoming overcrowded. In 1939 the average prison and Borstal population on any one day of the year was 10,000 to 11,000 out of a total population for England and Wales of about 40 million.

As the fateful years of the thirties slipped quickly by the threat of

(*left*) Building an air-raid shelter in a London garden.

(*below, left*) A V1 flying bomb over London in 1944.

(*below, right*) The war disrupted the lives of thousands of children, who were evacuated to safe areas of Britain.

PLATE 17

PLATE 18

(*above*) 16th November, 1940, the morning after the devastating raid on Coventry. The spire of the cathedral can be seen in the background.

(*below*) After an air raid on London in 1940. A policeman takes stock of the damage.

PLATE 19

(*above*) Ely during the 1947 floods.

(*below, left*) George Bernard Shaw (1856–1950).

(*below, right*) Mr. Tommy Watson, now in his nineties, one of the last of the old knife grinders who used to be a common sight in the streets of London.

(*above*) Mr. Attlee and Commonwealth statesmen in the garden of Number 10, Downing Street.

PLATE 20

(*right*) The wedding of Princess Elizabeth and Prince Philip of Greece on 20th November, 1947.

PLATE 21

(*above*) The Festival of Britain, 1951, designed to show the world that Britain still had ingenuity and inventiveness. In the foreground is the Festival Hall and beyond are the Dome of Discovery and the Skylon.

(*below*) King George VI and the Royal Family at the opening and dedication of the Festival Hall.

PLATE 22

(left) The new Coventry Cathedral, a triumph for the city which took so much punishment in the Second World War.

(below) One of the very popular Promenade Concerts which take place in the Royal Albert Hall during the summer.

(*above*) The Windscale Plutonium Station in Cumberland.

PLATE 23

(*below*) The General Election, 1964. B.B.C. television prepares for an 18-hour broadcast of results.

The New Britain.
(*above*) The Chiswick Flyover, part
of the M4 Motorway.

PLATE 24

(*right*) An Electronic Computer.

war loomed ever larger and armament factories developed their weapons. The League of Nations, on which such high hopes had been set after the First World War, maintained its prestige and authority till the end of the twenties, with its permanent International Court of Justice and its numerous works of humanitarianism. In 1932 President Hoover put forward a strong plan for worldwide armament reductions, which held out real hope for a permanent world peace, and at the new disarmament conference which followed fifty nations were present. The proposals were firstly, to reduce the offensive character of all land forces, which would involve the abolition of all tanks, all chemical warfare and all large, mobile guns; secondly, the abolition of all bombing planes and the total prohibition of bombardment from the air; thirdly, the reduction by one-third of the numbers of battleships and submarines permitted by previous treaties and by one-quarter of aircraft carriers, cruisers and destroyers, with a maximum of 35,000 tons submarine tonnage for any one power.

Mr. Baldwin had been prepared to go even further than this and agree to total abolition of all military aviation, capital ships, aircraft carriers, submarines and heavy, mobile guns and tanks; but members of the Cabinet did not agree with him and he was overridden. The compromise proposals put forward by Sir John Simon were not acceptable and by the time the League of Nations met at the next session for further discussions it was too late, for Hitler—with his complete disregard for all international agreements and treaties—had come to power.

In 1934, Lord Cecil organized the Peace Ballot in Britain, in which every citizen over the age of eighteen was invited to record his opinion on the questions of international disarmament and economic and military sanctions against aggressors. Eleven and a half million voters filled in forms and the ballot proved that 90 per cent were in favour of the League, of disarmament and the abolition of the private manufacture of arms. Over 80 per cent were for the abolition of air forces, over 90 per cent for economic sanctions against possible aggression and 74 per cent for military sanctions; but by the time the votes had all been collected and counted Mussolini had invaded Abyssinia. All was muddle and faint-heartedness and the sanctions, as we have seen, were applied only nominally. The method of collective resistance by peaceful nations against an aggressor was thereby made to look futile and the League of Nations became the home of lost causes and forlorn hopes.

The British people had made it abundantly clear that they did not want war and when the *Daily Express* assured them it would never happen most of the readers, against their better judgment, were reassured. Nevertheless all the nations concerned very soon began to

Lord Rutherford.

re-arm and take what precautions they deemed necessary, though having only the haziest idea of what might be coming—bombing, gas attacks or bacterial warfare. Rumour and supposition spread and the prospect became more horrible and alarming each month. The weapons of 1918—the guns, the tanks, the submarines, the destroyers, the warships and the aircraft—were hurriedly manufactured, all larger and deadlier than had ever before been conceived. The only thing missing was the airship. Germany had developed her zeppelins and from 1931 the Graf Zeppelin was making regular crossings of the Atlantic at a speed of sixty miles an hour; but when Great Britain launched her famous airship, the R.101, disaster befell its maiden voyage to Karachi. It crashed in flames near Paris and all aboard, including the Air Minister and many distinguished members of the aviation industry, perished. After that tragedy airships as a means of travel were everywhere abandoned.

The vitally important scientific discoveries of the thirties, which before long were to play so great a part in world affairs, were not yet considered by the arms manufacturers; but in 1932, which has been described as the most spectacular year in the history of science, Sir James Chadwick discovered the neutron, Sir John Cockcroft succeeded in splitting the atom and Lord Rutherford was evolving the science of nuclear physics.

It was the literary world of the thirties which expressed most vehemently the thoughts and fears that were beginning to assail the perceptive people of Britain, as the situation in Europe steadily worsened, for poets and writers alike were concerned and many of them saw in the socialism of Russia a solution for the people not only of Britain but of the whole world.

As early as 1922, when T. S. Eliot published his poem *The Waste Land*, the thinking of the younger generation was turning from the sufferings of the immediate past to a contemplation of the present and the future. Their generation had been sacrificed and they were determined to change the old order so that such a thing could never happen again.

> What are the roots that clutch, what branches grow
> Out of this stony rubbish? Son of man,
> You cannot say, or guess, for you know only
> A heap of broken images, where the sun beats,
> And the dead tree gives no shelter, the cricket no relief,
> And the dry stone no sound of water

wrote T. S. Eliot in *The Waste Land*, and again, in *The Hollow Men*:

> We are the hollow men,
> We are the stuffed men
> Leaning together,
> Headpiece filled with straw....

Eliot was concerned that individual men, possessed of the wrong kind of genius, could be free to make use of the forces of evil to pervert the world. Appalled by the power of this aggressive individualism, he retreated into the shelter of the High Church, expounding the dangers of an age which had no regard for orthodoxy and tradition. The "inner light" of the individual he described as "the most untrustworthy and deceitful guide that ever offered itself to wandering humanity".

W. H. Auden, the first of the Communist poets, saw things differently, and in protest at the conditions of the working classes of Britain wrote of a time when:

> The few shall be taught who want to understand,
> Most of the rest shall love upon the land;
> Living in one place with a satisfied face
> All of the women and most of the men
> Shall work with their hands and not think again.

Many young poets and writers wanted to change the world and thought it could be done easily, by writing and talking. They passionately desired a world commonwealth, where all social evils would be removed, but they had little real contact with the working classes and strove to fan the flames of a revolution which in Britain did not exist. They argued that the sudden cataclysm of twentieth-century civilization, with its unprecedented situations and vastly increased population, could not be governed by moral, economic and social laws which had evolved during past centuries, when such situations had neither existed nor been contemplated. For the new situations new values and new laws must be established.

Their thinking was often muddled and their ideas impractical; and their impact was slight. After the shock of the brief marriage between Communism and Fascism, with the Molotov-Ribbentrop pact of August 1939, they suffered the final disillusionment which had been nagging since the confused time in Spain, when they had tried to reconcile what they had hoped was going to be achieved with what they actually saw happening. Their mission had been nothing but a pipe dream; and though some matured into distinguished men of letters, never again did they try to wed their art to politics or any social message.

Of the novelists, Evelyn Waugh, Aldous Huxley, Charles Morgan, Somerset Maugham and Hugh Walpole were all at work throughout the thirties. A number of writers, including Virginia Woolf, Lytton Strachey, E. M. Forster and George Orwell, belonged to a group known as the Bloomsbury circle, which also included J. M. Keynes, the economist, and the artists Vanessa Bell and Duncan Grant.

There was a wealth of Left Wing literary magazines and Victor Gollancz had great success with his Left Book Club and its associated magazine, *Left News*. The club was formed early in 1936 and by the end of 1937 the number of members had risen to 50,000, all of them avid readers of the Left Wing books, which were chosen each month by John Strachey, Harold Laski and Victor Gollancz himself, and included Stephen Spender's *Forward from Liberalism* and George Orwell's *The Road to Wigan Pier*. The club's avowed intention in the first place was to create a popular front to oppose Fascism and its members included Socialists, Communists and Liberals, but in the end its sympathies were frankly Communist.

But there were not many months left now before all the efforts of the pacifists, the appeasers, the Socialists and the Communists in Britain came temporarily to an end. On 4th November 1938 a short news item appeared in the *Daily Express*: "The Cabinet plan to provide work for many thousands of unemployed in digging A.R.P. trenches in towns all over Britain. The work will be paid for at the usual rates."

News for the unemployed at last, but hardly welcome. Less than a year later the lights of Europe went out once more and for the next four and a half years all was darkness and confusion, destruction and mortal fear.

CHAPTER ELEVEN

The Second World War (1939–1945)

During the morning of 1st September 1939, as soon as news came that Hitler had crossed the frontier into Poland, the mobilization of all British land, sea and air forces, despite many dissenting voices from the Labour benches, was immediately ordered. For many of us those memories of the early days of September 1939 are a confusion of rapidly built air-raid shelters, of the sudden black-out, of hurrying figures groping their way through familiar streets which had become unfriendly, of darkened trains arriving in still darker stations, of the issue of gas masks, which we were ordered to carry with us at all times, and of the dozens of silver barrage balloons which appeared, shimmering and beautiful in the early autumn sunshine, as they hung low and protectively over the spires and domes and rooftops of London. Young men who the day before had seemed schoolboys appeared overnight in uniform, strangely transformed, faintly self-conscious, older, more serious and already a little remote. Girls exchanged their summer dresses for the khaki and blue of the service uniforms. Hundreds of bewildered schoolchildren, each carrying the inevitable gas mask in its cardboard box, and shepherded by harassed schoolteachers, gathered at the London railway stations for destinations which were unknown even to the weeping mothers who had come to see them go.

There was an air of tension everywhere and a fear of the unknown terror which might at any moment descend on us all. We said goodbye to family and friends not knowing when or where or how we should ever see them again. The familiar had suddenly become strange and we knew that our world would never be quite the same again. Our lives were no longer our own. We had become part of a war machine and must henceforth do as we were told; and dominating all the personal anxieties and sorrows, the upheavals of family life and the anguish of saying goodbye to husbands, sons and lovers as they departed for the fighting, there was a hastily improvised but highly efficient organization which very quickly gave people a sense of purpose and direction.

The conscription bill had been passed earlier in the year and the call-up of men and women proceeded smoothly, with a relentless rhythm. People were recruited for the army, navy and air force, for munition and aircraft manufacture, for civil defence, for work in essential services such as transport and the production and distribution of food, for the greatly expanded ministries and civil service and for the essential professions such as medicine, nursing and teaching. Every man had to satisfy the recruitment and labour officers that he was doing his utmost for the war, according to his mental and physical capabilities, and before long every woman, too, was called upon to contribute as far as her strength and family responsibilities would allow.

The appeasement of Munich had given Mr. Chamberlain and his Government, as well as the rest of us, a brief twelve months to prepare for all this. We all knew that this war was going to be, in some ill-defined way, more terrible than the last, and that this time the danger would come from the air, so that civilians and combatants alike would be in constant and mortal danger. In Abyssinia the Italians had used poison gas and there was no knowing what other plans for human destruction the Germans might have been secretly inventing. No one knew the strength of their air force and other equipment. Absurd, hysterical rumours were abroad that their tanks, for all their appearance of armour and strength, were light and useless, that their aircraft were inefficient, their pilots untrained. This was wishful thinking at its most dangerous and we were very soon to learn the folly of it. The British navy was undoubtedly considerably stronger than the German, and with the co-operation of the French navy we hoped we could be invincible on the high seas, but we gravely underestimated the strength of the German U-boats and the effectiveness of German air attacks on our shipping.

As the Government was expecting an immediate and heavy aerial bombardment, and had already prepared some 250,000 hospital beds for air-raid casualties, its first concern was to send all schoolchildren and expectant mothers or mothers with very young children out of the obvious danger areas of the big cities—particularly London, the most likely target of all—into the country. People in country districts were warned and a register was made of the number of evacuees which they could board. Many people, distracted with personal worries, by no means welcomed the idea of filling their homes with strangers, but generally speaking the billeting officers were tactful as well as persuasive, and as the busloads of children arrived in villages and country towns from the nearby railway stations, they were very soon sorted out, claimed by their temporary foster parents and introduced to their new homes, while their school-teachers, travelling with them, made arrangements with the local headmasters and headmistresses for classroom accommodation in the little country schools.

For many of London's children, as well as some of the young mothers, it was their first taste of the country, for they had been born during the lean years of the twenties and thirties, when many households were so poor that there had never been any money to spend on holidays or even on day trips to the seaside or the country. Everything was strange to them—the quietness, the food, the farmyard animals, even the birds and flowers and trees. There were cases of children who had never eaten green vegetables or fruit, or drunk fresh milk, having existed on the working-class diet of fish and chips or cold meat and bread, washed down with strong tea and condensed milk. Some had no change of clothing, no night clothes or dressing gowns. They knew nothing of discipline outside school or of going to bed at a reasonable hour. Life in the country taught them a great deal. Some disliked it and longed for the crowds, the shops and the cinemas, the cheerful squalor of the old life in the city streets, but most of them soon settled down happily and fell naturally into the ordered rhythm of rural life.

Country people were shocked at first by the poverty of many of the townspeople. It was something they had heard about in a vague way but were experiencing for the first time. They were generous and patient, and with the deepened perception and heightened emotion of wartime, the people of Britain learned at last to know one another. The sharp cleavage between rich and poor, town and country, was bridged in a way which had never before been possible. There were inevitably a few failures but generally speaking the experiment was a great success, many long-standing social barriers were broken for all time, lasting friendships were made, and in not a few cases it led to whole families, who hitherto had never thought of living anywhere but in a town, settling down in the country after the war.

A relatively few people, who had friends in Canada or America, decided to send their children there for the duration of the war, but most preferred to keep their families intact for as long as possible. Moreover, the Atlantic crossing at once became highly dangerous, for the Germans began their submarine warfare on the very first day of the war, and on the evening of 3rd September they torpedoed the liner *Athenia*, outward bound for America with many British women and children, as well as Americans, on board. A hundred and nineteen lives were lost, amongst them twenty-eight Americans, who were as yet not involved in the war. It brought a sharp realization of the tragedies to come, but nevertheless the expected bombing did not happen.

Shortly after Mr. Chamberlain had announced the declaration of war, the first air-raid warning wailed forth over London and the counties of the south-east. Air-raid wardens, nurses and members of the Fire Service all ran to their stations, ready to perform their first wartime duties, and members of the population dutifully hurried to the shelters which had been allotted to them. It was a false alarm. A solitary plane had been flying in across the Channel. A quarter of an hour later the "all-clear" sounded and everyone heaved a mighty sigh of relief.

It was to be another eight months before the air-raid sirens were heard again in London and that winter many women and children, against Government advice, returned home to London. As the flow of returning children increased, some of the London teachers had to return too, to re-open the schools: but they were badly understaffed, which meant that the numbers in the individual classes were too high for effective teaching. Conditions for the teachers were extremely difficult, and despite all their efforts the general standard of education in the elementary schools inevitably declined.

That first winter of the war nothing much seemed to be happening. It was the twilight war—a period of tension and apprehension, with both sides waiting and watching. Germany and Russia were making gigantic preparations for the battles ahead. In Britain, Winston Churchill had been appointed First Lord of the Admiralty and was urging us to prepare in like measure, but the Government was still of one party and the Labour opposition was strong and critical, with many members still urging a negotiated peace.

The submarine war, however, was intensive, particularly in the Atlantic. Hitler was using his first secret weapon, the magnetic mine, and during the first seven months of the war Britain lost, by U-boats, mines, surface raiders, aircraft and other unknown causes, between half and three-quarters of a million tons of shipping. An average of more than five British merchant vessels were lost each week. Food and most other commodities, such as petrol, fuel, building materials and paper, were rationed almost from the beginning of the war, and a year or two later Britain had clothes rationing too.

From the outset Britain was faced with the possibility of famine, and within twenty-four hours of the declaration of war the Government had taken control of the farming industry, for at this time more than two-thirds of British food was imported and the situation was highly dangerous. Through the policy of importing cheap grain from America and the Commonwealth in exchange for manufactured goods, farmers had long since been forced to abandon arable farming, and though Britain had large numbers of livestock, she could feed them only by importing between seven and eight million tons of animal feeding stuffs each year.

What Britain needed was more ploughed land for wheat and cereals and less grassland for livestock, for ten acres of grassland will support cattle to feed only twelve or fourteen people for a year but ten acres of wheat will provide a year's bread for two hundred. With the war already being waged and shortages of everything, including labour, becoming daily more apparent, British farm land, neglected for so many years, had suddenly to be turned from pastoral country to arable. Britain had to sacrifice half her pigs and more than a quarter of her poultry in order to concentrate on grain, potatoes and sugar-beet; and of the livestock which remained, milk had first claim, then beef cattle and sheep, and last of all pigs and poultry.

Eighty per cent of British farms consisted of only a hundred acres or less, and there were entire parishes which did not possess a plough or an acre of ploughland, so that some farmers, particularly in the Midlands, had actually to be taught how to use a plough. Since the lean days of the twenties thousands of acres of potentially good land had become waterlogged and overgrown with weeds and scrub, the home of hundreds of rabbits and unused by the farmers. Hundreds of miles of farm roads had to be cleared of thorn and scrub in order to get the machines on to the fields. Ditches had to be cleaned and drains cleared. Every acre of available land was now brought into use. Some of the commons and parks, even golf courses and playing fields in Britain were ploughed, and hills and swamps turned into fertile land again, while on established farms pastures were converted to corn land or to better grass for the dairy herds.

Within four years Britain had increased her arable land from some twelve million acres to nearly nineteen million, while the area under permanent grass had been reduced from over nineteen million acres to less than thirteen million. These results were possible only through the extensive use of modern farm machinery, two-thirds of which Britain made herself, the rest being imported from Canada, Australia and the United States of America.

In order to maintain the nation's health under the stringency of wartime rationing, the Government ordered the issue of cheap or free milk to children and nursing mothers. It meant that the consumption of milk rose by 40 per cent, but dairy farmers, though still losing their pastures to the plough, managed to meet it.

The farming industry, now consisting of 400,000 farms of all shapes and sizes, was made self-governing. Committees, responsible to the Ministry of Agriculture, were set up in every county, under an independent chairman and a technical expert, acting as executive officer. Each committee member had an average of eight square miles to supervise. He had to visit the farms in his area and, where possible, schedule extra land for ploughing. He had compulsory powers to enforce cultivation, and though he seldom had to use them three thousand farmers did in fact have their tenancies terminated during the war years because they could not or would not produce the minimum of food required of them.

County committees were subdivided into district committees. These were sometimes divided again, so that there might be a committee even for a single parish. This arrangement was highly successful, for the men giving the advice knew the local conditions and the men with whom they were dealing, and the farmers in their turn knew the committee members and respected them for their practical knowledge. Farming was back to the days of the nineteenth century, for the farmers now had a guaranteed market and were being paid a reasonable price for their produce.

Between the wars some 300,000 men had left the land, and by 1939 only 600,000 remained. With the outbreak of the 1939 war labour, for the first time for many years, had a scarcity value. A control of movement was ordered for farm workers to prevent their moving to more highly paid work. Farm workers of twenty-one and over were free from military call-up, and by 1940 workers of eighteen and over were exempted, while employers in other industries were prohibited from employing men normally working in agriculture, unless authorized to do so by the Ministry of Labour.

A member of the Women's Land Army.

The Women's Land Army was recruited and did valuable work. At harvest time the army helped. People working in the towns came into the country at week-ends and holiday times to do what they could, and later prisoners of war were used. "Dig For Victory" was one of the most familiar of the wartime slogans, and in addition to helping the farmers people dug up their own gardens, turning lawns and flower gardens into vegetable patches and sometimes small poultry yards; and where they had enough room, people kept a pig and a few goats as well.

With the farming industry working to capacity to make Britain self-supporting in food, with factories converted from peacetime industries to the manufacture of guns, tanks, ammunition and aircraft, the shipyards and dockyards, coal mines and iron foundries alive again and working as hard as they ever had, the people of Britain soon became accustomed to the wartime régime. Life was spartan and grim, but there was a new comradeship and unity of purpose in it all which made for a strange exhilaration. People were more friendly and warm-hearted, more sympathetic to those in distress and less selfish.

Britain could no longer declare war in the name of the countries of the Commonwealth, as in the 1914 war, but in 1939, when war came, Australia, New Zealand and Canada declared themselves at war with Germany and soon the reassuring, stalwart figures of their armies and air forces were to be seen once more in the streets of London. South Africa also declared herself for Britain, for she was still a member of the Commonwealth, though the vote to enter the war was won largely by the influence of General Smuts and by a very narrow margin in the Parliament at Cape Town. Eire, also still a member of the Commonwealth, remained neutral, and so did India, which was already in process of achieving its independent partition, though many of the Indian army volunteered and throughout the war maintained their tradition as gallant and brave fighters.

During the first winter of the war the fighting on land seemed very remote. British troops were sent to France and the French were hastily completing the fortifications along their defensive Maginot Line, but no shot was fired. In Poland, however, the German attack was the first example of the modern "blitzkrieg". The way was prepared by a carefully organized system of spies and traitors. The attack was then launched by an air bombardment of such concentration and destruction as had hardly before been conceived, with dive bombers in use for the first time. The planes bombed communications, power stations and industrial towns, choosing always sites where they could produce the maximum disorganization. There followed a concentrated land attack by tanks and heavy armour, and to add to the confusion and terror parachutists were dropped, who quickly linked up with the fifth column, the traitors on the ground, who were waiting for them. Poland was attacked on three sides and the Polish army was hopelessly outmatched in numbers and equipment, the cavalry facing tanks and armoured cars with the swords and lances of another age long since departed. Within a fortnight it was almost over and then Russia moved in from the east to complete the massacre. Warsaw held out even then, for a few more days, till a merciless bombing reduced the city to a mass of smouldering ruins.

Russia was beginning to sharpen her claws. After her joint occupation of Poland with Germany she obtained naval and military bases and airfields in Estonia, Latvia and Lithuania. She attempted to acquire similar bases in Finland, and when the Finns refused them she copied the German tactics and invaded. It was on 30th November 1939 that the news of the Russian invasion of Finland reached Britain. Russia was expelled from the League of Nations and plans were discussed for sending help to Finland, but Sweden and Norway, anxious to maintain a strict neutrality, could not give permission for Allied warships to enter their territorial waters. Moreover, many members of the Opposition were fiercely opposed to British intervention, still anxious to keep Britain out of the fighting war and hoping for a last-minute negotiated peace.

There were many British volunteers for the Finnish campaign, but by March 1940, before they could be sent to the battlefield, Finland collapsed and it was too late. Finland was occupied by the Russians and the next month Germany attacked both Norway and Denmark, using the same blitzkrieg methods and with the same success, despite the initial victories of the British navy, which raced to Norwegian waters as soon as Norway's neutrality had been violated. Had Norway allowed Britain to help sooner, when the attack seemed imminent, the outcome might have been happier, but she maintained her strictly correct neutrality till the last minute, so that when Britain arrived the damage, accelerated by the activities of her fifth column, led by the traitor Quisling, was too far advanced, though Britain held on to Narvik for a while.

With the capitulation of Norway came the real explosion in Europe for which the world had been waiting and watching for eight months. In France the Communists were extremely active, and in their attempts to undermine the morale and will to fight of the army and the people were assuring them that the war was an "imperialist and capitalist crime against democracy". In Britain the Communists, under direction from Russia, were preaching the same message, but there were not many of them and their impact was slight. Nevertheless, the war was still being run by a Conservative government, and from the Socialist opposition and the trade unions there still came talk of trying to end the war by a conference.

The successful German invasion of Norway caused great alarm in Britain. Everyone thought they could run the war better than Mr. Chamberlain, and the Opposition called for a debate. Mr. Chamberlain's account of the disaster in Norway roused the antagonism of many Conservatives as well as the Opposition, and the criticism and vituperation were merciless, Mr. Amery rising to quote to the Prime Minister the words spoken by Oliver Cromwell three centuries earlier: "You have sat too long for any good you have been doing. Depart, I say, and let us have done with you. In the name of God, go!"

The debate continued on 9th May and Mr. Chamberlain confided to his ministers that he was convinced the time had come for a coalition government, in which all parties would be represented, and that if Labour would not serve under him he was prepared to resign in favour of someone who was acceptable to them. The following day, without the slightest provocation, and after renewed avowals of friendship, Germany launched a savage attack on Holland and Belgium. While news of this fresh disaster was coming in, Mr. Chamberlain resigned and Winston Churchill was appointed head of a new coalition government, in which members of the Labour and Liberal parties had a strong representation, Mr. Attlee, the leader of the Labour Party, becoming Mr. Churchill's deputy.

The German army pressed on into France. The Maginot Line was by-passed and the French army too thinly dispersed along it surrounded, within a few days between four and five million British, French and German soldiers were fighting one another. It was a totally different story from the static trench warfare of 1914. Preceded by heavy aerial bombardment, the German blitzkrieg technique of mass attack with heavy tanks and dive bombers was once more successful, and within three weeks the French army had collapsed and the British army had been ordered to retreat to Dunkirk, to avoid certain annihilation. The British First Armoured Division had lost sixty per cent of its tanks and neither Britain nor the French possessed any dive bombers at this stage. Britain had ten fighter squadrons of Hurricanes, eight of Battles, six of Blenheims and five of Lysanders, and with these she covered her retreating armies, as they gathered on the sands of Dunkirk to await transport across the Channel.

The deliverance of the British army from Dunkirk was one of the greatest epics of the war. In nine days, under merciless bombing from which there was no respite, nearly 340,000 soldiers were transported safely back to Britain from Dunkirk, in an assortment of ships ranging from destroyers to sloops, corvettes, gunboats, trawlers, tugs and naval motor-boats; 851 ships were recorded as taking part in the operation, of which 243 were sunk, but there were also unrecorded rescues by dozens of ships' lifeboats and small privately owned boats which their owners took across the Channel to help as best they could. During the last days of the evacuation Britain also rescued thousands of French soldiers, who preferred to join the Free French army, hastily being assembled in Britain, rather than submit to the Germans.

It was during these momentous days that the Royal Air Force won its first laurels of the war. Outnumbered by the Germans as it was, it showed incomparable courage and skill, fighting tenaciously and tirelessly, outmanœuvring its opponents time and time again, and inflicting such heavy losses on the Germans that it achieved the first real halt to Hitler's European conquest.

The bulk of the British army was safely back in Britain, but France, Belgium, Holland, Denmark and finally Norway were now in German hands, for during the evacuation of Dunkirk Britain had also withdrawn the last of her troops from Narvik. Then, on 10th June 1940, Italy entered the war on the side of Germany, creating an immediate threat to Malta and British interests in the Middle East and Africa.

Britain was entirely alone. Winston Churchill's task was the heaviest that any British statesman had ever had to face, and he rose to the occasion with a strength and grandeur which have become one of the proudest stories of British history. With inspired courage he addressed the House of Commons: "Even though large tracts of Europe and many old and famous states have fallen or may fall into the grip of the Gestapo and all the odious apparatus of Nazi rule, we shall not flag or fail. We shall go on to the end. We shall fight in France, we shall fight in the seas and oceans, we shall fight with growing confidence and growing strength in the air; we shall defend our island, whatever the cost may be. We shall fight on the beaches, we shall fight on the landing-grounds, we shall fight in the fields, and in the streets, we shall fight in the hills; we shall never surrender: and even if, which I do not for a moment believe, this island or a large part of it were subjugated and starving, then our Empire beyond the seas, armed and guarded by the British fleet, would carry on the struggle, until, in God's good time, the New World, with all its power and might, steps forth to the rescue and the liberation of the Old."

There was no comfort in this stirring rhetoric. It was a rallying call, for Britain was in dire peril. Where would Hitler strike next? Britain was the obvious target. He made his plans for invasion, and Britain prepared to fight back. The Local Defence Volunteers, afterwards called the Home Guard, were quickly recruited, from older men in civilian jobs, and they drilled enthusiastically in their few hours of spare time. They had no arms during the first few weeks and uniforms were mostly hasty improvisations. The Air Raid Precaution service was rapidly enlarged and rosters of duties for fire-watchers compiled. Tank traps and road blocks to hamper the invaders appeared on all the coast roads. The treasures of London's museums were dispatched to secret places of safety in the country. Magna Carta, the symbol of British democracy, was sent to America. Stores of emergency rations —tinned food, sugar and tea—were dispersed throughout the country, in warehouses, storage sheds, and even in the cellars of private houses, so that, if communications were cut, each remote village or hamlet would be able to survive for a while.

In preparing for the invasion the Germans knew that they must first win air supremacy over the English Channel, putting the British air force out of action, so that it would be unable to hamper their embarkation in France and their landings at the Channel ports. The next battle of the war, therefore, was between the Luftwaffe and the Royal Air Force. It opened on 10th July 1940, the Germans directing their attack mainly against the Kent coast. During July there were heavy losses of fighters on both sides, but no decisive victory. On 15th August the Germans launched their heaviest daylight raid of the war, sending eight hundred planes to the south coast and another hundred Heinkel bombers, with an escort of forty Messerschmitts, to Tyneside. In the northern raid thirty Heinkels were shot down for the loss of only two injured British pilots. In the South the Germans lost forty-six planes to Britain's thirty-four.

The Germans, surprised and somewhat disconcerted, began to have second thoughts about their invasion, but they still hoped to wear down British resistance by intensive bombing. Between 24th August and 5th September they launched incessant attacks on British airfields in southern and south-eastern England, inflicting terrible losses and straining British resources to their utmost limits. The factories worked night and day to provide replacements of aircraft, but Britain was losing the battle in numbers alone. The airfields at Manston and Biggin Hill were cratered with bomb holes and ruined. During that disastrous, tragic two weeks 103 British pilots were killed, with 128 gravely wounded, and 466 Hurricanes and Spitfires were lost or seriously damaged. Of a thousand British pilots, nearly a quarter were lost and had to be replaced by younger, less experienced men. But as the situation seemed to be fast becoming untenable, the Germans suddenly changed the attack to London and the docks. From 7th September onwards they attacked each night and by 14th September it looked as though the whole of the London docks were on fire. The great timber sheds of the Surrey Docks, on the south bank, were ablaze. As night fell the darkening sky turned brilliantly, terrifyingly crimson, and the slow ripples of the oily black river gleamed angrily as they reflected the stabs of flame which leapt ever higher from the gigantic piles of wood crackling and roaring their way to total destruction.

The following day, Sunday, 15th September, the Germans made a heavy daylight raid on London. Londoners watched a score of dog-fights taking place above the rooftops simultaneously and incendiaries by the score pattered down on to the pavements. The Germans lost fifty-six planes that day and the following evening Bomber Command attacked their shipping lying at anchor in the French Channel ports, waiting to set forth on the invasion of Britain. The Battle of Britain was won by the Royal Air Force, and on 17th September Hitler decided to postpone the invasion indefinitely. The following month Italy invaded Greece from Albania, but, helped by the Royal Air Force based on Crete, the Greeks fought back gallantly and Mussolini suffered a severe rebuff.

The Germans, though postponing their plans for invasion, did not stop their air raids on Britain. They made attacks on the provincial cities but concentrated on London, and from 7th September until 3rd November London was raided every night by an average of two hundred bombers. The autumn nights were made hideous with the whine and crump of bombs, the rattle of falling bricks and masonry, the crackle and bark of the anti-aircraft guns, the clatter of breaking glass, ambulance bells, fire engines, cries for help from the injured, confusion, urgency and fear. Yet there was seldom panic. Their privations seemed to give people an added strength. They grew used to taking normal safety precautions and spending their nights in air-raid shelters. They installed Anderson shelters in their back gardens or the small Morrison shelters—reinforced steel-topped tables with wire sides—in their cellars, under the stairs or anywhere else they thought safest. Special brick and concrete shelters were built in the streets, some large enough to accommodate up to seven thousand people, and bunks were installed on the platforms of Underground railway stations, to which many people descended each evening after work, remaining there till the following morning, regardless of warning or all-clear, in order to secure a good night's rest. When it became apparent that bomb damage was causing serious losses among civilians, many of whom were losing businesses and livelihoods, Mr. Churchill arranged that compensation should be paid to them under the War Damage Act.

By the middle of September the Germans had devised a new terror —the delayed action bomb— and a new courage was demanded by the bomb disposal squads, whose task it was to dig out the bombs, explode them or make them harmless. The following month the Germans were dropping land mines by parachute. Then, on 17th October, 480 German aircraft dropped on London not only 386 tons of high explosive but 70,000 incendiary bombs. They caused so many fires that firewatching became compulsory and Londoners took it in turn to spend their nights on the rooftops, putting them out as quickly as possible.

On 3rd November 1940 London had its first raid-free night for weeks, for the Germans switched their attention to other industrial centres of Britain once more, this time with renewed ferocity. On 14th November Coventry was devastated by five hundred aircraft, which droned over southern England and the Midlands in relentlessly regular droves all through the night, dropping six hundred tons of explosives and thousands of incendiaries. The centre of the city, including the ancient cathedral, was laid waste, four hundred people were killed and many seriously injured, but the factories went on working, and within a week the life of the city was stirring into action once more. Birmingham was the next target and on three successive nights of raids nearly eight hundred people were killed and two thousand seriously injured. Bristol, Southampton, Liverpool, Plymouth, Sheffield, Manchester, Leeds and Glasgow were all heavily attacked and then, on 29th December, came the fire raid on the City of London, when acres of historic buildings were lost for ever and eight Wren churches and the ancient Guildhall were either totally destroyed or badly damaged.

With the New Year the raids on London continued and people were becoming weary with constantly broken nights and the senseless destruction and carnage. The Air Ministry became aware of the fact that German bombers were flying to their targets by means of a radio beam, which gave their bombing great accuracy. Very soon, however, British technicians had learnt to deflect the beam, so that German pilots, following it blindly, flew off course and dropped their bombs several miles away from the intended target, usually in open country. Moreover, the beam enabled British fighters and anti-aircraft batteries to locate the raiders and estimate their courses, so that, as the winter of 1941 gave way to spring, the toll of German casualties steadily mounted. The German High Command became increasingly concerned at their bomber losses and in May 1941 called off the raids on Britain. Once more the Royal Air Force had won a resounding victory, and for the next three years Londoners had a respite.

During these long years life in Britain was austere. Everyone worked long hours and the amenities of life were few. Food was scarce and dull but adequate, and prices were pegged, so that all could afford to buy the rations. There was inevitably a black market, but the majority of decent folk did well enough without recourse to it. The war, with its victories and defeats, its moments of wild hope and near despair, of triumph and anguish, was everyone's principal concern, for there were few families who did not have someone very close to them engaged in the fighting.

In the eastern Mediterranean the Germans infiltrated through the Balkans, by way of Rumania and Bulgaria. There was disaffection in Yugoslavia and the Germans made a sudden attack. Yugoslavia quickly collapsed and was occupied by the Germans, who then attacked and quickly overcame Greece, the 45,000 British troops who had landed to help the Greeks during the attempted Italian invasion being evacuated from Thermopylae under conditions which were even more perilous than those at Dunkirk. Germany's next target was Crete, which she invaded with airborne troops. By 28th May 1941, after the most terrible slaughter, Crete was in German hands; and in North Africa Italian troops were preparing to invade Egypt and seize Suez.

In June 1941 Hitler made the fatal mistake of attempting to invade Russia, turning on her treacherously. After the first few weeks of German success the fighting became hideous and terrible, and as the news of the appalling losses on both sides arrived in Britain that following winter, the British people knew that Germany was receiving wounds from which it would take her a generation or more to recover. Then, at the end of the year, Japan attacked America and the whole world became locked in mortal combat.

In 1942 the outlook for Britain was at its blackest. In the Far East the Japanese had inflicted grievous losses on the Americans, and with bewildering speed occupied the Dutch East Indies, Hong Kong, Singapore and Rangoon. In Africa the British had turned the Italians out of East Africa and Abyssinia, but had had to retreat in the north from the Germans and Italians, under the leadership of General Rommel, to El Alamein, which was only a few miles west of Alexandria.

In Britain the armament factories were working night and day to produce the weapons needed to fight back from this frightful predicament. Britain was not alone now, however. Help was coming from America and American soldiers and airmen were soon landing in Britain in thousands.

With the Russians successfully holding the Germans before Stalingrad, the turn of the tide in the general conduct of the war came in October 1942, when General Alexander and General Montgomery launched their attack on the Germans and Italians at El Alamein. They had built up an army of 150,000 men against Rommel's 100,000, with 1,050 tanks against Rommel's 500. The British now engaged in their own version of the blitzkrieg, opening the battle with the most intense artillery barrage that the world had ever known. The attack was launched on 23rd October 1942, and after ten days' fighting the Germans fled and most of the Italians surrendered. By 12th November the Germans and Italians had been expelled from Egyptian soil and during the last days of that year and the spring of 1943 the British advanced steadily along the North African coast, until there were no more German or Italian armies left on African soil. At the end of 1943 Allied armies invaded Sicily and then the mainland of Italy. The fighting was hard and slow, for the Germans in Italy put up a stubborn

Lord Montgomery of Alamein

resistance, but the Russian campaign had sapped their strength and by May 1944 Rome and Florence had been captured.

In Britain excitement was mounting every day. Britain's air attacks on Germany had been relentless and devastating, and in southern Europe the Germans were in full retreat. Despite these successes, however, for total victory it was essential that the Allies launch a second front in northern Europe. Now it was the turn of Germany to await the invasion of Europe, as four years earlier Britain had waited for Germany. Preparations were made in absolute secrecy. People hazarded many guesses as to where and when the fateful attack would be made, but none save those in the highest places of the War Office had any idea.

It was on 6th June 1944 that the Allies landed in Normandy, with General Eisenhower as Supreme Allied Commander and General Montgomery in command of the British and American armies during the landings. There followed days of agonizing anxiety, for into this hazardous venture had been thrown thousands of British lives—a vast civilian army—and the three years' labour of the armament workers.

The Germans fought desperately, but now their armies were fighting on two fronts. The landings were successful and the advance into Europe steady. Gradually the Allies approached Berlin from the west, while the Russians advanced from the east, and on 4th May 1945, when the two great forces met in Berlin, the German Government surrendered.

Britain, however, was to suffer more trials during that last year of the war. As the Allied troops landed in Normandy the Germans launched from the French coast pilotless robot planes filled with explosive. The air-raid sirens wailed once more over London and south-eastern England as these monstrosities chugged their way through the summer skies. The Government found it difficult to find a name for them. "Manless machines" and "pilotless aircraft" had too sinister a sound, but these flying bombs were soon dubbed "doodlebugs"—and very unpleasant they were, particularly at night-time, as they roared noisily overhead, trailing smoke and flames. Suddenly the engine would cut out, there was an ominous silence for a moment and the plane hurtled to the ground, exploding with a sickening, shattering crump to spread death and destruction.

More sinister still were the long-distance rockets which followed a few weeks later, fired from the French coast and landing on London and the Home Counties. They were Hitler's last secret weapon and the attacks continued until the rocket-launching sites along the French Channel coast had all been captured by the Allies.

In the Far East the Japanese were also in a slow retreat and by 3rd May 1945 Rangoon had been recaptured. The war was brought to an abrupt end by yet another secret weapon, devised this time by the Allies and more terrible than any that had yet been used—the atom bomb. It was dropped by the United States air force on Hiroshima in August 1945, killing 60,000 people, wounding 100,000 and rendering 200,000 people homeless, its devastating power making all previous methods of warfare obsolete. The Japanese surrendered and the killing was over.

The ethics of dropping the atom bomb are still debated. By bringing about the end of the war so quickly it may indirectly have saved more lives than it destroyed. On the other hand, the Japanese were already considering capitulation and it has been argued that, had they been warned of what was coming, there is little doubt that they would have surrendered immediately in order to avoid the frightful massacre of Hiroshima.

The end of the war had come at last, but with it the British people found themselves in an altogether different world from the one they had known five and a half years earlier, and it was with feelings of sober wonder rather than rejoicing that they faced the future and the dawn of the mid-twentieth-century Atomic Age.

CHAPTER TWELVE

Life in Britain during the Second World War

During the five and a half years of the war the social life of Britain grew steadily more austere. Dress was drab and utilitarian. Clothes rationing, which was introduced in June 1941, meant that women's coats, suits and dresses had to last for years, and fashion as it had been known in the old days, with each season introducing a new line or colour, fad or fancy, disappeared. "Utility" clothes were manufactured at a reasonable price and were good value, but they were all very similar and the days of individualism in dress were over. Non-utility clothes were available, but they were expensive, and their cost steadily mounted. However, sufficient supplies of the utility clothes were available for all who had the wisdom to spend their clothing coupons wisely.

Skirts remained short, mainly because they took less material, and shoulders were squared, to give everyone a vaguely military look. Hats were not rationed but most women discarded them for head scarves, varied by mackintosh or "pixie" hoods in cold, wet weather. Both housewives and war workers took to slacks and pullovers during their waking hours, which were also, for the most part, their working hours, and some took to versions of Winston Churchill's siren suit, an ingenious and useful one-piece garment like a child's romper suit, zipped up the front, and the perfect answer for nights spent in and out of air-raid shelters, for it was draught-proof and extremely comfortable, if hardly elegant. Silk stockings were expensive and rare and nylons were not yet on the market in Britain. Good shoes were also difficult to come by. Women took to sheepskin-lined boots in the winter, if they could find them in the shops, and towards the end of the war shoes with clumsy wedge-soles appeared.

There was little food and drink available for entertaining in the home. Wine and spirits were virtually unobtainable for several years. Tea, sugar, butter, meat, bacon and eggs were all strictly rationed, the egg ration being down to one egg every two months during the worst period. In the restaurants, though one did not have to give up food coupons as in the 1914 war, a five-shilling maximum price was imposed for all meals. Most factories and other large establishments employing war workers had efficient canteens, and British Restaurants were established, where people who had no canteen facilities could obtain a reasonable midday meal, but the meals were indifferent and the queues for seats long and tedious. People with friends in America, Canada, Australia or South Africa were glad of the food parcels which began to arrive and even the forces in some areas abroad were sending luxury foods to their families in Britain.

With petrol strictly rationed many people sold their cars or put them away for the duration of the war. There was no pleasure motoring and only people who were able to prove that they could carry out their work more efficiently by car than by public transport were allowed any supplies above the bare minimum allotted, particularly in country districts, for such matters as driving to the nearest station or taking young children to school.

Paper and newsprint were in very short supply. Newspapers and magazines became progressively smaller. The publication of books was severely restricted and their price rose. Productions were far less attractive, with poor quality paper, smaller print and narrower margins, and many books appeared with paper backs because of the difficulties and expense of obtaining board covers. At the same time a certain number of mushroom publishers appeared on the scene, who had managed to acquire black market supplies of paper on which they printed books of no literary merit and a very dubious entertainment value—highly spiced romances, thrillers which hid inconsistencies of plot with scenes of sadistic violence, and indifferent children's stories, with plots which bore a monotonous resemblance to one another and were both unimaginative and improbable.

The principal diversion for most people was the radio. In their blacked-out homes they listened for hours, particularly to the news bulletins, which were read every few hours throughout the day, from early morning till midnight. The B.B.C. did splendid work during these years, offering constant amusement to people of all tastes, from Tommy Handley's brilliant *ITMA* programmes to symphony concerts, from the *Brains Trust* to the singing of the Forces' sweetheart, Vera Lynn.

It was during these years that the radio was first used as a means of mass indoctrination. Propaganda, both subtle and blatant, poured forth daily into nearly every home in the country. The B.B.C. also extended its services to cover very nearly every country in the world, sending hope to those in the enemy-occupied countries brave enough to risk their lives to listen and broadcasting ingenious code messages to members of the resistance movements. They broadcast propaganda and news of Allied victories to the German people and Germany retaliated, particularly with the broadcasts of the Irish traitor Joyce, who because of his strange, pretentious English accent became known in Britain as Lord Haw-Haw; instead of striking terror into British hearts, as was the intention, he proved himself an unfailing source of amusement and entertainment. The B.B.C. also broadcast to the neutral countries, such as Turkey, Portugal and South America, with the British version of the news, to counteract the propaganda and news services of the enemy.

The B.B.C.'s television service, too young in 1939 to have got into its stride, was closed down at once on the outbreak of war and the majority of the technicians were directed to the development of radar. Cinemagoing remained immensely popular and during the latter part of the war the British film industry enjoyed a boom. At first, however, all cinemas were compulsorily closed. The film industry and factory managers protested at this sudden ending of what had been so popular a diversion, and they were soon reopened. Throughout the war the British public went to the cinemas in increasing numbers, the weekly attendances rising from 19 million in 1939 to 30 million in 1945.

At the beginning of the war the British film industry had a hard struggle to keep going, for many of the big studios, including Pine-wood, were requisitioned, and most of the personnel called up for the forces or the engineering industry, so that soon only one-third of its technicians and nine of its twenty-two studios were left. Britain was far slower than the Germans to use either documentary or feature films as war propaganda. Within the first few months of the war the Germans were showing "terror" films of their attack on Poland to neutral countries, as well as cunningly devised anti-British feature films. During 1940 and 1941 Britain made several films with war themes, such as *Pimpernel Smith, Contraband, Freedom Radio, Convoy, Ships With Wings* and *Dangerous Moonlight*, the theme music of which was the popular Warsaw Concerto; but the majority were second-feature films which are best forgotten—farcical comedies featuring music-hall artists. They managed to pay for themselves and provided a little harmless amusement for those who could stomach them, and that is the best that can be said.

However, it was not long before the Ministry of Information organized its films division and produced a number of short films, many of which were included in the public cinema programmes. Some were instructional, some designed to boost morale. At the same time the films division of the British Council produced films for overseas consumption, which were intended to show Britain to the rest of the world and were made by companies specializing in documentary films.

The first Ministry of Information documentary to impress America profoundly was *London Can Take It*, made by the Crown Film Unit, and this was followed by the memorable *Target For Tonight*. It was so effective, its story so moving, and the telling of it so dramatically simple, that this documentary technique was used for the next two or three years in many British films which, though fictional, had a war theme, such as *The Foreman Went To France, One Of Our Aircraft Is Missing, Next Of Kin, The First Of The Few, In Which We Serve, The Gentle Sex, Millions Like Us* and *San Demetrio, London*. At last Britain had produced a distinctive style of film making, in contrast to some of the earlier films, which had been bad American copies. "Britain has stopped trying to imitate us", remarked the shrewd Sam Goldwyn on seeing these films for the first time. "They have begun to use a method of their own, applying a broader viewpoint and getting closer to the people."

By 1944 the Rank Organisation owned 619 cinemas and the Associated British Corporation another 442, the two groups thereby owning a third of all the cinema seats in the country, in addition to two-thirds of the studio space. Some people deplored this monopoly and the Government appointed the Palache committee to investigate the position. They commented in their report that "Already the screen has great influence both politically and culturally over the minds of the people. Its potentialities are vast, as a vehicle for expression of national life, ideals and traditions, as a dramatic and artistic medium, and as an instrument for propaganda"; and in order to ensure that independent film producers would be able to survive and obtain adequate distribution for their work, they proposed the Government-sponsored

Film Finance Corporation, from which money could be borrowed for worth-while ventures.

Arthur Rank himself was well aware of the power of the film as a propaganda instrument for good. During the war years he was financing the Religious Film Society and its films for education in the various aspects of the Christian religion, and he also launched Children's Entertainment Films for showing on Saturday mornings at the Odeon and Gaumont cinemas.

As the war passed into its closing phase, the supply of American films increased. Many were concerned with the war, and British studios were also turning out a great many more dramatic war documentaries.

Towards the end of the war there was a feeling in the industry that the British public had had more than enough of war films and from the Shepherd's Bush and Islington studios of the Rank Organisation there now emerged a series of sexy melodramas, in which the stars under contract, Phyllis Calvert, Margaret Lockwood, James Mason and Stewart Granger, startled their audiences into shocked delight at their uninhibited and outrageous goings-on. The films included *The Man In Grey, Fanny By Gaslight, Love Story, Madonna Of The Seven Moons, A Place Of One's Own, They Were Sisters* and, at the end of 1945, *The Seventh Veil* and the most shocking of them all, *The Wicked Lady*. At the same time, however, Arthur Rank helped to finance some films of real quality, such as Laurence Olivier's productions of Shakespeare's *Henry V*, and *Hamlet* and he also backed an expensive adaptation of Shaw's *Caesar and Cleopatra*. A successful film of 1944 was *Waterloo Road* and C. A. Oakley rightly comments that it is "remembered principally because of a tremendous fist fight between Stewart Granger and John Mills—an early pointer perhaps to the new 'toughness' making its way into the cinema."

Some theatres closed at the outbreak of war and others were bombed, while those which re-opened after the first few weeks began their performances at 6.30 p.m., so that few people were abroad in the West End after ten o'clock. Yet theatres were soon booming and several long runs were established, notably *Arsenic And Old Lace*, Terence Rattigan's *While The Sun Shines*, Noël Coward's *Blithe Spirit* and Ivor Novello's *Perchance To Dream*, all of them excellent light entertainment and completely remote from the hazards and miseries of war.

It was during the war years that the Council for the Encouragement of Music and the Arts (CEMA) was founded, under the chairmanship of J. M. Keynes, with money granted in the first place by the Pilgrim Trust and later supplemented by the Treasury. With this financial backing the Old Vic, bombed out of its old home in the Waterloo Road, was able to send four or five companies out with Shakespeare and other classical plays, opera and ballet to remote parts of the country, particularly the hard-worked industrial areas which hitherto had had no opportunity of enjoying them; and their London company they established at the New Theatre. Here, in 1945, Ralph Richardson and Laurence Olivier, on their release from the Fleet Air Arm, launched a series of memorable productions which were so successful that the Treasury decided to continue its grant to CEMA, henceforth known as the Arts Council of Great Britain. It was the first time in British history that the State had given official patronage to the arts.

Sadler's Wells escaped the bombing and under the direction of Ninette de Valois the school of ballet not only kept going, under difficulties of every conceivable kind, but grew in stature and developed a style so individual that it established for Britain, during these difficult years, a true ballet tradition.

The other main diversion for people during the war was dancing. Night clubs kept going in the West End of London and there was dancing at most of the big hotels and restaurants; but also, on a far simpler scale, there were dances in all the towns and villages throughout the country week after week, mostly in aid of some wartime charity. Men and women were usually in uniform, on leave or awaiting embarkation, but for those who were not in the services there was no dressing up, and evening dress, both for men and women, virtually disappeared.

The rate of scientific advance, which had begun a century or more earlier, was maintained throughout the war years. Armaments and bombs grew heavier and more lethal. Tanks developed into the great Shermans and Centurions, and within a few years Hurricanes and Spitfires were fighting German Junkers and Dorniers at 140 miles an hour. These were all natural developments from well-established principles. British scientists, however, working during the 1930's, developed two major inventions which were to contribute inestimably to the eventual winning of the war—radar and jet propulsion. When the possibility of war drew closer, these two phenomena were studied very closely. Could they in any way be used for air defence?

Radar (Radio Detection and Ranging) is based on the principle that though wireless waves travel in straight lines they can be intercepted and reflected back along the line in which they have been passing. As early as 1924 it was first noticed that wireless waves were reflected back from the atmosphere when they reached a certain region, known as the Heaviside layer, and scientists were able to measure the actual height of this barrier. Then, early in the 1930's, Post Office radio engineers saw that when aircraft were flying in the vicinity there was a change of wireless signals.

The Air Ministry appointed a committee to investigate the matter, for whom a report was prepared by Robert Watson-Watt, a distinguished meteorologist specializing in "atmospherics" at the National Physical Laboratory. He and his assistants invented a way of observing atmospherics by the flicks of light they produced on a cathode-ray screen. He reported to the committee that the way to detect and locate aircraft was "to put up a short-wave radio frontier" which they must penetrate. Once the aircraft met the barrier they would reflect back waves, which could be detected on the cathode-ray screen. Watson-Watt assured the committee that it would also be possible to tell not only the direction of an enemy aircraft but also its position, and by installing in all British aircraft instruments which affected the radar detection screens in a distinctive way, it would be possible to distinguish between friend and foe.

The Air Ministry asked Watson-Watt to develop his ideas and with a team of scientists he set to work. By May 1936, at his research station at Bawdsey Manor in Suffolk, he had already established his Radio Detection System, as it was then known, and soon afterwards the team had devised small radar machines which could be carried by both aircraft and ships at sea; and a means was devised whereby information received on the more powerful and wider ranging radar ground screen could be instantly transmitted to an aircraft in flight.

Watson-Watt was appointed to the Air Ministry as Director of Communications Development and his successor at Bawdsey was A. P. Rowe, who discovered a method of overcoming any possible enemy jamming of the equipment. These discoveries were a closely guarded secret until the outbreak of war, and then the W.A.A.F. did valuable service as R.D.F. operators. The whole of Britain was screened for radar detection during the war, and as the system was perfected it became possible for a ground operator, who could see both the British and enemy aircraft on the screen in front of him, to tell a British pilot the course to follow till his less powerful apparatus could detect the attacking aircraft itself.

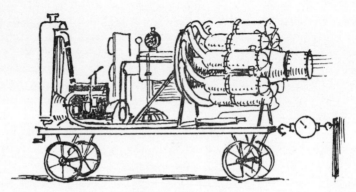

The first jet engine.

Radar helped to save the day during the Battle of Britain, and in the Battle of the Atlantic, against British shipping, a surfaced submarine could also be detected by ship's radar. When Britain was on the offensive and bombing Germany, fresh developments enabled her bombers to be guided to their targets by radar and brought home again. This method was tried out on the thousand-bomber raid on Cologne in May 1942 and was used with increasing effect as the war continued, culminating in D-day, when Allied aircraft were able to destroy the German coastal batteries, which they could see on their radar screens, with bewildering speed; the invading ground forces were also able to direct their gunfire with deadly accuracy.

Frank Whittle was responsible for the invention of jet propulsion. When he began his work the highest speed for an R.A.F. fighter was 150 miles an hour. Whittle argued that for greater speed an ordinary propeller and piston engine would not be strong enough, and he sought a more effective means of propulsion. Throughout the thirties, with a sequence of setbacks and disappointments which would have daunted a lesser man, he worked on the design of his new engine, the motivating force of which was a gas turbine engine heating a powerful jet of air. By 1941 the first test was made, and at 25,000 feet the test pilot reached a speed of 370 miles an hour. Three years later jet-propelled aircraft were being delivered to the Royal Air Force, just in time to prove a ready and effective answer to Hitler's much-vaunted secret weapon, the flying bomb.

As always happens during a war, the medical and surgical professions, presented with many more cases of disease and injury than are usual in peacetime, made striking advances. In regard to the civilian population, the Ministry of Food organized the rations with great skill. Though they seemed meagre enough, they proved sufficient not only to maintain the nation's health but actually to raise the standard of physique amongst many children and young people; the issue of cheap or free milk, fruit juices and vitamin pills to schoolchildren and mothers with babies helped a great deal to bring about this satisfactory result.

Shortly before the war, the sulphonamide series of drugs was produced—the best known being M and B 693, which proved of great value in checking a number of streptococcal infections—and then came the discovery of the antibiotics, including penicillin. One of the first uses of penicillin was the treatment of injured pilots during the Battle of Britain, and it has since saved thousands of lives. With the increasing use of antibiotics, however, strains of bacteria have developed which are resistant to them, so that although the antibiotics remain an important weapon in the fight against disease, their effectiveness has been found to have certain limitations.

Blood plasma gave life to casualties who otherwise might have died from loss of blood. D.D.T., which was discovered in Switzerland and passed on to the Allies in 1942, checked insect-borne diseases, and the scrub typhus vaccine checked typhus. Vitamin pills and specially planned hard rations reduced the danger of malnutrition for troops fighting a long way from base, particularly in the Far East jungle warfare, and mepacrine, introduced in 1944, reduced malaria casualties to 26 per thousand from the appallingly high figure of 740 per thousand which was recorded for 1943.

The Royal Air Force possibly suffered more casualties from severe burns than any other of the fighting services, and thousands of airmen alive today, who had been so terribly disfigured that they could scarcely have faced moving in ordinary society again, owe their rehabilitation to a normal working and social life to the skill and devotion of the plastic surgeons. Sir Archibald McIndoe, whose hospital at East Grinstead became so famous, Sir Harold Gillies, working at Park Prewett, near Basingstoke, the unit at St. Albans, working on dental and jaw injuries, and the team at Stoke Mandeville hospital, who while dealing with all manner of injuries made special investigations into the treatment of burns, all did magnificent work.

Airmen and other casualties arrived at these hospitals in desperate condition, with foreheads, noses, jaws and cheeks shot or burnt away. By grafting skin, bone and muscle from other parts of the body, or even from other human donors, the surgeons built new faces for these victims. The process was long and painful and it usually had to be undertaken in several stages, at intervals of two or three months. There were times, when new skin and underlying fat had been grafted, that these men looked puffy and grotesque and remained so for several weeks, till the fat had been absorbed into the underlying tissue, but as they were otherwise physically fit they were encouraged to meet the rest of the world and overcome their self-consciousness, as a preliminary to their total rehabilitation. Sometimes, when the surgeons had done all they could, building new noses and jaws, new eyelids and ears, the patients were unrecognizable for a while, but they were restored to an appearance which was at least normally human, and with the help of the doctors and nursing staff, as well as their own families, they gradually learned to adjust themselves. Shattered limbs were often restored in the same way, and where this proved impossible artificial limbs were devised which were astonishingly useful and effective.

Operative techniques were developed in other spheres, particularly in brain and thoracic surgery. In the treatment of tuberculosis it was found possible to collapse a lung for a period, and when it was incurably dieased, as in the case of lung cancer, to remove it altogether. Fresh treatment for fractured limbs and spinal injuries was devised, which meant that many victims who a few years earlier might have been lifelong cripples were restored to normality.

The improved medical and surgical treatments and the different nature of the fighting meant that the total number of casualties during the war was considerably less than during the First World War. The

British total for dead and missing, presumed dead, of the armed forces was 303,240, and for the Dominions and Colonies 109,000, making a total of 412,240; 60,500 civilians were killed in air raids in the United Kingdom and 30,000 fishermen and men of the Merchant Navy were lost.

Not only was the technique of the fighting different. The members of the forces were themselves different, for they were men and women of the twentieth century, who had been born into an age when the levelling process of the classes was already under way. This vast civilian army had no time for the spit and polish of the old army tradition nor for the "ours not to reason why" mentality. They fought none the less heroically, but they had a sense of purpose which was directed beyond the day of victory into that vague and sunny period of "after the war". Their horizons had been extended beyond their wildest dreams, for they had travelled far and wide and seen many lands and peoples. Some had received their training in Canada, America or Australia. The deserts of North Africa, which a few years earlier had been explored by only a handful of travellers finding their way by compass, they now knew as a cockney taxi driver knows his London. They had fought in both the western and eastern Mediterranean, in Malta, Sicily, Italy and Crete. They came to know Egypt, South Africa, India, Indo-China, Japan and the Dutch East Indies; and from the summer of 1944 thousands took part in the victorious advance across Europe from Normandy through France, Belgium and Holland to Germany.

During the First World War there had been no radio to keep them in touch with the rest of the world and no airmail letters and newspapers. Now they knew each day how the war was being waged and they were in constant touch with home. The army commanders were quick to understand the mood and outlook of this new army and the old feudal spirit, which had persisted longer in the regular army, perhaps, than anywhere else, gave way to a more democratic approach. General Montgomery in particular dispensed with many of the old formalities, without sacrificing discipline. "Every single soldier", he declared, "must know, before he goes into battle, how the little battle he is fighting fits into the larger picture, and how the success of his fighting will influence the battle as a whole." Not only did each army group on its own particular front have its own newspaper, edited by a soldier journalist and containing news supplied by the Ministry of

Information News Service, but the Army Bureau of Current Affairs organized educational courses and published pamphlets on current affairs, and there was also a welfare organization to help and advise members of the forces with personal and family problems.

Among these fighting men were many who in 1939 had been unemployed and unwanted and had known the soul-destroying hopelessness of the dole queues; and it was small wonder that they were determined that, once the war was over and they were returned to civilian life, such

Sir William Beveridge, the instigator of the National Health Service.

a state of affairs should never happen again. Horizons were broadening at home, too, for everyone now had a part to play and was being well paid for it, and many who had been unemployed or had subsisted on near-starvation wages knew for the first time in their lives the comfort of living in financial security. With labour at a premium, the power of the trade unions had greatly increased, and with it the strength of the Labour Party.

As the war proceeded, the coalition government made its plans for post-war reconstruction. Committees were set up and reports issued on the possibilities of an extended National Health Service; secondary education for all was considered, as well as schemes for rebuilding London and the creation of new towns. Then came the Beveridge Report. It created nation-wide interest and hope for all those who had been dreading a future which might mean a return to the bad old days. Sir William Beveridge had a deep knowledge of the needs of the people, for, like Clement Attlee, he had worked in his younger days at Toynbee Hall, the university settlement in Whitechapel. In his report he declared that the five great evils to be conquered were "Want, Disease, Ignorance, Squalor and Idleness". He outlined the principles for a social insurance which should be the right of every citizen, and which would include a complete health service as well as a system of family allowances. "The scheme proposed here", he wrote, "is in some ways a revolution, but in more ways it is a natural development from the past. It is a British revolution."

The report showed how, without any extreme measures, want could be abolished and a "national minimum" of living be assured for all, for social security, he said, "was not a matter of politics but of common sense". His plan depended on full employment and he charged the Government with the responsibility of maintaining employment and also, so far as lay in their power, for preventing and combating disease. It was basically an insurance scheme. In return for weekly contributions benefits would be paid, as of right and without a means test, during periods when, through illness, disability, unemployment or old age, earnings stopped. Medical and hospital treatment would be given as part of the insurance, and—because the birth rate was falling—special family allowances where there was more than one child.

Sir William was at pains to point out that "the plan is not one giving to everybody something for nothing . . . or something that will free the recipients for ever thereafter from personal responsibilities . . . [it] leaves room and encouragement to all individuals to win for themselves something above the national minimum, to find and to satisfy . . . new and higher needs than bare physical needs."

When the Government discussed the report many received it enthusiastically, for, as *The Times* commented: "Sir William Beveridge has succeeded in crystallizing the vague but keenly felt aspirations of millions of people." Some, however, were not prepared to go the whole way. There were those who argued that such protection for the individual would result in "moral ruin". Others wondered whether the State could stand the expense. Ernest Bevin declared that the way to social security lay in Socialism and big wages, rather than in a "social ambulance scheme". However, as early as 1943, in a speech by Sir John Anderson, the Government pledged its acceptance of a good deal of the Beveridge plan, particularly in regard to the health service, family allowances and the unemployment insurance scheme; and *The Times* commented that "no speech ever delivered in the House of Commons has committed a Government to more far-reaching measures of social advance".

There had been no general election in Britain since 1935, when Mr. Baldwin had become Prime Minister with a large Conservative majority of 247. When, two years later, he retired through ill health, Mr. Neville Chamberlain had taken over, and in 1940, on his enforced resignation, Winston Churchill had formed the coalition government, still with a Conservative majority. A new election was long overdue and within a few weeks of the end of the war in Europe election day was announced. Conservatives and Socialists both began energetic canvassing. Millions of men and women were voting for the first time, and many of them were still serving overseas. They were bombarded with propaganda from both sides, and for twenty-six nights in succession there were party political broadcasts on the radio.

Winston Churchill was at the height of his popularity, acclaimed everywhere not only as the saviour of his country but of the free world. He had saved us from Fascism. He had saved us from invasion. He was a hero figure, the upholder of democracy. His stalwart bulldog figure and broad, confident smile, his power of inspired rhetoric and his superb command of the English language, had led and strengthened the British people through days of dire peril to ultimate victory. It seemed inconceivable that he should not continue to steer them into the new era of peace.

But—and it proved to be a very big but—he was a member of the Conservative Party, and many were unconvinced of the Conservatives' intentions in regard to the social reforms of the Beveridge plan, despite the Government's pledge. Conservatism they associated with the miseries and privations of the thirties, the years of appeasement and vacillation, of unemployment and the old class distinctions. The Socialists, however great their share of responsibility may have been for Britain's appeasement policy, presented no doubts in regard to their enthusiasm for the Beveridge plan—and it was this, above all, that the people wanted. It had assumed the proportions of a People's Charter, which they must have at all costs. Some, indeed, were so ignorant politically that they believed that Winston Churchill could still, with a Socialist government, remain Prime Minister; and as people weighed the claims of the two parties the *Daily Mirror*, the most widely read newspaper in the country, ranted in flaring headlines against the "treacherous, upper-class riff-raff" who had made the period between the wars "such an ignoble page of English history".

Election day came, and when the booths closed the ballot boxes were duly collected throughout Britain. Then came a pause of nineteen days, while the service votes from all over the world arrived by post. At last the count began, and it very soon became clear that the poll was swinging to the Left. By the end of the day the results were published. It was a devastating defeat for the Conservatives and Labour had won with a majority of 145 seats over all other parties. That evening Winston Churchill drove to Buckingham Palace to hand his Government's resignation to King George VI, and half an hour later Clement Attlee arrived to take office as Britain's new Prime Minister.

Later Winston Churchill, writing of his appointment in 1940 and his resignation in 1945, said: "Thus then, on the night of the tenth of May, at the outset of this mighty battle, I acquired the chief power in the State, which henceforth I wielded in ever-growing measure for five years and three months of world war, at the end of which time, all our enemies having surrendered unconditionally or being about to do so, I was immediately dismissed by the British electorate from all further conduct of their affairs."[1]

The new parliament met on 1st August 1945. The war in the Far East ended a few days later and it was now the task of the Labour government to bring about, in war-torn, disorganized Britain, the long-awaited peace and prosperity for which all had been hoping and planning.

[1] Winston Churchill, *The Second World War*. Vol. I, *The Gathering Storm* (Cassell, 1948).

CHAPTER THIRTEEN

After the War

Hopes ran high during the summer of 1945. For millions of British people the bad old days were over. After five and a half years of war Britain stood on the threshold of a new way of life, in which there would be an opportunity for everyone to live fully and with dignity. This was a time for rejoicing and few were in the mood to take any notice of Mr. Attlee's sober warning that there were difficult days ahead.

The truth of the matter soon became apparent, however. During the war Britain had sold £1,100 million worth of investments to foreign countries to buy the materials of war. The income from that money, now gone for ever, had been used to finance one-fifth of her pre-war imports, particularly food. The export of manufactured goods, which had formed the foundation of her national income, had of necessity been greatly curtailed during the war years and she had been subsisting largely on money borrowed from America. From America, too, she had been taking 25 per cent of her imports, with another 20 per cent from Canada.

After the war America announced that the Lease-Lend arrangement must end. This was an agreement by which the United States had provided Britain and other allies with armaments and other necessities of war, including food, without immediate payment, the conditions of their supply being left for later consideration.

With her overseas investments nearly all gone, her export trade shrunk to less than a third of its pre-war volume, half her merchant shipping sunk and a debt of £3,000 million hanging over her, Britain faced bankruptcy. The way to recovery was by stricter economies and harder work. Britain had to increase production and manufacture goods at an economic price in order to re-establish her export markets.

The prospect was bleak, for world markets had changed since 1939 and in the scramble for world trade Britain was back almost where she had been at the beginning of the nineteenth century, before she had been first in the field with industrial development, thereby gaining such great economic and financial advantages. Now Britain was no longer the world's workshop, for the United States had become a bigger producer of steel than the whole of Europe had ever been. The Dominions which once had supplied cheap food were developing their own secondary industries at an increasing rate. They wanted fewer British manufactured goods and, with their own increasing populations, had less food for export. India and the Argentine were also becoming indus-

The prefabricated house was intended as a temporary measure to help solve the terrible accommodation problem after the war.

trialized and needed more of their home-grown food for their growing urban populations, which meant that smaller supplies of rice, tea and beef were forthcoming and they were charging more for them. British manufacturers needed all their skill and salesmanship to sell enough goods abroad to pay for the essential imports of food and raw materials, and the days of cheap food were gone for ever.

So in Britain during the early post-war years there was no end to food and clothes rationing. Life became grimmer and, for the first time, even bread and flour were rationed. Meat, butter and sugar were all scarce, as well as cigarettes, wines and spirits; and there were small children in Britain who had never in all their lives seen a banana.

Through these dreary months the demobilization of the forces proceeded steadily and factories changed from war to peacetime work. Men who had left their jobs were legally entitled to receive them back; and for those who had been too young to work when they were called up or had been unemployed there were government training schemes for a wide variety of trades. The story of 1919 was not repeated, and this time, with every branch of trade and industry being called to a maximum of production, few people had any difficulty in finding work.

The housing shortage was perhaps the greatest social problem of this time. Housing had been neglected in Britain for many years before the war and the bombing had intensified the problem, for there had as yet been no time, labour or materials for rebuilding. Temporary prefabricated bungalows had been hastily produced for a certain number of bombed-out families, but the plight of those young people now wanting to marry was dire. The price of houses soared far above their means and rents of flats and houses rose at the same rate. In an attempt to curb the rocketing prices the Government put a strict check on private and speculative building and helped local councils to build small houses of a strictly limited size and price, which were allotted to people on a points system based on the urgency of their need. It was a fair system but for a long time to come the demand for these houses far outstripped the supply.

The first year of the peace was no fun for anyone, but very gradually there appeared signs that better times were on the way. In the autumn of 1946 the Council of Industrial Design, which had been formed late in the war, held its first exhibition of the new fabrics and materials which Britain was now designing and manufacturing. Though at that first exhibition they were for export only, and Britons could only gaze at them wistfully, like children pressing their noses to a shop window, the fact that such things were actually being made again was encouraging. Nevertheless, during that summer and autumn of 1946 even the weather turned against Britain, bringing disaster to the farmers, who were still working to capacity to produce nearly half the nation's food.

When the corn was ready for harvesting freak storms swept over many counties, battering and ruining the crops. Some were washed right out of the ground and in Suffolk farmers had absolutely nothing left in their fields to harvest, though elsewhere the flattened corn was cut by scythe and the harvest eventually gathered. In the North, on the mountain slopes of Wales and on the southern moors, the wet summer meant that the hay crop was a complete failure. The farmers knew that they would be hard put to it to feed their flocks and herds throughout

"Well, and what can I do for you good people?"

The housing shortage, 1948.

the coming winter, and by November, though the valley farmers and the Government did what they could to help, sending emergency supplies of such feeding stuffs as could be spared, some of the hill farmers were forced to sell off their cattle, numbers of which were already unfit for slaughter and sale to the butchers.

A few weeks later, in January, came the snow. It fell for weeks on end, in most parts of the country for just on three months. By the end of January many hundreds of farms in the North, the Midlands and North Wales were isolated. Food supplies to the towns were interrupted. The men on the milk lorries would cut roads through the snow, but still it came, the gales quickly blocking the roads again. Farms and villages ran short of food and fuel. Farm carts were broken up to keep the farmhouse fires alight. Half-starved stock was slaughtered in the byres and despite all the efforts to bring hay and straw to the hill farms, some had not a forkful left. The hill sheep, trapped in the snow, were dying in tens of thousands. Day after day farmers and shepherds struggled through snowdrifts twenty or thirty feet deep to try to rescue them, but that winter four million sheep and lambs, more than a quarter of Great Britain's total flock, were lost. Three million of them were hill sheep, which meant that two-thirds of Britain's valuable hill wool was lost too. Thousands of farmers lost their entire flock of sheep and thirty thousand head of cattle died of hunger or cold, or had to be shot, during that black winter.

As Britain shivered, fuel ran short everywhere, in homes, offices, shops and factories. Coal and boiler fuel had to be strictly rationed and there were power cuts of electricity and gas which lasted for hours at a time.

In the middle of March came a final gale of driven snow, followed by frozen rain, which killed off hundreds more of the surviving sheep as they lay frozen to the ground, their fleeces turned to heavy blocks of ice which tore away from their skin. Snow and rain fell in prodigious quantities. It could not sink into the ground because the whole country was gripped by frost and the soil frozen hard, but when the thaw did come it was accompanied by even heavier rain. The snow melted. It still could not seep into the frozen ground but ran into the streams and little rivers and then on, gathering in volume, into the upper reaches of the main rivers and down towards the sea.

The scenes of disaster now moved from the hills to the valleys and particularly to the half a million acres of the Fenlands. On the night of 16th March a terrible gale blew across the Fens, blowing down trees, scattering the roofs of haystacks and tossing the tiles from farm buildings. The water rose in the dikes and the wind piled it against the banks until it began to flow, slowly at first and then in a torrent, from one embanked level to another. Men worked until sheer exhaustion brought them to a standstill. The army, with amphibious vehicles, moved in to help collect the livestock, but most of the fowls drowned, and as the flood gathered momentum hundreds of tons of root crops and clamps of potatoes had to be abandoned.

Families watched helplessly as the water lapped round the ground floors of their homes. With relentless speed it rose to the upper storeys and reached the eaves. Then the houses began to crumble and disintegrate, the cherished possessions of a lifetime floating away on the flood water. Seven hundred families moved out of their houses in a single day of that disastrous spring. Six weeks later ten-thousand-acre stretches were still eight feet deep in water and of some farms barely a trace remained.

The River Wissey, a tributary of the Ouse, burst its flood bank and the water flooded Hilgay Fen. Here it was checked for a few days by the heroic efforts of the men who built a wall of sandbags nearly a mile long, but then it burst through a culvert and flooded right across Feltwell Fens. The water tore through with such force that houses were shattered and the topsoil of farmlands swept away, leaving a ruined expanse of bare peat. The flood approached Crowland so quickly that the electricity supply was damaged before the warning siren could be sounded, but someone had the presence of mind to hurry into the abbey and give the alarm in the oldest way of all, by tolling the ancient bells.

The three main breaches in the flood banks of the Fens were in the banks of the Great Ouse, near Over, the banks of the Wissey and of the Welland. These breaches had to be filled in; water from the flooded fens had to be pumped back into the rivers; destroyed farms had to be rebuilt and re-equipped; reclaimed fields had to be cultivated and planted, so far as was possible, with a crop for the same year; and the flood banks which had been weakened though not actually breached had to be strengthened before the autumn and the hazards of the following winter.

The National Fire Service, the Admiralty, the army and the Metropolitan Water Board all sent pumps, and seventeen were lent from Holland. Their transport and erection alone was a major engineering feat and once they were in action the work forged ahead. The areas of shallow flooding were quickly cleared, but where the flooding was deep it was May or June before the crops could be sown, while at Haddenham, where the fen is so low-lying that the water was still being pumped away in July, the ground was not ready that summer and a whole season was lost.

As the pumps finished their work the farmers moved in. Homes and farm buildings were ruined, hayricks and farm implements lost. Hundreds of tons of potatoes had gone, as well as tons of seed potatoes for the spring sowing, and there was little livestock left. Frost, snow and floods that winter had cost the farming community £20 million. The Government subscribed £1 million. The National Farmers' Union formed an Agricultural Disaster Fund, and a week later the Minister of Agriculture announced that the Government would double whatever was contributed to it. The farmers set to work. Implements were collected and redistributed. Bulldozers were used to spread topsoil more evenly. Dikes and ditches were cleared and repaired.

Men ploughed by day, in the hot summer sun, and at night, by the light of searchlights and car headlamps. As each fresh strip of field was uncovered and dried, so it was cultivated. Behind the ploughs came the drills. Within a few weeks fields were green again with new-sown corn. Potatoes and sugar-beet were widely grown, and many sowed barley for quick ripening, as well as peas, turnips, cabbages and flax. While homes were being rebuilt and dams repaired and strengthened, the main job of the farmers went on, until land which two months earlier had been at the bottom of great lakes was growing food once more and supplying Britain's most vital need.

It was a story which was soon forgotten by the townsfolk not intimately concerned with its personal sufferings and hardships, for life was moving and changing very quickly elsewhere throughout the country; and though the newspapers made much of it for a while, they soon had news of a different kind to dispense.

As King George and Queen Elizabeth, with Princess Elizabeth and Princess Margaret, left for a tour of South Africa that winter, there were already rumours of a possible engagement between Princess Elizabeth and Prince Philip of Greece and Denmark, and when the Royal Family returned to London in the late spring the engagement was officially announced, the wedding taking place later in the year.

The British public, starved for so long of anything so romantic to read about in their newspapers as a royal wedding, seemed to take as much interest in it as in the social reforms which the Labour government, with furious energy, were introducing. By January 1946, eight months after they had taken office, they had introduced no fewer than seventy-five bills, fifty-five of which already had the royal assent; and that was only the beginning. The three State airlines were established. Cable and Wireless, Limited was nationalized, and also the Bank of England, which since its foundation at the end of the seventeenth century had been an independent company owned by shareholders. Now, after compensation had been arranged for the shareholders, the stock was transferred to the State, and the Treasury became its owner. Its governor, deputy governor and sixteen directors were all appointed by the Crown and it became the Government's bank, holding the vast account of the Exchequer.

The Beveridge National Insurance Bill was passed and then, in quick succession, Dr. Dalton's Investment Control Bill and bills for Coal Nationalization, National Health Insurance, New Towns, Housing and Trade Union Law. During 1947 there were bills for Industrial Organization and Development, the Nationalization of Transport and Electricity Production and for Town and Country Planning. The newly formed Transport Commission, now made responsible for organizing Britain's bankrupt and old-fashioned railways, also reorganized 3,000 road haulage firms, while the British Electricity Authority took over 550 electricity companies, which they organized into effective area boards. Throughout 1948 bills were passed for National Assistance, the Nationalization of Gas Production and Electoral Reform; and in 1951 the Iron and Steel Industry was nationalized.

In regard to education, the Board of Education, by the 1944 Education Act, became a ministry and the aim of the Act was "to secure for children a happier childhood and a better start in life, and ensure a fuller measure of education opportunity for young people and to provide means for all of developing the various talents with which they are endowed and so enriching the inheritance of the country whose citizens they are." About 12 per cent of the schools of England and Wales are still independent, receiving no grant from the Ministry of Education but supporting themselves on fees paid by the pupils, but the rest are supported almost entirely by public money, and to these schools 90 per cent of children go. Parents have a legal obligation to send their children to school at the age of five, and most go in the first place to a primary school, passing at the age of seven to a junior school, where they stay till they are eleven. They then pass to one of the secondary schools, which are mainly of two kinds, grammar schools and secondary modern, the grammar schools taking the children who are likely to benefit from an academic education, the secondary modern schools those for whom a more general and practical education seems more suitable. There are also an increasing number of secondary technical schools, which give an education in various aspects of industry, commerce and agriculture.

Most grammar school pupils stay at school till they are sixteen, some till they are seventeen, eighteen or even nineteen. In the secondary modern schools most leave at fifteen but an increasing number are staying on for at least another year.

The development of these different types of school was a logical piece of planning but trouble soon arose over the vexed question of deciding which school a child should attend after leaving its junior school. Was a test given at the age of eleven years to decide a child's whole future course of life? The arguments for and against the system seemed equally plausible and the problem is still not solved, some county authorities relying solely on the teachers' reports of a child's work and waiving the examination entirely, others taking the child's record into account as well as his eleven-plus test result. By the beginning of the sixties, about one in four children was going to a grammar school and the rest to secondary modern schools. Some were contented enough, others bitterly disappointed. Some parents worried their children into a state of nervous exhaustion during the weeks before the test, in their anxiety that they should win places in grammar schools, and amongst the children themselves there was real distress if they failed to be sent to the same school as their friends.

In some parts of the country the solution to the problem of schooling for children after leaving their primary schools was solved by the establishment of "comprehensive" schools, which combined the facilities of both secondary modern and grammar schools; and some authorities, carefully watching the progress of the children in their secondary modern schools, offered opportunities for those who developed academic tastes and abilities during their teens to transfer to grammar schools at thirteen or even fifteen years of age.

The passionate desire for equality of opportunity led to arguments about the justice of allowing any fee-paying schools to exist at all, particularly the public schools. Those families whose sons and daughters had been going to public schools for generations remained unperturbed. The social climbers felt that they would lose a lot of fun if the top rungs of the ladder were suddenly removed, so that there were no longer anywhere to climb. And the rest continued to grumble.

Facilities for university education have been greatly extended and new universities formed throughout the country, most of them adopting, where possible, the invaluable tutorial system of Oxford and Cambridge. By 1960 there were some 106,000 full time university students in Britain, 80 per cent of them receiving scholarships or grants. For the rest the facilities for further education, either whole or part-time, in technological or training colleges were greatly extended, as well as for training in art schools and music schools, for those who had reached the standard of efficiency required for entrance.

The National Health Service was made available to everyone, whether insured or not. The purpose of the National Health Service Act of 1946 was "the establishment ... of a comprehensive health service, designed to secure improvement in the physical and mental health of the people ... and the prevention, diagnosis and treatment of illness", ensuring that "benefits once available only to insured persons or those who could afford to pay for them, or as a form of charity, should become available to everyone".

The service consists of the general practitioner service of doctors and dentists, the hospital service, with the consultation of specialists, and the local health service, which includes the district nurses, local welfare centres and baby clinics. When it was first introduced there was a storm of protest amongst both doctors and their patients who had hitherto paid for their treatment, for they declared that the old, friendly relationship between doctor and patient would be destroyed by the deadening impersonality of bureaucracy. However, the scheme got under way and, after its initial growing pains, began to work. There was no compulsion for doctors to take part in the service, or for patients to stop visiting doctors in private practice if they wished, though they had to contribute to the service. Today, however, there are very few people in Great Britain who do not belong to it. Most specialists have joined and the vast majority of general practitioners, as well as nearly all the dentists and chemists.

By 1960 there were 22,500 general practitioners in the service, with only 500 to 600 remaining in private practice. There were 12,500 dentists in and about 900 still independent, as well as 970 ophthalmic medical practitioners, 6,900 opticians and about 19,000 chemists.

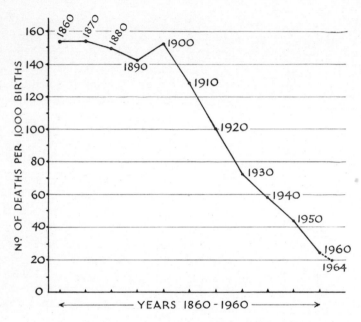

A chart showing the number of infant deaths before the first birthday over the last hundred years.

There were 3,000 hospitals, between them providing more than half a million beds, 174,000 full-time nurses and 46,000 part-time. The service was costing the country £697 million, about 3½ per cent of the entire national income, the money paid by individual contributions accounting for less than one-sixth of this amount.

At first the service, being entirely free, was abused. The hypochondriacs haunted the surgeries, delighted at the prospect of recounting their symptoms and receiving a free bottle of medicine. The lazy ones saw the chance of a few days' rest from work by thinking up some mild ailment and obtaining a medical certificate. At the same time, however, people who had long been in real need of medical attention, or should have been wearing spectacles or dentures, but had felt they could not face the expense, now benefited enormously. As the cost of the service mounted a charge of a shilling for each prescription was made. It raised a storm of protest but it curbed the malingerers, while the immigration authorities made it their business to check the flow of foreign visitors who had developed the habit of paying short visits to Britain for the sole purpose of benefiting from free medical treatment; it also eased the burden on the doctors, each of whom had an average of over two thousand registered patients on his books.

The National Insurance scheme which provided a retirement pension for women after the age of sixty and men after the age of sixty-five, as well as an income during unemployment, was generally welcomed. The Beveridge plan had allowed for an average unemployment rate of 8 per cent, but in practice the figure fell happily well below that, at times to less than 1·5 per cent, so there was little occasion for the amount of unemployment pay to come under discussion. However, as living costs steadily rose the pension paid to retired people was constantly under review and had to be frequently adjusted to provide the reasonable standard of maintenance which the Act had promised. As pensions were increased the amount of weekly contributions of those in work had also to be raised, and for those pensioners who still could not manage to make ends meet the National Assistance Board was created, which was, in effect, a continuation of the old pre-war Assistance Board which had derived from the Elizabethan Poor Law. Thus the Welfare State, planned by the wartime coalition government under Winston Churchill's premiership, came to pass within two or three years of the end of the fighting.

The Government, so intimately concerned with Britain's own social revolution, was quick to perceive the changing mood of the people of Asia, so soon to be followed by the rapid upsurge of Arab and African nationalism. In India Lord Wavell was succeeded as Viceroy by Prince Philip's uncle, Lord Louis Mountbatten, who was charged with the difficult task of steering India into her promised independence. The Indian Congress wanted an undivided, independent India, but the Moslem League insisted on partition, with the creation of the new and separate independent Moslem country of Pakistan. The problems of territorial division, with thousands of Moslems living in Hindu India and thousands of Hindus living in Moslem Pakistan, were manifold, but under Lord Mountbatten's guidance a working agreement was reached within a few months, and on 14th August 1947 India and Pakistan became two independent states, both electing to remain within the British Commonwealth of Nations. There followed months of riots, train wrecking, burning, looting and tragic, bitter bloodshed between the two nations, which made many wonder whether the decision had been too precipitate, but the forces of nationalism unleashed after the war were too strong to be denied or even to be delayed. Order was eventually restored and within a year both Ceylon and Burma had also been granted an unconditional independence. In the 1950's and 1960's, as the Pan-African movement swept through Africa, her peoples were also given their independence.

The Labour government had hopes of joining a united Europe but here they ran into troubles which gravely affected their plans and hopes. Talks at the Peace Conference were acrimonious. France was politically disorganized, Germany in ruins and Russia proving disconcertingly intractable.

In 1945 Russian, American and British troops had divided Berlin between them, Russia occupying the eastern part of the city, the British and Americans the western sectors. Many Germans, as well as hundreds of thousands of people in Central Europe, were starving and had to be fed. Britain herself was on the verge of bankruptcy, with hardly enough food for her own people, and in 1947 she was forced to turn once more to the United States of America for a loan. The outcome of these negotiations was the Marshall Plan, drawn up by General Marshall, the American Secretary of State during the Truman administration. It aimed to introduce more systematic American aid to Europe, particularly Britain and France. It was not clear at first whether Russia was to be included but it soon became apparent that American policy was decisively opposed to the Communism of Russia and the Socialist states of eastern Europe. Moreover, the Marshall Plan was not to be administered through the United Nations Organization, which had been planned during the war to succeed the League of Nations. The plan aimed to reorganize the economic resources of western Europe. The heavy industrial and agricultural engineering equipment needed was to be bought from the United States of America with dollar credit and a system created which allocated to the various countries, in accordance with their needs, a share of the resources of iron and steel, coal, transport and agricultural products which the countries between them possessed. The plan treated Europe as a whole, without regard to the individual economies of the separate countries. Thus Germany, being a country of great industrial resources, was to take its full place again as part of the new European workshop.

Russia, who had not been invited to take part in preliminary discussions, disagreed with the plan, arguing that it created an organization "over and above the countries of Europe . . . interfering in their internal affairs down to determining the line of development to be followed by the main branches of industry in those countries", and that "the European countries would find themselves placed under control and would lose their former economic and national independence because it so pleases strong powers".

The Marshall Plan was adopted by the countries of western Europe but Russia withdrew from the talks. In Berlin the American and British sectors were fused and Americans and Russians now faced each other—the capitalists and the Communists—each heartily disliking and distrusting the other. Communication between the two sectors became increasingly difficult until it virtually ceased and across the bomb-shattered city dropped the iron curtain of silence. News from east Berlin was sparse and few knew what the Russians were doing or thinking. Then, in 1948, the world was startled by the sudden death of Jan Masaryk, the Czechoslovakian minister of foreign affairs, and the Russian occupation of the country in a manner which was a sinister reminder of Hitler's methods of the thirties. Could it mean war again? There followed months of uncertainty and trepidation, as Britain was forced to suffer still more shortages and restrictions. Half a million young people applied for emigration to South Africa, the Rhodesias, Australia and New Zealand, but even shipping was short and the waiting lists grew ever longer.

By June 1948 all pretence of Allied co-operation in Berlin was over and the road between east and west Berlin finally cut. For the next twelve months there was deadlock and the United States, ready to wage war on Communism wherever it might appear, began sending troops to Britain, which served as its forward base of preparation for war if it should come. In September 1949 came the news that the Russians had exploded their first atomic bomb. The United States promptly retorted that they would go ahead with the tests of their new hydrogen bomb. And the threat of war seemed to be drawing very close.

In Britain the time for a general election was coming round again. The Labour government had worked hard to try to achieve the aims it had outlined in the 1945 election campaign, but in many ways it had failed to do so. "Of the promises made . . . to undertake drastic action to ensure an efficient industry; to prevent restrictive price rings; to introduce modern methods and materials; to maintain a due balance between housing, schools and factories; to institute centralized purchasing and price control; and to set up a Ministry of Housing and Planning; not one had been fulfilled. There were still hundreds of thousands of families without a separate home, and thousands still lived in slums. Men and materials which should have gone into housing had been used on non-priority work in hotels, offices, shops and other buildings. No more than a quarter of the building trade operatives had ever been working on new houses. And building costs had risen so high that the rents of new dwellings were often beyond the means of those who most needed them."[1] Over two million people—4 per cent of the population—were receiving National Assistance and the level of insurance benefits was lagging far behind the rising cost of living.

The election was held in February 1950 and showed a marked swing to the Right. Labour were once more returned to office, but the majority was only six—so small that it would clearly not be workable for long. Problems more serious than ever lay in store for them. After 1945 the peninsula of Korea had been partitioned between the Communists to the north and the Democrats of the south by the dividing line of the 38th parallel of latitude, under a mandate of the United Nations Organization. By the end of 1949 China's Red Army occupied the whole of China and Chiang Kai-shek's Nationalist forces retreated to Formosa, whereupon the American fleet arrived protectively in the waters between Formosa and the Chinese mainland. On 25th June 1950 North Korean forces, supported by Russian and Chinese Communist armies, moved south across the 38th parallel into South Korea. American forces, under the auspices of the United Nations, were

[1] D. N. Pritt, *The Labour Government, 1945–1951* (Lawrence and Wishart, 1963).

rushed into action, and the United Nations army also included two British battalions.

It was war again and no one knew where it would stop. Britain began a costly rearmament programme of £3,400 million. It meant more sacrifices and economies. Mr. Attlee warned the country that "the relief we have all been waiting for" would have to be still further postponed. Three months later, under the leadership of the American General MacArthur, the United Nations forces had pushed the Communist armies back across the border again and then, to the consternation of the whole of western Europe, he pursued them into North Korea to wage a further war, and President Truman announced that he was seriously considering the use of America's atom bomb. Mr. Attlee flew to Washington to remonstrate. The immediate danger was averted and the Americans were given orders to return to South Korea, but throughout that winter the war dragged on. Thousands of Korean peasants, utterly bewildered and at a loss to understand what was happening, were made homeless and starving, and at the battle of the Imjin river alone six hundred British soldiers of the Gloucesters perished.

The bill for the Korean war was crippling and in Britain plans for the development of the Welfare State had to be modified. It was at this stage that the small charge for spectacles and dentures, and the shilling fee for medical prescriptions, later raised to two shillings except in cases of real hardship, were imposed.[1] Aneurin Bevan, the Minister of Health, was so indignant that he resigned. Hugh Gaitskell, the Chancellor of the Exchequer, had to announce a rise in income tax and surtax, a property tax and increases in entertainment tax and petrol duties. Food and clothing were still strictly rationed, and though new houses were being built, finding one seemed as difficult as ever.

Against this background, inspired by the enthusiasm of Herbert Morrison, the Festival of Britain was planned for the spring and summer of 1951, exactly a century after Prince Albert's Great Exhibition at the Crystal Palace in Hyde Park. Many protested that it would be a waste of time and materials and that the gravity of the world situation made such a project unjustified. Nevertheless plans went ahead, and along the south bank of the Thames, from Battersea to Waterloo Bridge, rose the exhibition buildings and amusement park, the res-

[1] These charges were abolished by the 1964 Labour Government.

233

taurants and the skylon, the new and permanent Festival Hall and later the National Film Theatre. The last lingering vestiges of Victorian and Edwardian imperialism in Britain had no part in the exhibition. Instead it displayed all the resources and modes of the mid-twentieth century, which would lay the foundations of Britain's future culture and show the world that, though she was no longer a first class power, she had lost nothing of her ingenuity and inventiveness.

"Oh, I get plenty of tea now—Johnnie's just turned the blue ration book."

© Punch

234

"Making a virtue of necessity, the Festival's designers had taken the available materials, wood, plastics, glass, fabrics, asbestos, and combined them with imagination and skill. Aluminium brought lightness and sparkle; wood, showing its natural grain, contributed mellowness; great walls of glass, and light, unsupported ramps of concrete, gave a wondrous illusion of space. Even so ephemeral a material as canvas or perforated hardboard was used with highly civilized effect. Chairs, made from wire or bonded sheer-wood, would have baffled Chippendale, yet were strangely comfortable and, if some thought them precious, others found them elegant. Everything, the litter baskets, the signboards, the plant pots, the conical metal lampshades, seemed fresh and new. People soon began to sense that a common approach, a recognizable style, ran through them. It came, to some, as a revelation."[1]

Just as the 1851 exhibition had led to many mid-Victorian vogues in furniture and household decoration, so the 1951 festival began a number of trends. This time it brought colour, design and sometimes an elegant simplicity into the homes of the people, though it was not always successful. The craze which developed for gay wallpapers, for walls painted in different colours or papered with contrasting patterns, and for a multitude of indoor plants in gimcrack plant stands, sometimes tended towards an undesirable confusion and fussiness. Nevertheless, people plunged happily into the new fashion for redecorating their homes in the "contemporary" manner and began to take great pride in them.

Gradually the general living conditions in Britain began to improve. There was still full employment and wages were rising. Controls were relaxed. With improved foreign trading there was more foreign currency available for holidays abroad and more licences were issued for private building. Petrol came off the ration and then clothing. Britain began to smarten itself up and have some fun again.

The strength of the trade unions increased enormously during these post-war years and unofficial strikes, as well as official ones, for shorter working hours and increased wages, became increasingly frequent. As wages went up the cost of living rose with them and nothing was solved. In November 1950 Hugh Gaitskell, in an effort to stabilize wages and prices, protested that "the increase in wages should not go beyond what is justified by increases in production, after allowing for other claims,

[1] Harry Hopkins, *The New Look* (Secker and Warburg, 1963).

especially the claims of exports and defence", but the unions, ever suspicious of anything that suggested the policy of a wage freeze, and conscious of the enormous bargaining power they now wielded, would have none of it.

The report of the International Labour Office on the trade union situation in the United Kingdom, published in 1961, says that: "There are many examples in which an unofficial strike has been mainly due to the impatience of the rank and file, lack of understanding of economic and political problems, and obstinacy in taking the short-term view, in spite of explanations and assurances given by responsible representatives of the trade unions. In such cases it may be doubted whether the union members fully realize that they are doing harm to their organizations and are acting contrary to their own interests in weakening their unions. . . ."

By the summer of Festival year the impracticability of running the Government with such a small majority grew so apparent that a new election became inevitable. Election day was 25th October 1951. Labour announced during their campaign "Welfare at home, peace abroad, a constant striving for international co-operation—this is Labour's aim. The Tories . . . promise no light for the future. They would take us backwards into poverty and insecurity at home and grave perils abroad. . . ." The Tories, on the other hand, emphasized the need for a stable government which, untrammelled by party politics, would guide and direct the nation through the perils of international politics. They promised a continuance and development of the country's social amenities, as far as the Exchequer could afford. They supported the Labour government's rearmament programme but promised an end to nationalization and the return of the steel industry to private ownership.

The British electorate considered these two programmes, took a chance on Labour's warning that the Conservatives would lead them back to poverty, and went to the polls to vote them back to power. The Conservatives won a small but working majority, the actual figures being Conservatives 321, Labour 295 and Liberals 6.

So by the end of 1951 Winston Churchill was back as Prime Minister, though by now he was an old man in his late seventies. In 1955 he handed over office to Anthony Eden, who quickly held an election and won an increased majority for the Conservatives.

In February 1952 Princess Elizabeth and her husband set out on a Commonwealth tour, but less than a week later the country was shocked to learn of the sudden death of King George VI. Princess Elizabeth and Prince Philip flew back from Kenya and the following year, in June 1953, the young princess was crowned Queen Elizabeth II of Great Britain and became "Head of the Commonwealth and Her other Realms and Territories".

Throughout that year the cold war with Russia continued—a war of words and threats involving the spending of vast sums of money on armaments which each year became more terrible and destructive. In Britain, however, industry continued to revive. Prices were high but so were wages and the Government honoured its promise to maintain full employment.

The year 1954 saw the beginning of a new prosperity. Meat, the last of all the commodities to be still rationed, was freed. Trade boomed. Britain was establishing her overseas markets again, and though in the realms of international finance she seemed constantly to be running into "balance of payments" crises, there was little evidence of this in the people's pay packets or in the shops, which were now piled high with goods, many of a type which people had not seen for years —carpets, curtains and furniture, wines and spirits and exotic food, clothes and electrical equipment of all kinds, radios, television sets, washing machines, spin dryers, cookers, mixing machines and electric irons. There were cars in abundance and during the fifties the number on the roads doubled. There was so much to buy that people were soon buying too much, despite their bulging pay packets. They embarked on the biggest orgy of spending the country had ever known and the facilities offered by hire purchase proved an added temptation. The national hire purchase bill began to mount steadily. In 1959 it had reached £725 million and by 1964 it had passed the £1,000 million mark. By 1965 the average expenditure in a British household had risen to £19 a week, and for those who still had money to spare, after they had bought their full quota of motor cars, motor bicycles, electrical equipment, record players and the like, there were still the football pools, the betting shops and the bingo halls on which to spend it.

Everywhere there was change—a clearing away of the old and a replacement by the new. Coal mines were modernized and reorganized. The North and the Midlands were working to capacity. In South

237

Wales new industries arose, such as nylon spinning and watch-making, and new steel and tinplate plants were installed.

Anthony Eden's brief term of office was notable for the Suez Canal crisis. The 99-year lease of the Suez Canal Company, the shares of which were held mainly by France and England, was due to expire in 1968, when the canal was to be handed over to the Egyptian government. In 1956, however, President Nasser seized the canal. British troops landed in protest, but a few days later world opinion declared itself so clearly in favour of the Egyptians that the British were ordered to retire.

In 1957 Anthony Eden had to resign through ill health, and the premiership passed to Harold Macmillan. In the General Election of 1959, the Conservatives, basing their campaign on the theme of growing prosperity, increased their majority to 100.

In 1963 Mr. Macmillan also had to resign for health reasons. He was succeeded by Lord Home, who gave up his peerage in order to become Prime Minister. Sir Alec Douglas-Home (as he then became) held a General Election in the following year. On this occasion, however, the Conservatives, after thirteen years in office, were defeated. The Labour Party, which had fought the election largely on the issue of Britain's slow economic growth, was returned to power, and Harold Wilson became Prime Minister. Labour obtained 317 seats, the Conservatives 304 and the Liberals 9, so that the overall Labour majority was only 4.

In March, 1966, Harold Wilson's Labour government was returned with a greatly increased majority.

CHAPTER FOURTEEN

The New Britain

By 1945 the continuity of tradition in Britain had been badly disrupted. By way of the Press, the radio and films people had been bombarded with propaganda of every angle of opinion from Left to Right. Standards of ethics had crumbled away. Treaties had been broken and promises dishonoured. Only one person in seven now went to church and half the population claimed that they no longer believed in a personal God, though most admitted that such private ethical codes as they retained were derived from earlier Christian teaching. Psychiatry, though only imperfectly understood, was immensely popular. People justified their behaviour by explaining that they were the victims of their own subconscious instincts. They could not help themselves or their actions, for they were subjected to forces within themselves which they could not control. In this way they denied every human being's most vital freedom—the freedom of will to decide between right and wrong and behave accordingly.

During the succeeding years life has in many respects become increasingly difficult. Artists have painted pictures which to many people have meant nothing and writers have written poems and plays which people could not understand. Scientific device has proceeded at such a breathless pace that inventions are outdated within a matter of months. The Brabazon airliner, designed at a cost of £12 million to fly non-stop to New York, was launched in 1951 and scrapped within a year. Then came the de Havilland Comet, the world's first jet airliner, setting off for South Africa at a speed of five hundred miles an hour; and very soon Rolls-Royce were turning out jet engines as renowned as their motor-cars.

By 1956 labour-saving devices were being introduced into factories and workshops which would relieve workers of much of the old, grinding, monotonous toil, but this "automation" was regarded with deep suspicion. Men feared for their jobs and protested, as the Luddites had protested early in the nineteenth century during the Napoleonic wars, when new machinery had been installed in the factories of Nottingham, Yorkshire and Lancashire. Automation did not, in the end, result in unemployment but merely in the creation of a different kind of work in the same factories, but many are still disgruntled and uneasy with it. Harry Hopkins[1] quotes the case of George Mee of Derby, who left his job at a new "fully automated" ground mica factory. "All he had to do all day, he explained to reporters, was to watch gauges, making an occasional adjustment. In six months of automated existence he had put on three stones. 'Automation', declared Mr. Mee, 'may be perfectly all right for some people, but it bores me.' "

When electronic brains and computers were first introduced these mammoth mechanical calculators were discussed in awed tones, as though they were robots which had actually acquired some esoteric, spiritual property. Then there were the alarming warnings of the dangers of the side effects of nuclear fission and the risks of undue exposure to radiation from fallout after nuclear tests. There was great concern when, in 1954, the Atomic Energy Authority proposed to dump its radioactive waste in the old mine workings of the Forest of Dean. Large nuclear power stations were built in remote parts of the country to develop electric power from nuclear fission for peaceful industrial purposes, as a substitute for the increasingly expensive coal and oil; but the ultimate effects of nuclear fission are still not known, though a careful watch is kept on the level of units of strontium 90 in the bones of people living in the possible danger areas.

Medical science has been producing new drugs at an astonishing rate, the effects of which are still not fully known, and it has seemed for many years as though the entire human race is being used as a guinea pig. Cortisone, the wonder drug and panacea for a variety of human ills, including arthritis, arrived from America in 1949, and a few years later came the tranquillizers. The antibiotics in curing one condition are in some cases creating others which have so far defied treatment. The tragic effect of thalidomide, given to expectant mothers, was not discovered until hundreds of babies had been born with the most cruel deformities.

In 1957 the Russians began the Space Race, when they launched their satellite, the Sputnik, into outer space. It made many of the science fiction stories seem out of date, but no one yet knows the effect these space flights may ultimately have on the human mind.

Ordinary men and women, trying to settle down in this new world

[1] Harry Hopkins, *The New Look* (Secker and Warburg, 1963).

from which so many of the bad old things had been swept away, found it by no means the cosy life they had been expecting. On the contrary, in regard to the wider issues it was becoming more restless and incomprehensible each day, with the lengthening shadow of the atom bomb ever present. Within the family circle, however, and not looking too far afield or ahead, life for many people was a good deal more comfortable than it had been. They had financial security, more money, more leisure. What new fashions in clothes and art, in social habits, manners and customs were to evolve and what would happen to those who had not the mental equipment to assimilate the facilities for education and culture which were now becoming available?

When in 1945 the fighting was over and demobilization under way, men changed from their uniforms into Government-issued "demob" suits, and women made the best use they could of their wartime wardrobes and clothing coupons to achieve some sort of style again. Women had had a hard time during the war and there had been no opportunity to nurse the illusion that they were frail creatures, to be protected and cherished from the harsher aspects of life. Now, though clothes were still rationed, they decided that it was high time to discard their old pullovers and short, shapeless skirts for something more elegant and attractive. In 1947 Christian Dior introduced the New Look. The square, military cut disappeared and in its place came dresses and coats with natural curves and small waists. Hips were padded and skirts were cut long and full, sometimes almost down to the ankles, swirling and graceful again. To rediscover their waists women had to take once more to corsets, which were still regarded by the austere Board of Trade as a luxury, but they won their point. The fashion was startling at first. Some thought it ridiculous and retrogressive, entirely unsuited to the harshness of the times. It would take too much material. It was extravagant. Women were truly emancipated at last, they argued, and during the war had proved themselves the equal of men intellectually and often physically. If they returned to such obvious femininity, would they not be jeopardizing the place in society they had won for themselves so dearly? Were not these long, hampering skirts and confined waists symbolic of the years of subjugation and confinement to the home? When the country was short of labour they had been told that their services in industry, commerce, the professions and the forces were not only important but vitally necessary. When jobs were in short supply they had been told that women's place was at home, in the kitchen and nursery. Now surely was the time to take a strong stand, establish themselves firmly where they wanted to be and stop this business of being swept every few years from work to home and from home to work, on the uncertain tides of economic expediency.

However, no amount of argument can ever change the fundamental difference between the sexes and women in 1947 decided to make the best of both aspects of their much-discussed personalities. They liked

© *Punch*

The New Look of 1948.

the New Look and they adopted it. The fashion spread from the West End of London to the suburbs and then throughout the whole country with astonishing speed. It was gay and interesting, but it remained wearable, adapted from the more extravagant Paris version to a form more suited to the life of the average Englishwoman, which included travelling by trains and buses and Underground railways; for although many women were only too glad to return to their homes and become housewives again, many remained at work, particularly the newly married ones.

The New Look was adapted to a form more suitable for the life of the average British woman.

The New Look and longer skirts were popular for several years and before long nylon stockings were on the market, to be followed very soon by underclothes and blouses in all the labour-saving, easily laundered, man-made fibres. As the economic position became easier and clothing came off the ration, the fads and fancies of fashion reasserted themselves. By the middle fifties waists had disappeared and skirts were shorter. There was the season of the sack, the spring of the H line and the summer of the A line. Apart from slight variations in the length of the skirt, however, and in the position of the waist line, fashions for women during the post-war years have not altered fundamentally. Wool jersey suits with top coats for winter and printed cotton dresses for summer, with silk dresses and matching jackets for special occasions, have been the rule for many years.

Evening dress soon came back again but more often than not it was short and practical, though long dresses appeared for occasions of pomp, such as civic receptions and banquets. Cocktail dresses have become the usual wear for dining out, for the theatre and for private parties, and except for the fashionable first nights neither men nor women now wear evening dress for the theatre. In the country the twin set and tweed skirt have become almost a uniform and during the winter, in both town and country, women wear what is most comfortable and warm—thick, knitted cardigans, slacks or tweed skirts, fur-lined jackets and boots.

Girls growing up and just discarding their school uniforms usually adopt the styles of the currently most popular film or television star for a year or two, wearing their hair in elaborate beehives or in straggling, unkempt, wispy locks, taking to black stockings and spike heels, pale lipstick and heavy eye make-up, suede jackets and black tights in such rapid succession that they can completely transform their appearance in a matter of days. Bathing costumes have at the moment reached the point where they are so scanty that their only future, assuming always the eternal process of change, is for them to become more substantial or be entirely discarded.

After the war the Savile Row tailors decided to try to make men as conscious of fashion as women. They introduced a new Edwardian cut in their suits, with narrow trousers and a shorter, squarer jacket. Youths from the suburbs and working-class districts, finding themselves with large pay packets from the time they left school, and uncertain what to do with the money, observed the fashion and took to it themselves, to the chagrin of its designers, who in the interests of exclusiveness had to drop entirely or drastically modify their own plans. It was Britain's working-class youth which became clothes conscious and took to elaborate dressing in tight trousers, short jackets, often with velvet collars, and elaborate, brocaded waistcoats; and with this uniform they began to wear their hair long on the nape of the neck and side whiskers. These Teddy boys were intensely proud of their newly acquired expensive elegance, but in contrast university students and the sons of the professional classes took to duffle coats and loose, ungainly sweaters. Older men remained loyal to their traditional conservatively cut dark suits for most occasions, though even in these there has crept a hint of the more elegant Edwardian line, with narrower trousers, and men have become far more interested in their appearance than they were between the wars, while an increasing number of youths have taken to long hair.

During the latter part of the 1940's, though food was still short and houses difficult to find, the entertainment industry offered plenty of diversion. Cinema-going was still the most popular form of mass entertainment and in 1946 the average weekly total of cinema audiences in Britain was over thirty-one million, the highest it had ever been. The industry was booming and the outlook bright. Denis Forman, the director of the British Film Institute, wrote at this time that British film makers had "emerged from the war full of confidence in their new-found powers . . . and for the first time there is a truly British school of production, which has gained worldwide recognition", and in the United States an Indiana newspaper reported that "the more intelligent people here like British films".

One of the first important films released after the war was the Noël Coward-David Lean production of *Brief Encounter*. It was beautifully written, acted and directed and for the next ten years remained the best-known British film on the Continent and in America. The films which followed were less successful. There was something missing from them—a vitality and truth—and Paul Rotha wrote that "the realism and fidelity to life of the best of the wartime films have been replaced by an escape into romanticism and historical setpieces. Once more we have turned back to adaptation of successful plays and novels instead of stories written for the screen. For all their cunning use of camera magic these new films are theatrical and literary in conception."

Arthur Rank was now the most important figure in the business. He owned a very large circuit of cinemas in Britain and had acquired wide interests in the Commonwealth; he also possessed large and splendidly equipped studios capable of turning out some hundred films a year. Provided his films had a proper showing in America and pleased American audiences, the prospects were never better. The Rank Organisation set to work with high hopes, but 1946 was a year of disaster. The Organisation lost a million pounds on a musical which was a failure and did not even reach the States. Another half a million was dissipated in an attempt to establish a cartoon film industry in Britain under the direction of David Hand, who had been trained in the Disney studios at Hollywood, and even more in experimenting with a new type of production—the independent frame method— which attempted to economize studio space and time by using small and fragmentary foreground sets against back projection.

In 1947 the Labour government, being short of dollars, imposed a duty of 75 per cent on all American films coming into Britain. Hollywood promptly retaliated by withholding its films altogether. This meant a shortage of films for the British cinemas and a new chance for the Rank Organisation, which announced a £9 million programme. The studios set to work, but just as the new films were ready for launching the tax on imported American films was removed and the British films had to compete with a flood from Hollywood.

Two of the best British films of this time were *Great Expectations* and *Odd Man Out*. Most of them, however, were not outstanding and many showed an increase in the violence and sadism which had already become so apparent in both British and American films. An opinion poll run by a popular film magazine voted Herbert Wilcox's romantic story *The Courtneys Of Curzon Street* the most popular British film of 1947, and at the time Wilcox said it appealed to British audiences because it was "about nice people". "The public appreciate a change from gloomy horrors", he continued. "They want sentiment not sadism, and certainly not studies in psychiatry." Public taste is well-nigh impossible to gauge and whether or not they wanted sadism and psychiatry that is what they were to get for a very long time to come. Herbert Wilcox was to have few more successes and in 1964, during his examination in bankruptcy, he was to attribute his losses in part to the public's changing tastes.

In 1947 Alexander Korda re-established London Films, and in 1948 Associated British re-opened the Elstree studios and went into steady production again; but it was Arthur Rank's enchanting film *The Red Shoes* which re-established the British film both in America and on the Continent. Olivier's *Hamlet* and Korda's *The Fallen Idol* were also widely acclaimed, as well as *Oliver Twist* and *The Winslow Boy*; but apart from these films, neither Rank, Korda nor Associated British produced any more winners, though from Ealing Studios were coming the first of the brilliant series of comedies, distinctively British in their humour, which were to delight audiences for several years to come, as for example *Passport to Pimlico*, *Whisky Galore*, *The Lavender Hill Mob* and *The Titfield Thunderbolt*.

In October 1948 Rank had to announce to his Odeon shareholders that their company had borrowed £13½ million from the bank. The Government's import duty on American films had lost Britain the

American market and though the duty had been rescinded she had not been able to recover it.

But there was another vitally important factor which brought disaster to the film industry—the sudden popularity of television. The B.B.C. resumed television broadcasting in 1946 and by 1947 18,000 combined TV and radio licences had been issued. Interest was keen but television sets were expensive and with so many other things to be bought for the household, to replace wartime wear and tear, their sales were at first relatively slow. It was in 1949 that people stopped going regularly to the cinema. They became more selective, going only to films they particularly wanted to see and missing the others. Old hands in the industry said it was just a temporary decline in interest. Slumps, they declared, had happened in the business every seven years. One had been due in 1939 but the war had given the industry an artificial boost. Now a decline was long overdue but things would right themselves before long. They were wrong. While cinemas grew steadily emptier, television became increasingly popular. With the boom year of 1954 and the opening of commercial television in 1955, the television mania swept the country and the cinemas, neglected and forgotten by their old devotees, stood more than half empty.

Television watching became such a craze for a while that it changed people's living habits. Night after night families sat in darkened rooms watching the screen, neglecting their friends, their old hobbies, their local cinemas and pubs. They even took to eating their suppers from a tray, sitting round the small grey screen, so as not to miss a moment of this new entertainment, which was so little different from a film show in many respects, though infinitely more trying on the eyesight.

From a weekly attendance of over thirty million, cinema audiences had dropped by 1962 to 7.9 million. Between 1950 and 1959 a thousand cinemas closed and those that managed to remain open depended to a large extent on the sales of ice cream and peanuts for their profits. By 1962 nearly another thousand had shut down, many having been converted into dance halls, bowling alleys or bingo halls, and a large number of the smaller country towns were left with no cinema at all. At the same time the number of television licences soared and by 1959 ten million were being issued each year.

Britain had changed her habits. With better housing conditions amongst the working classes the need to escape into the spurious luxury of the cinema was less acute. Moreover, new houses were being built in the ever-spreading suburbs, increasingly far removed from the town centres where the cinemas were sited. Television was in the home itself, providing a diversion without the trouble of a bus journey.

The film industry struggled on but in 1949 Gainsborough studios closed and the Lime Grove studios at Shepherd's Bush were sold to the B.B.C. for television production. Denham was sold but Pinewood survived. The film industry tried many ways to revive the public's flagging interest, introducing, with all the publicity blare of show business,

"She's done thirty thousand miles, most of it looking for somewhere to park."

© *Punch*

248

stereoscopic films, which had to be viewed through polarized spectacles, and the wide screen of Cinemascope.

During the 1950's many excellent films appeared, including the memorable *The Bridge On The River Kwai* and other war subjects, such as *The Battle Of The River Plate, Reach For The Sky, Sink The Bismarck, The Dam Busters, Dunkirk, Carve Her Name With Pride, A Town Like Alice, The Cruel Sea* and *The Man Who Never Was.* There were also some very successful comedies, notably *Genevieve, Doctor In The House* and its sequels and the *Carry On* series.

Towards the end of the 1950's a new type of British film began to emerge, the main features of which were a realistic portrayal of working-class life and a frankness about sex. It was partly influenced by the "angry young man" movement in the theatre (see p. 251), and some of the films, including *Look Back In Anger* and *A Taste Of Honey*, were based on plays. Other notable films of this type were *Room At The Top, Saturday Night And Sunday Morning, A Kind Of Loving* and *This Sporting Life*—all based on novels. They were well made and were generally well received by the public. There were also, of course, a number of good British films of the late fifties and early sixties which did not come into this category, including *Tom Jones, The Servant* and the Peter Sellers comedies.

The number of cinemas in Britain and the size of audiences continued to decline throughout the first years of the sixties, but now show signs of remaining fairly steady, the industry making about seventy feature films a year compared with the pre-war two hundred; but those seventy earn more money abroad, for film production has declined in Hollywood and on the Continent in just the same way, and fewer films are available to fill the programmes of the surviving cinemas of the world.

In British homes the mania for television is abating somewhat but the average time each member of the household looks in is still two and a half hours a day. The B.B.C. opened its second channel in 1964 and competition between the B.B.C.'s two channels and the various commercial companies is fierce. The advertising programmes on the commercial channels have brought American selling techniques into British homes for the first time. Both the B.B.C. and the commercial companies have good news services and sports programmes, as well as educational programmes for adults and for schools. They both have quiz programmes and run soap operas which are innocuous enough and amble on week after week with such purposelessness that there seems no reason why they should ever end until death overtakes one or other of the principal characters.

The drama programmes, however, are the subject of much controversy. A few excellent television playwrights have emerged and the B.B.C.'s adaptations of the classics have been widely acclaimed, but far too many plays are concerned with crime.

It has been argued that the violence and sadism which came into British films after the war, particularly in the second features, lost the industry three-quarters of its audience; but this is hardly logical, since the programmes the public are now seeing in their homes have followed the same trend. The companies have long hours of programme time to fill and there is no doubt that crime stories and spine chillers are far easier to write than plays concerned with a somewhat more intellectual conflict; nor do they demand so much mental effort on the part of the viewer. From time to time people protest at the low standards of human behaviour displayed on the screen; usually they are told they are being puritanical and hypocritical. They argue that the programmes are bad for their children to watch and are told that they should exercise more control over their families, either sending them out of the room or to bed or else switching off their sets.

Just as during the 1930's the Government was aware of the influence of films on the rising generation of British youth, and in the 1940's the Palache Committee reported that "culturally the screen has great influence both politically and culturally over the minds of the people", so they are equally concerned about the influence that television has over the minds of the viewers. From time to time committees are appointed to investigate these matters and all the old, well-tried arguments are brought forth yet again. One school of thought claims that watching scenes of crime and violence can do no harm to young people and helps to drive their baser instincts out of their systems. The other claims that it is highly dangerous and helps to implant base urges that otherwise they might not have. The fact remains that a number of young delinquents have admitted to magistrates that the crime they have committed was copied from one they had seen played on television.

The popularity of radio listening declined with the rising passion for television but there are signs that it is returning to favour, though the well-loved *Children's Hour* was brought to an end because of the decreasing number of listeners. The explanation put forward for this was that children have become so used to listening to adult television programmes that they now have no time for the less sophisticated entertainment which a few years ago was considered suitable for their age. However, introduction of the highly convenient transistor radios has undoubtedly given a fillip to radio listening and there are few households which do not possess one.

The theatre has gone through the same phase as the cinema and television drama in its emphasis on realism. A new school of dramatists came to the fore in Britain—the "angry young men"—who wrote their reports, in dramatic form, of the seamy side of life amongst Britain's lower middle and working classes. The first of them was John Osborne, with his plays *Look Back In Anger* and *The Entertainer*; and Shelagh Delaney, with her play *A Taste Of Honey*, won fame as the first "angry young woman". This type of play, however, though it received a great deal of publicity, never formed more than a small proportion of the theatrical offerings on view; and serious playwrights such as Terence Rattigan, whose work had nothing in common with the new school, maintained their popularity.

Government subsidies for the theatre have slowly increased, and a number of theatres also receive support from civic councils. Britain now has a National Theatre, replacing the former Old Vic. Other leading companies include the Royal Shakespeare Company, with theatres at Stratford-on-Avon and in London, and the English Stage Company, which introduced the work of many new authors (including John Osborne) to British audiences.

The enthusiasm for ballet and opera at Covent Garden and Sadler's Wells was unabated and the new operas of Benjamin Britten and Michael Tippett were eagerly awaited and assessed. Though the Queen's Hall had been destroyed during the bombing, the Promenade concerts began again at the Albert Hall, under the direction of Sir Malcolm Sargent, and their devoted followers, amongst whom are a high proportion of young people, have created a first night and last night tradition of their own; the concerts given by international artists at the Royal Festival Hall have also become a source of great joy and inspiration to music lovers. Many people who never before had had the money or opportunity to hear music and opera at first hand or watch ballet have come to love them dearly, and the sale of long-playing records is a clear refutation of the allegation that the British are an unmusical nation.

An odd feature of the craze for blown-up realism was that realism in art was regarded for a while as effete and worthless. During the late forties and throughout the fifties, though solid work was being done by Britain's serious artists and sculptors, particularly Henry Moore, it was the abstract artists who achieved the publicity, and their work became so obscure that in the end one could only take the artist's word for the meaning of the strange patterns and shapes which were presented to the wondering world as works of art. Nevertheless, for a while they became immensely popular and sold for high prices. The galleries bought them as examples of contemporary art, and the dealers flourished on the intellectual snobbery of purchasers who felt that pictures which so few could understand must somehow be of significance.

Late in the 1950's a young artist replying to his critics protested thus: "I do not 'draw' horizontal lines on canvas. I apply polyvinyl and polythene tapes to boards which are treated with plastic emulsion paints; also of the three paintings I am exhibiting, two are horizontal with vertical readings across the plane of the painting."

These abstract artists became obsessed with the feeling, texture and colour of raw materials. "The resulting amorphous unfocused paintings, invariably giant in size . . . were not painted. The paint (or whatever was introduced on to the canvas—often it wasn't paint) was dribbled on, hurled on, flicked on a horizontal canvas from above. Sometimes, the size of the canvas being so vast, the colouring matter was ridden over by a bicycle for the sake of the tyre marks and effect of pressure."[1]

An exhibition of post-war art and sculpture was held early in 1964 at the Tate Gallery, consisting of sixty-five pieces of sculpture and three hundred paintings, in which the work of British and American artists predominated, though France and Germany were also well represented. There were paintings by Picasso, Braque, Léger and Matisse, but an important part of the exhibition was devoted to the younger abstract artists. Some critics took these pictures seriously but others dismissed them as incomprehensible rubbish. Thus Nigel Gosling, writing in the *Observer*, said that "there are rooms where the artists

[1] Pearl Binder, *The English Inside Out* (Weidenfeld and Nicolson, 1961).

think new thoughts in new materials and rooms where they talk to us in commercial language that we hardly like to listen to. . . . There are weirdies and solemnities, high spirits and intellectual space-probes. Not for a moment are we offered the comfort of cliché and the gentle declivities of convention. . . . To give people what they want is to feed them on stones: this is the great fallacy behind the socialist-realist doctrine. It is a more elusive doctrine which must be made good. This exhibition is rich in nourishment."

Terence Mullaly of the *Daily Telegraph*, however, writing of the same exhibition, said that: "Art's latest manifestations have done nothing to bridge the gap between the artist and the majority of those who care about art. Equally sad, those whose interest is very slight, or who feel antipathy, are further alienated by much contemporary painting and sculpture. . . . The visitor to this exhibition—and remember it is supposed to be a solemn statement about what is most characteristic of the art of our time—moves from a crude machine, which traverses a short track with the maximum of noise, to a wash-basin. If he avoids tripping over metal cones on the floor, which pass as sculpture, he will have his eyes hurt, quite literally hurt, by tricky patterns of straight lines, which are 'pictures'."

The vogue for abstract art seems to be declining. In Paris alone eight galleries which had been selling these pictures have closed recently through lack of patronage. Norman Wilkinson, applauding this decline, wrote recently in a letter to the *Daily Telegraph* that "fostered by critics and boosted by dealers, acres of canvas have been covered with this utter rubbish and one hopes that its purchasers now realize that they have been 'had for mugs'.

"At a rough guess I would say that one in five hundred abstract pictures painted is by an artist who is sincere in his attitude to this form of painting, and that is probably a generous estimate. The yearly exhibition by the 'Young Contemporaries' is a demonstration of utter futility by young artists who should be learning their craft, but who follow the cult in the hopes of quick notoriety."

Young artists today, according to *The Times* report of a recent Young Contemporaries exhibition, are developing a "new manner, sharply flavoured with the signs, slogans and mordant humour of Metropolitan life . . .".

With the rage for modern art in its most bizarre forms at its height, there was also, as a counter movement, a great revival of interest in the eighteenth-century artists, and as, with the deaths of the older members of great families, estates were broken up and heirlooms came on the market, being sold to pay death duties, the sales of pictures and furniture were crowded with buyers, who paid increasingly high prices for them. Along with the fashion for modern interior decoration, with

These contemporary homes, although they have the appearance of matchboxes, are light and airy.

its bright colours and bleakly functional lines, there was an equally strong fashion for "period" furnishing, either with genuine pieces or good reproductions of the eighteenth-century and the best of the early nineteenth-century styles.

Contemporary architecture has come in for much criticism, principally because the plain rectangular blocks of flats and offices, with their steel and concrete frames and acres of plate glass, have become monotonous, and where they are built in the midst of pre-war shops and houses they look incongruous and out of harmony. Where they are massed together, however, the general appearance can be impressive, and these skyscrapers seem the only solution for the housing of a rapidly increasing population in a small island which is losing hundreds of acres of its countryside each year to the encroaching suburbs of the towns. I have even heard a youngster who had known one of these stark blocks of flats all his short life describe it by the unlikely adjective of "cosy", presumably because he was so familiar with it.

For the new schools and hospitals which have been built since the war few have anything but praise. The first important modern post-war building was the Festival Hall and the most impressive, attaining true grandeur, the new Coventry Cathedral.

There was a great revival of interest in books after the war and people began to read as they never had before. In 1950 it was estimated that half the population were readers of books and that Britain was the best read nation of the six leading democracies. Book clubs helped and also the issue of paperbacks, the sales of which reached 60,000,000 in 1958. In that year the public libraries of Britain recorded the issue of 392,000,000 books. Publishing flourished and became big business. The public taste for non-fiction was increasing. History proved extremely popular and the works of Winston Churchill, Arthur Bryant and G. M. Trevelyan all became best sellers. The nineteenth-century classics were eagerly read as they appeared in their new cheap editions, as well as biography and autobiography. Travel, anthropology, authentic adventure and wartime exploits all sold well, and also science fiction. The novel as a vehicle for social comment seemed in decline and those published and becoming best sellers were mainly stories of good entertainment value with well-documented backgrounds, such as Nicholas Monsarrat's *The Cruel Sea* and the stories of Hammond Innes, C. S. Forester and Nevil Shute. Among the more serious writers to emerge since the war are Iris Murdoch (*The Sandcastle, The Bell*), Angus Wilson (*Anglo-Saxon Attitudes*) and Kingsley Amis, whose *Lucky Jim,* with its rude and discontented "hero", was one of the most famous novels of the 1950's. Pre-war novelists who enhanced their reputations included Graham Greene (*The Heart Of The Matter*) and C. P. Snow, with his *Strangers And Brothers* series.

After 1945 the birth rate in Britain rose rapidly and by the early 1960's there were five million young people between the ages of fifteen and twenty-one, a large proportion of whom had left school at fifteen and were earning their own livings. Physically they are adult but mentally they are still immature, some with little intellectual ability and no desire for further education or the capacity to assimilate it. Many indeed are barely literate and it is a sobering fact that even today in

Britain there are three million adults who have derived so little benefit from their education that they can neither read nor write.

These young people earn their weekly wage easily, in dead-end jobs which require little skill and a minimum of mental effort. Their parents, who are often themselves earning good wages, ask little or nothing of them for their board and they often have several pounds a week to spend on their clothes, bicycles, motor bicycles, pop records, record players, cinema seats, confectionery, cosmetics, tobacco, alcohol, dancing, magazines and holidays. Their collective spending power amounts to £900 million a year, which is a quarter of the total amount spent by the entire country on consumer goods. Two-thirds of them do not belong to any youth organization and they have few hobbies, apart from dancing and motor cycling. They favour the jazz clubs and worship the pop singers, who, like the pop artists, make fortunes without acquiring a true technique. Most of them, in fact, cannot read music at all, but put across their numbers by means of a sense of rhythm and sheer animal vitality, which arouse their listeners to hysterical frenzies of enthusiasm which in their abandonment are both alarming and depressing to watch. The sales of their records have risen phenomenally in recent years, and it is mainly the teenagers who buy them.

These youngsters, having few inner resources, are bored and constantly in search of new diversions and new ways of self-assertion. They are badly in need of guidance and control and too often their parents tend to spoil and indulge them, thereby aggravating their boredom and retarding their development as responsible citizens, for it is a fundamental truth that the things we strive for give us more satisfaction than those we receive without effort. It has long been argued that one of the dangers of the Welfare State is that a passage through life made too easy will sap the people's will to strive and turn contentment into apathy, wherein lie the seeds of decay. This is not necessarily true, but the behaviour of these young people has rung the danger signals. Some have taken to drugs for "kicks", others to rowdyism and crime, particularly violence and assault, wilful damage to property and breaking and entering.

In 1958 the number of crimes reported in England and Wales was 120 per cent higher than in 1938, the increase being greatest amongst young people between the ages of seventeen and twenty-four, and for several years after the figure rose rapidly. In 1959 the increase was 7·8 per cent, in 1960 10·1 per cent. The problem has been treated with responsibility and skill by officials of the Home Office, welfare officers of the prisons and wardens of Borstal institutions, detention centres, remand centres and hostels, and though the figures are still increasing the rate of increase is tending to slacken.

Moreover, there are positive signs of the re-establishment of moral standards. Forty "Rockers"—the name for one of the teenage gangs of the early sixties—have recently turned to philanthropy by taking twenty needy children for a day by the sea, paying all the expenses out of their own pockets. "We want to make ourselves wanted in the community", explained the eighteen-year-old chairman of the club. "Most people don't think very highly of Rockers. We want to raise our public image. We thought the best way to do this was by helping people."

Despite the materialism of the times, engendered by high wages and the multiplicity of goods to be bought, the conscience of the people of Britain, which has shaped so much of her history, has never for long been still. With an average income which is the sixth highest in the world, individuals have responded generously with contributions to the vigorous Oxfam fund and the War on Want campaign for helping the under-privileged countries of the world. The Campaign for Nuclear Disarmament began in England in 1957 and less than two years later twelve countries of western Europe had become affiliated to it, establishing their protests by processions and demonstrations. The churches, very slowly, are gaining a certain amount of ground again, particularly the Roman Catholic Church, which between 1950 and 1960 had an increase of membership in Britain from under four million members to well over five million.

The journey for Britain from 1900 into the middle years of the twentieth century has been tumultuous and revolutionary, but the vigour within her people has given them the strength to adapt themselves, without losing their essential character, to a constantly changing spiritual, physical and economic environment, and this power of adaptation, which will carry them into the future, is the essence of all true living.

> ". . . naught shall make us rue,
> If England to itself do rest but true."[1]

[1] Shakespeare, *King John*, V. vii.

257

Bibliography

ADBURGHAM, ALISON, *A Punch History of Manners and Modes*, Hutchinson, 1961.

BARNETT, CORRELLI, *The Sword Bearers*, Eyre and Spottiswoode, 1963.

BINDER, PEARL, *The English Inside Out*, Weidenfeld and Nicolson, 1961.

BLOOM, URSULA, *The Elegant Edwardians*, Hutchinson, 1957.

BLYTHE, R., *The Age of Illusion*, Hamish Hamilton, 1963.

BRUCE, MAURICE, *The Coming of the Welfare State*, Batsford, 1961.

BUCHAN, JOHN, *History of the Great War*, Nelson, 1921.

CHURCHILL, WINSTON, *The Second World War*, Cassell, 1948 onwards.

COWLES, VIRGINIA, *The Kaiser*, Collins, 1963.

CUNNINGTON, WILLETT, *The Art of English Costume*, Collins, 1948.

DIBELIUS, WILHELM, *England*, Cape, 1930.

DUTTON, RALPH, *The Victorian Home*, Batsford, 1954.

EVANS, I. O., *Inventors of the World*, Warne, 1962.

GREEN, J. R., *A Short History of the English People*, Macmillan, 1921.

HALÉVY, E., *A History of the English People*, Benn, 1951.

HARRISON, MICHAEL, *London By Gaslight*, Peter Davies, 1963.

HOPKINS, HARRY, *The New Look*, Secker and Warburg, 1963.

LAVER, JAMES, *Edwardian Promenade*, Hulton, 1958.

MACDONALD, J. R., *The Socialist Movement*, Williams and Norgate, n.d.

MASTERMAN, C. F. G., *The Condition of England*, Methuen, 1909.

MONTGOMERY, JOHN, *The Twenties*, Allen and Unwin, 1957.

MUGGERIDGE, MALCOLM, *The Thirties*, Hamish Hamilton, 1940.

OAKLEY, C. A., *Where We Came In*, Allen and Unwin, 1964.

POLLARD, A. F., *A Short History of the Great War*, Methuen, 1920.

PRITT, D. N., *The Labour Government, 1945–1951*, Lawrence and Wishart, 1963.

RAYMOND, JOHN, *The Baldwin Age*, Eyre and Spottiswoode, 1960.

ROBERTS, DAVID, *Victorian Origins of the Welfare State*, Yale University Press, 1960.

SYMONS, JULIAN, *The Thirties*, Cresset Press, 1960.

TREVELYAN, G. M., *History of England*, Longmans, 1926.

TUCHMAN, BARBARA, *August 1914*, Constable, 1962.

WEST, V. SACKVILLE-, *Knole and the Sackvilles*, Heinemann, 1922.

Index